Opposing Viewpoints in Social Issues

OTHER BOOKS OF RELATED INTEREST

Opposing Viewpoints in Social Issues

William Dudley, Book Editor

David L. Bender, Publisher
Bruno Leone, Executive Editor
Bonnie Szumski, Editorial Director
David M. Haugen, Managing Editor

OPPOSING
VIEWPOINTS®
SERIES

Greenhaven Press, Inc., San Diego, California

Cover photo: Photodisc

Library of Congress Cataloging-in-Publication Data

Opposing viewpoints in social issues / William Dudley, book editor.
    p.   cm. — (Opposing viewpoints series)
   Includes bibliographical references and index.
   ISBN 0-7377-0122-6 (pbk. : alk. paper). —
ISBN 0-7377-0123-4 (lib. bdg. : alk. paper)
   1. Social problems. I. Dudley, William, 1964–   . II. Series:
Opposing viewpoints series (Unnumbered)
HN59.2.S624 2000
361.1'0973—dc21

99-30912
CIP

Greenhaven Press, Inc., P.O. Box 289009
San Diego, CA 92198-9009

"Congress shall make no law...abridging the freedom of speech, or of the press."

First Amendment to the U.S. Constitution

The basic foundation of our democracy is the First Amendment guarantee of freedom of expression. The Opposing Viewpoints Series is dedicated to the concept of this basic freedom and the idea that it is more important to practice it than to enshrine it.

CONTENTS

WHY CONSIDER OPPOSING VIEWPOINTS?

> "The only way in which a human being can make some approach to knowing the whole of a subject is by hearing what can be said about it by persons of every variety of opinion and studying all modes in which it can be looked at by every character of mind. No wise man ever acquired his wisdom in any mode but this."
>
> John Stuart Mill

In our media-intensive culture it is not difficult to find differing opinions. Thousands of newspapers and magazines and dozens of radio and television talk shows resound with differing points of view. The difficulty lies in deciding which opinion to agree with and which "experts" seem the most credible. The more inundated we become with differing opinions and claims, the more essential it is to hone critical reading and thinking skills to evaluate these ideas. Opposing Viewpoints books address this problem directly by presenting stimulating debates that can be used to enhance and teach these skills. The varied opinions contained in each book examine many different aspects of a single issue. While examining these conveniently edited opposing views, readers can develop critical thinking skills such as the ability to compare and contrast authors' credibility, facts, argumentation styles, use of persuasive techniques, and other stylistic tools. In short, the Opposing Viewpoints Series is an ideal way to attain the higher-level thinking and reading skills so essential in a culture of diverse and contradictory opinions.

In addition to providing a tool for critical thinking, Opposing Viewpoints books challenge readers to question their own strongly held opinions and assumptions. Most people form their opinions on the basis of upbringing, peer pressure, and personal, cultural, or professional bias. By reading carefully balanced opposing views, readers must directly confront new ideas as well as the opinions of those with whom they disagree. This is not to simplistically argue that everyone who reads opposing views will—or should—change his or her opinion. Instead, the series enhances readers' understanding of their own views by encouraging confrontation with opposing ideas. Careful examination of others' views can lead to the readers' understanding of the logical inconsistencies in their own opinions, perspective on why they hold an opinion, and the consideration of the possibility that their opinion requires further evaluation.

EVALUATING OTHER OPINIONS

To ensure that this type of examination occurs, Opposing Viewpoints books present all types of opinions. Prominent spokespeople on different sides of each issue as well as well-known professionals from many disciplines challenge the reader. An additional goal of the series is to provide a forum for other, less known, or even unpopular viewpoints. The opinion of an ordinary person who has had to make the decision to cut off life support from a terminally ill relative, for example, may be just as valuable and provide just as much insight as a medical ethicist's professional opinion. The editors have two additional purposes in including these less known views. One, the editors encourage readers to respect others' opinions—even when not enhanced by professional credibility. It is only by reading or listening to and objectively evaluating others' ideas that one can determine whether they are worthy of consideration. Two, the inclusion of such viewpoints encourages the important critical thinking skill of objectively evaluating an author's credentials and bias. This evaluation will illuminate an author's reasons for taking a particular stance on an issue and will aid in readers' evaluation of the author's ideas.

As series editors of the Opposing Viewpoints Series, it is our hope that these books will give readers a deeper understanding of the issues debated and an appreciation of the complexity of even seemingly simple issues when good and honest people disagree. This awareness is particularly important in a democratic society such as ours in which people enter into public debate to determine the common good. Those with whom one disagrees should not be regarded as enemies but rather as people whose views deserve careful examination and may shed light on one's own.

Thomas Jefferson once said that "difference of opinion leads to inquiry, and inquiry to truth." Jefferson, a broadly educated man, argued that "if a nation expects to be ignorant and free . . . it expects what never was and never will be." As individuals and as a nation, it is imperative that we consider the opinions of others and examine them with skill and discernment. The Opposing Viewpoints Series is intended to help readers achieve this goal.

David L. Bender & Bruno Leone,
Series Editors

Greenhaven Press anthologies primarily consist of previously published material taken from a variety of sources, including periodicals, books, scholarly journals, newspapers, government documents, and position papers from private and public organizations. These original sources are often edited for length and to ensure their accessibility for a young adult audience. The anthology editors also change the original titles of these works in order to clearly present the main thesis of each viewpoint and to explicitly indicate the opinion presented in the viewpoint. These alterations are made in consideration of both the reading and comprehension levels of a young adult audience. Every effort is made to ensure that Greenhaven Press accurately reflects the original intent of the authors included in this anthology.

INTRODUCTION

"I believe in individualism . . . up to the point where the individualist starts to operate at the expense of society."

—Theodore Roosevelt

Pick up any newspaper in the United States today, and one can find evidence of the constant conflicts that result from the tension between the rights of the individual and the needs and desires of the common good.

Protecting individual rights is the cornerstone of the founding principle of the United States. The Declaration of Independence proclaims that all men are created equal, and the Constitution's Bill of Rights enumerates the most important of the citizenry's individual rights. Yet the state must, and does, curb individual rights on a daily basis, through laws and the courts. How much the state should curb individual rights, and in what areas the state should get involved, however, is a never-ending, constantly shifting debate that gets played out in the media and in politics.

In this book, *Opposing Viewpoints in Social Issues,* a multitude of debates emphasize this tension. Should gun rights of citizens, for example, be curbed to protect the type of senseless massacre that occurred in Littleton, Colorado, where thirteen people were killed by two student gunmen who also took their own lives. For some, including President Bill Clinton and a host of others, the answer is an emphatic yes. Only by curbing certain types of ammunition and weaponry, insisting on background checks on buyers, and imposing stiff fines on those that violate these rules, can this type of violence be curbed. Essentially, those that favor involvement of the state believe that the state can and should become involved in solving social problems. The state should go beyond punishing perpetrators to preventing possible infractions, which necessitates laws that place curbs on the right of individuals to purchase guns. As sociologist Amitai Etzioni argues, "no right is absolute and all must be balanced against the common good."

Those who favor individual rights believe that the state cannot fix problems that essentially reside in the human heart. Using the Littleton, Colorado, example, these people would argue that laws, curbs on ammunition, or any other such measures could not have stopped those teenage gunmen. Aberrant, terrible crimes will happen, but they are the cost of freedom. Freedom cannot be predicated on the actions of the insane, the radical, or the twisted in society. Individual rights must, by their very nature, guarantee the freedoms of the average, law-abiding citizen. When the state gets involved, it punishes all for the crimes of a few, and this cannot be acceptable to the citizenry as a whole, many argue. In fact, fear of tyranny, of the state overstepping its bounds, is the essence of what America's founders attempted to prevent. As philosophy professor Tibor R. Machan proclaims, "The only truly public good is the protection of individual rights, nothing else."

Because the United States is based on democratic principles, an uneasy balance exists between those that believe individual rights must take precedence in society and those that believe the state must place limits on those rights. This balance has factored into nearly every issue under public debate. Thomas Jefferson foresaw the conflict, but believed that the nation should err on the side of the individual, arguing that a government "shall restrain men from injuring one another," but "shall leave them otherwise free to regulate their own pursuits of industry and improvement." As the viewpoints in this volume reflect, the definition of what constitutes the common good, what Jefferson would term "improvement," is much in debate.

CHAPTER 1

CAN GUN CONTROL LAWS PREVENT VIOLENCE?

CHAPTER PREFACE

The United States stands out among developed nations in both the high number of guns it has in circulation and the number of its people that are killed in gun-related homicides each year. The number of firearms in circulation in the United States has increased from about 54 million in 1950 to 192 million in 1998, according to *U.S. News & World Report*. In 1996, almost 36,000 Americans were killed with firearms in homicides, accidents, and suicides. A 1997 study published in the *Journal of American History* stated that the number of people in Western Europe killed with guns in a year is less than the number of Americans killed in a week.

Some people believe that the prevalence of guns in America and America's high numbers of gun fatalities are directly related, and ascribe the comparatively low rates of violence in countries in Europe and elsewhere to laws making it more difficult for people other than police officers to carry firearms. "Most countries in the Western world do not let people have handguns, and they certainly don't let people have military weapons," states Wendy Cukier, a Canadian professor and expert on international gun control issues. In 1996, for example, Australia passed several gun control measures following a mass killing of thirty-six people by a person armed with an assault rifle. The new laws banned the sale and possession of all semiautomatic and pump-action firearms (handguns were already regulated), introduced a comprehensive gun registration system, and required that gun owners store their firearms and ammunition separately. The regulations also made it more difficult for private citizens to acquire a permit for gun ownership, requiring a reason other than self-defense to own any firearm, a twenty-eight-day waiting period, and firearms training for first-time gun owners. Gun control advocates in the United States have called for similar measures. "Foreign nations . . . that limit firearms control gun violence more effectively," asserts a *Los Angeles Times* editorial. "Gun crime is by no means unheard of in those nations, but . . . the incidence of gun homicide, accidents, armed robberies and other violent crimes is much lower than here."

However, the major trend in recent years in the United States has been to encourage rather than discourage private gun ownership. Twenty-two states between 1986 and 1996 reformed their laws to make it easier for adults to obtain a permit to carry a concealed weapon—usually a handgun. State legislatures replaced "may-issue" laws—under which local law enforcement officials were given broad discretionary powers to grant or withhold such permits—with "shall-issue" laws, under which all people who applied and met specific criteria (such as no criminal record) were issued permits to carry weapons.

Opponents of these laws argue that permitting and encouraging people to arm themselves for their own self-defense does not solve the problem of gun violence and may make it worse. "Arming a society does not create civility nor does it produce solutions to gun violence," asserts the Coalition to Stop Gun Violence, an association of gun control organizations. Proponents, however, contend that such measures do in fact enable people to effectively defend themselves and bring down crime rates. Social researchers John R. Lott Jr. and David B. Mustard studied the effects of concealed weapons laws and concluded that "allowing citizens to carry concealed weapons deters violent crimes and it appears to produce no increase in accidental deaths." Attorney Jeffery R. Snyder asserts that "it is not the number of guns [in circulation] but their distribution—that is, the people who have the guns and what they are using them for—that matters." The viewpoints in this chapter examine the relationship between guns and violence and whether public policies should restrict or encourage private gun possession.

"The one 'casual' factor that sets us apart from the rest of the world is the huge arsenal of handguns . . . that makes it possible to settle with finality the passionate domestic arguments and street disputes that produce most of our homicides."

THE PREVALENCE OF GUNS CONTRIBUTES TO VIOLENT CRIME

Richard Harwood

While the United States has similar crime rates to those of other developed nations, it has much higher incidents of homicide. More than twenty thousand people are murdered in the United States every year. In the following viewpoint, Richard Harwood examines why the United States faces such an epidemic of violence. While the ultimate reasons for America's high levels of violence remain a mystery, an obvious contributing factor in his view is the 50 to 70 million handguns found in the United States—a much higher number than in other countries. The easy availability of handguns may help escalate disputes and confrontations into fatal incidents. Richard Harwood is a columnist for the *Washington Post* newspaper.

As you read, consider the following questions:

1. How many people have been murdered in the United States between 1980 and 1997, according to Harwood?
2. What countries have homicide rates that exceed those of the United States, according to the author?
3. Why does Harwood believe it is not rational to argue that Americans have a unique propensity for murder?

Reprinted from Richard Harwood, "America's Unchecked Epidemic," *The Washington Post National Weekly Edition*, December 8, 1997, with permission. © The Washington Post.

A mericans have invested a great deal of wealth and effort in this century to keep death at bay, and they have had a lot of success. Cholera, smallpox, typhoid have been eliminated in this country. Other diseases that once killed millions now are cured easily or prevented. The average American's life span has been extended by nearly 30 years.

Health and medical care have become our leading industry. We spend more on these services than we spend for food, housing, automobiles, clothes or education.

But neither money nor science has brought us any closer to solving or even moderating one epidemic in American life: violence. For at least a century and probably longer we have been the most murderous "developed" society on earth. From 1980 to December 1997 nearly 400,000 Americans have died at the hands of fellow citizens—more than the number of Americans who died on the battlefields of World War I and World War II combined. It would take eight Vietnams to fill as many graves.

AMERICA IS NOT A LAWLESS SOCIETY

Our propensity to violence cannot be explained by the cliche that America is a uniquely "lawless" society. [Criminologists] Franklin Zimring and Gordon Hawkins of the University of California write: "The reported rates [per 100,000 people] of both violent and nonviolent crime in the United States . . . are quite close to those found in countries like Australia, Canada and New Zealand." The rate of criminal assault is higher in those countries than here. In robberies, the United States is second to Poland and similar in rate to Italy, Australia, Czechoslovakia, Canada and England. Scandinavian robbery rates are not strikingly lower than those in this country. A study in 1992 revealed that London had a higher overall crime rate than New York City, including 66 percent more thefts and 57 percent more burglaries. But New York has 11 times as many murders.

So it is not crime that sets us apart. We have no more pickpockets, shoplifters, burglars, robbers or brawlers than Western Europe or the British Isles. But we have a surplus of killers—a large surplus. Our homicide rate is 20 times the rate in England and Wales, 10 times the rate in France and Germany and is exceeded only by a few Latin American countries, notably Colombia, Mexico and Brazil.

Why this is so is a mystery to medical scientists (psychiatrists and psychologists included) and to anthropologists and social scientists as well. Politicians have no answers. They wage futile "wars" on crime, expand the police forces and the offenses punishable by death, keep a million citizens in prison, beef up law enforcement agencies and equip them with everything from tanks to helicopter gunships. Through it all, the homicide rate remains almost constant—roughly eight to 10 murders for every 100,000 people in the course of a year.

AMERICA'S MURDER PROBLEM

When 20,000 to 25,000 people are being murdered every year, you've got a problem. It's not a huge problem in the context of death in America; more than 2.25 million of us die every year from all causes—including 30,000 to 40,000 from AIDS, 40,000 or so in automobile accidents and about 30,000 as a result of suicide.

But even in that context, murder is a serious problem. It poisons society with fear and suspicion, turns large areas of our cities into combat zones and contributes to urban flight.

Still, despite our cowboy image in much of the world, it is irrational to assume that a propensity for murder is rampant in the American character; 99.99 percent of us never murder anyone. And there is no uniformity among those who do. Some regions have more violent traditions than others, the South in particular: Louisiana's murder rate today is 20 times the rate in Vermont. Men are more murderous than women. Cities have proportionately more murders than suburbs and rural areas. The 20 largest U.S. cities have 11.5 percent of the American population but account for 34 percent of the reported homicides. African Americans, heavily concentrated in these cities, are at far more risk of death by homicide than nonblacks. They are 13 percent of the American population, but they account for 45 percent of homicide victims and 55 percent of suspects charged with homicide, according to calculations by Zimring and Hawkins. Many theories are offered to explain the relatively high level of lethal violence in these urban communities, but none has been validated. Whatever the "causal" factors, the number and percentage of blacks charged with homicide in the age groups most prone to violence—15 to 34—is tiny, roughly a tenth of one percent. And if black homicides were ignored in the calculations, the U.S. homicide rate still would be three to five times greater than the rates in Europe and Britain.

THE GUN FACTOR

Zimring and Hawkins conclude that the one "causal" factor that sets us apart from the rest of the world is the huge arsenal of handguns—estimated at from 50 million to 70 million—that makes it possible to settle with finality the passionate domestic arguments and street disputes that produce most of our homicides. Eliminating handguns would not eliminate rage or conflict but certainly would lower the life-threatening consequences of these encounters.

People will argue that other deadly weapons—knives, blunt instruments, poison and the noose—will remain available to people who want to kill. Sure. They're available all over the world, too, but nowhere else is murder so commonplace.

It would take political courage to do anything about the gun problem, and it is in short supply in Washington. But no other remedy—medical, chemical, technological or spiritual—is at hand or even on the horizon.

"The so-called 'instrumentality theory,' which connects the prevalence of guns to high rates of death by violence, has virtually collapsed."

THE PREVALENCE OF GUNS DOES NOT CONTRIBUTE TO VIOLENT CRIME

Daniel D. Polsby

In the following viewpoint Daniel D. Polsby argues against what he calls the "instrumentality theory"—the idea that the mass prevalence of guns in America accounts for the country's high rates of lethal crimes relative to other countries. This theory has been embraced by gun control advocates, the federal government, and by major newspapers and television networks, he contends, but is not supported by the facts. Research indicates that guns are used lawfully for defense far more than they are used for crimes. Interspousal homicide rates have fallen in the United States, contrary to what one would predict with the instrumentality theory. Additional evidence against the theory, he argues, comes from the declining murder rates in states that have relaxed laws permitting people to carry concealed weapons. Guns appear instead to have a deterrent effect on violence. Polsby is a law professor at Northwestern University in Evanston, Illinois.

As you read, consider the following questions:

1. What does Polsby state to be the origins of the instrumentality theory of gun violence?
2. How freely available are guns today compared to thirty years ago, according to the author?
3. What has been the experience of Florida following the passage of liberalized concealed weapons laws, according to Polsby?

Excerpted from Daniel D. Polsby, "From the Hip," National Review, March 24, 1997. ©1997 by National Review, Inc., 215 Lexington Ave., New York, NY 10016. Reprinted by permission.

In a democracy, public policy is tailored to what people believe, no matter what the facts might be. For weapons policy, the point is not the connection between guns and extreme violence, or between gun-control laws and the prevalence of guns, but rather how people *see* the connection. We know that many crimes, murder and robbery especially, are committed with guns—many more, both proportionately and absolutely, than in the Eisenhower decade. In recent years, the homicide-victimization rates for young males, especially young black males, have skyrocketed, with most of the increase attributable to firearms wounds. We also know that guns have been increasing their market share as a means of suicide.

But are these trends the byproduct of there simply being too many guns available to people? And would banning handguns or assault rifles reduce this availability and thereby drive down rates of murder and suicide? If your answer to these questions is "yes," then cheerleading for gun rights will look mighty like cheering for murder and suicide and opposing common decency. But "yes" is the wrong answer, at least without a load of qualifications. Firearms violence does not correlate with how many guns there are in a given population; it correlates with how they are distributed in that population—that is, who has them and for what purpose. Gun-control laws characteristically ignore that distinction, and usually aim only to limit the number of weapons in circulation. This is why their effects have usually been disappointing if not counterproductive. There is plenty of evidence to substantiate this case, and little to dislodge it. But who ever heard of evidence when the gun-control winds begin to blow?

Politicians of both parties have tended to play firearms issues as a straight interest-group bidding contest. The sources from which most people get their information—television networks and major newspapers, above all the *New York Times*—have done no better. They have chosen sides—and almost all the same side. They have helped the public to believe that private ownership of firearms, of handguns especially, is the major reason why America's homicide rate exceeds those of other industrialized nations. The case is closed so far as they are concerned, closed so completely that they have left a genuinely big firearms story all but uncovered. That story is that the so-called "instrumentality theory," which connects the prevalence of guns to high rates of death by violence, has virtually collapsed.

Until the late 1960s the connection between firearms and violence was not much of a public issue, and certainly not a partisan one. American liberalism's greatest postwar figure, Hubert

Humphrey, was a devoted shooter of game birds, but his views about guns were not limited to sport. He also believed something that in today's liberal circles would be received as in essence psychotic, namely that, in having institutionalized widespread private firearms ownership, our country had bought itself an insurance policy against tyrannical government.

But so far as the Democratic Left was concerned, the days of that sort of thinking were already numbered. The tocsin for the change was probably Ramsey Clark's *Crime in America*, published in 1970, which laid out what American liberal, and Democratic, thinking on virtually all crime questions would become. "Total casualties from civilian gunfire in this century exceed our military casualties in all the wars from the Revolution through Vietnam," Lyndon Johnson's attorney general intoned. "It is not hysteria that demands gun control; it is 8,900 murders, 12,000 suicides, 65,000 assaults, 99,000 robberies—all committed with guns in the single year of 1968. The toll will rise until we act." Yes, but act how? "If government is incapable of keeping guns from the potential criminal while permitting them to the law-abiding citizen, then government is inadequate to the times. The only alternative is to remove guns from the American scene."

The intellectual groundwork for Clark's dramatics had been laid two years before, by George Newton and Franklin Zimring, authors of the 1968 staff report of President Johnson's National Commission on the Causes and Prevention of Violence, entitled *Firearms and Violence in American Life*. Newton and Zimring carefully traced the growth of gun sales in Detroit following a series of riots, and fitted an overall increase of firearms crimes to the general expansion of firearms possession. They repeated the exercise in eight widely separated American cities, with the same result: the proportion of guns used in violent transactions is a function of the overall gun-possession characteristics of a given population. Their most influential contribution may have been comparing violence in the United States with violence in England and Wales, something that ever since has been a stock element in the argument for suppressing firearms sales. England and Wales, which tightly restrict the private possession of handguns and other firearms, have among the lowest murder rates in the world, less than 1 in 100,000 of population for each of the last twenty years, compared to the American rate of 9 or 10 in 100,000, ten to twenty times worse. If one considered only gun murders, Newton and Zimring pointed out, America's record was forty times worse.

This is the outline for what is commonly known as the instrumentality theory of guns and violence. Its claim is not so much that guns "cause" crime as that they make the outcomes of whatever crimes there are going to be more deadly rather than less deadly. The claim has a basis in common sense. It is reasonable to think that a certain number of intentional killings would be unfeasible without a gun. And many killings develop out of a domestic brawl or an argument between neighbors and not a specific intention to kill. Murder resulted simply because a gun was handy; without a gun the offender would have used a chair or a knife, and his victim in all probability would have lived. In some number of cases, these intuitions are undoubtedly correct. The question is, How many? And how many offsetting cases are there, in which the presence of a gun averted trouble rather than making it worse?

Ramsey Clark's argument became the most influential framing of the firearms-and-crime problem of its time, and indeed it is influential still, nearly thirty years later. . . . It became a fixture of public discourse that "science knows" that a gun in the home is 43 times more likely to kill its owner or a family member than to kill an intruder, that guns have become "the new polio," a calamity which now accounts for more premature deaths of younger Americans than anything this side of AIDS. A rationally ignorant public, most of it two or three generations remote from rural life and daily familiarity with guns, went along. And here we are today.

PROBLEMS WITH THE INSTRUMENTALITY THEORY

Almost from the beginning there were nagging anomalies in the instrumentality theory. In 1979, David Bordua, a University of Illinois sociologist, and his student Alan Lizotte published a study of Illinois counties that seemed to show that where guns were found in the greatest percentage of households, the rate of gun crimes was lower, and where they were found in the lowest percentage of households, the rate of gun crimes was higher. The Chicago Metropolitan Crime Survey replicated this result as recently as 1996. And the international comparisons in their own terms raise serious questions. After all, even if one sets firearms murders (about 55 per cent of the total in this country) to one side, our domestic-murder rate is still seven or eight times that of England. What accounts for the difference here? Once the door is open for considering the rather substantial differences between the cultures and populations of the two countries, it is open also for asking whether those differences might explain some of the firearms murders. Surely not all those murders are instrumentality effects; some must be written down to other causes.

Indeed, the whole matter, fairly weighed, is much more complicated than the standard account supposes. There are firearms effects on both sides of the violence equation. An accumulation of survey research points to the conclusion that guns are used defensively and lawfully much more often than they are used in crimes—twice as often, according to a Police Foundation survey coauthored by Florida State University criminologist Gary Kleck and Duke University criminologist Philip Cook, who found at least a million and a half defensive uses per year. Guns do inflict wounds that tend to be much more medically dangerous than the wounds inflicted by knives, but as Kleck found, when guns are used, whether by criminals or by the law-abiding, they make confrontations much less likely to result in woundings in the first place.

But the anomalies run much deeper than that sort of cost accounting allows. After all, it is wrong to pretend that handguns or any other sorts of firearms are "more available" today than they were in prior generations. Thirty years ago, handguns, shotguns, rifles, and ammunition could be bought over the hardware-store counter almost anywhere in the country by almost any adult. Anyone, sight unseen, could mail-order guns and ammunition and have them delivered by the United States Postal Service, COD, a fact that anyone with some 1950s vintage *Popular Mechanics* magazines can corroborate. In fact, firearms have been less available since the Gun Control Act was passed in 1968, followed by the proliferation, at every level of government, of new restrictions and sometimes outright prohibitions on the legal possession of guns.

GUNS AND MURDER

The availability of guns aside, if the instrumentality theory were going to hold anywhere, it should be in the home, because people spend more time there than anywhere else, and because guns are kept there more than they are kept anywhere else. It appears, moreover, that despite increasingly restrictive legislation, between 1980 and 1992 the national handgun stock increased by 40 per cent and the proportion of households in which a firearm is present has held at somewhere above 40 per cent. The instrumentality theory makes a distinct prediction about this state of affairs, namely that the interspousal homicide rate would increase considerably in that period. In fact it has not, but rather has been steady or falling throughout this period, according to a study by James Mercy and Linda Salzman in the *American Journal of Public Health*. . . .

Chicago statistics, carefully kept and released annually by the Detective Bureau of the city's Police Department since 1965, bear witness to the same general drift. Over the course of the past thirty years there has been a striking trend away from homicides among relatives, romantic interests, step-relatives, in-laws, quasi-in-laws, neighbors, and friends. Domestic and acquaintance homicides accounted for nearly half of all killings in Chicago thirty years ago; recently they have been around 15 per cent of the total. Indeed, an interesting fact of record—which of course has never been published in either of Chicago's socially responsible, gun-control-favoring newspapers—is that the actual number of these sorts of killings per annum has diminished in thirty years, from 183 such killings in 1965 to 147 in 1994, which is more than proportionate to the city's population decline. To be sure, city murders have increased very dramatically—930 in 1994, compared to 395 in 1965. But every bit of that increase has been among "non-friend acquaintances," strangers, or persons unknown. In other words, gang killings with illegal guns.

GUNS AND SUICIDE

Though international comparison is a favorite device of instrumentality theorists, this artifice is usually kept in modest seclusion when the subject of suicide comes up. No doubt this is because some of the highest suicide rates in the world are found in countries, like Japan, Hungary, and Germany, that have some of the toughest and most effective prohibitions on civilian gun possession. . . .

According to a report published in the August 9, 1995, issue of the *Journal of the American Medical Association*, between 1980 and 1992—while the handgun stock in the United States increased by approximately 40 per cent—suicide rates among persons aged 25 and younger declined from 5.7 per 100,000 to 5.4 per 100,000. This is, of course, the very age group whose homicide victimization has exhibited the most startling spike in this same time period. The instrumentality theory is in ruins. And the worst of it has not yet been told.

CONCEALED WEAPONS

In the last year or two before 1997, Texas, Virginia, Tennessee, Kentucky, and a number of other states have relaxed their restrictions on the carrying of concealed handguns by civilians. When the late returns come in, these changes may yet save the instrumentality theory from the dustbin, but the early returns are not encouraging. "I'm detecting that I'm eating a lot of crow on this issue," Harris County District Attorney John Holmes recently professed. Holmes's jurisdiction, the third most populous county in the United States, includes Houston. Holmes was one of many who predicted that "blood would run in the streets" when the Texas concealed-carry law came into effect 14 months ago. It hasn't happened. In fact, with 112,000 new concealed-carry permits issued, there have been all of 57 "incidents" recorded among licensees, mostly, according to The Texas Lawyer, involving possessing while intoxicated or failing to conceal the weapon. Eating crow is "not necessarily something I like to do," Holmes told The Texas Lawyer, "but I'm doing it on this."

It is a remarkable story, when one thinks about it. After all, the instrumentality theory is not completely vacuous. A good deal of deadly violence is indeed of the impulsive variety, and adding guns to tantrums must often lead to a certain amount of trouble. And if rational rather than impulsive behavior is the issue, relaxed concealed-carry laws do raise a real concern, what strategy theorists call the "first mover" problem. Suppose an angry quarrel breaks out between two strangers. Neither one knows whether the other is armed, but each knows if he himself is. Because whoever gets his gun out first (the "first mover") has a strategic advantage, an armed man in this situation might well think it better to go for his gun first and ask questions afterward. If both players are armed, both should reason thus. The Gunfight at the O.K. Corral is the predicted result. Yet such incidents seldom occur. Evidently the reality is more complicated than the model allows.

The problem with the "first mover" formulation is that it focuses on two people only and assumes away the whole rest of the world. But an antagonist cannot make such an assumption. What if he pulls a gun on an unarmed man? What if bystanders, themselves armed, arrest him or finger him for the police? What if he shoots his antagonist, and armed bystanders gun him down? For rational actors, these are pacifying incentives. Better keep one's shooting iron put up unless and until the end is nigh. Call this the "strategic pacification" effect of firearms.

The Florida experience with liberalized concealed-carry laws is the proper place to end our excursion. As of 1988, when it liberalized its law, Florida had one of the country's highest murder rates. As happened two years ago in Texas, Florida public officials and newspaper editorialists outdid themselves with lurid predictions: blood in the streets, the O.K. Corral, High Noon, John Wayne, and so on. As in Texas, nothing of the sort resulted.

Within a few years something like 150,000 permits were out-standing, but fewer than ten felony offenses have been committed in all this period of time with properly authorized guns, none involving homicide. And in fact, the state's murder rate has fallen in every single year since the law was changed, and now is below the national average.

"For most violent crimes like murder, rape, and aggravated assault, the new concealed-weapon laws had the greatest deterrent effect in counties with high crime rates."

ALLOWING PEOPLE TO CARRY CONCEALED HANDGUNS REDUCES VIOLENT CRIME

Jeffrey R. Snyder

In recent years many states have liberalized laws allowing people to legally carry concealed weapons. Between 1986 and 1996 the number of states in which it is legal to carry such weapons grew from nine to thirty-one. In the following viewpoint, Jeffrey R. Snyder argues that while many gun control proponents who opposed these reforms predicted disastrous increases in violence, these laws instead have saved lives and prevented murders, rapes, and other crimes. They give law-abiding citizens the means to assert their right of self-defense, while creating a deterrent effect for potential criminals. Licensing systems which objectively screen potential permit holders are the most effective form of gun control yet devised, he concludes. Snyder is a New York attorney.

As you read, consider the following questions:

1. How are the new gun licensing laws different from those they replaced, according to Snyder?
2. In Snyder's opinion, why can't people rely on the police for protection against criminals?
3. What twin goals do licensing systems for concealed weapons accomplish, according to the author?

Reprinted from Jeffrey R. Snyder, "Easing Handgun Licensing Laws: Helping the Public Fight Back," USA Today magazine, September 1998, by permission of the Society for the Advancement of Education, (c) 1998.

A little over a decade ago, a controversial "concealed-carry" law went into effect in Florida. In a sharp break from the conventional wisdom of the time, the law allowed adult citizens to carry concealed firearms in public. Many people feared this quickly would lead to disaster and that blood literally would be running in the streets. Today, it is safe to say that those dire predictions were completely unfounded. Indeed, the current debate over concealed-carry laws centers on the extent to which they can reduce the crime rate.

To the shock and dismay of gun control proponents, concealed-carry reform has proven to be wildly popular among state lawmakers. Since Florida launched its experiment in October, 1987, numerous states have enacted similar laws, with positive results.

REFORMING THE LICENSING SYSTEM

Prior to 1987, almost every state either prohibited the carrying of concealed weapons or permitted concealed carry under a licensing system that gave government officials broad discretionary power over the decision to issue a permit. The key feature of the new licensing laws is that the government must grant the permit as soon as the citizen can satisfy specified, objective licensing criteria. In general, these laws provide that a permit must be issued to any adult state resident who has not been convicted of a felony; has no history of drug or alcohol abuse and/or mental illness; has not committed any violent misdemeanor within the last three to five years; and, in most states, has taken a firearms training course. In nearly all of these instances, the applicants' fingerprints are recorded and the license seekers are subjected to a background check.

In most instances, the new shall-issue laws replace concealed-weapon statutes dating from the 1930s and 1940s that granted the licensing authority (usually the police) broad, undefined discretion to issue permits to "suitable persons" or individuals of "good moral character" who had "proper cause" or a "justifiable need" to carry a weapon. Such laws still continue in about 15 states. As written, they suggest that only certain people, in "special" circumstances, are entitled to defend themselves from deadly violence with lethal force, and that those who face just the "ordinary" risk of criminal violence do not deserve the right to carry the means with which to defend themselves. The implicit suggestion that some lives are more worth protecting than others is morally repugnant and insupportable.

In large metropolitan areas with high crime rates, these older licensing laws typically have been administered to deny the issuance of permits to ordinary citizens. From 1984 to 1992, the city of Los Angeles refused to issue a single permit. In a metropolis of 3,500,000 people over a period of nine years, not one applicant was found to have both "good moral character" and "good cause" to carry a handgun for protection. In Denver, Police Chief Ari Zavaras granted a mere 45 permits in a city with a population of 500,000. The detective who administered Zavaras' program explained that "Just because you fear for your life is not a compelling reason to have a permit." Among those denied a permit was Denver talk-show host Alan Berg, who had received death threats from, and later was killed by, white supremacists.

In New York City, the list of permit holders strongly suggests that licenses are issued on the basis of celebrity status, wealth, political influence, and favoritism. Such luminaries as journalist William F. Buckley, Jr., real estate mogul Donald Trump, publisher Michael Korda, comedians Bill Cosby and Joan Rivers, and radio shock-jock Howard Stern are among those who have been granted licenses. Meanwhile, taxi drivers, who face a high risk of robbery and murder, are denied permits because they carry less than $2,000 in cash. A Federal district court in California upheld similar class-based discrimination in Los Angeles County's policy of issuing permits to carry firearms almost entirely to retired police officers and celebrities, "because famous persons and public figures are often subjected to threats of bodily harm."

THE RIGHT OF SELF-DEFENSE

The point is not that celebrities, the wealthy, or influential citizens do not deserve to protect themselves; they most certainly do. The crime victim rolls in this country are not populated predominantly by the rich and famous, though, but almost entirely with the names of ordinary citizens, who equally are entitled to defend themselves and protect their lives. The frustration of the common, law-abiding citizen's desire to protect himself (and, increasingly, herself) from violent crime due to law enforcement's arbitrary refusals to issue permits under the older licensing systems has led to vociferous demands for licensing based on satisfaction of nondiscretionary, objectively verifiable, and specified criteria.

Shall-issue licensing systems are based on a recognition that an individual's safety is his or her personal responsibility and on the right of self-defense. Every state recognizes a right of its citizens to use lethal force to repel a criminal assault that threatens imminent danger of death or grievous bodily injury. Self-defense, so defined, is not lawlessness; it is in accord with the law. It is, in fact, in accord with the same law the police rely on in using lethal force. The right of self-defense belongs to each person, not merely those who the police or other licensing authorities believe "deserve" to have that right. Yet, this right is a hollow promise if a state deprives its law-abiding citizens of one of the most effective means to exercise it.

According to Department of Justice statistics, about 87% of violent crimes occur outside the home. Despite the fact that Americans possess approximately 70,000,000 handguns, one is not armed if one does not have a weapon at hand when, and where, needed. Perversely, discretionary licensing regulations and prohibitions against the carrying of weapons succeed in disarming only those who respect the law. By ensuring that those who abide by the law will not carry weapons outside the home, licensing regulations aid and abet criminals by assuring them that they will find unarmed, easy victims. Shall-issue concealed-carry laws, by contrast, deprive criminals of that peace of mind.

Critics who advocate that citizens should remain defenseless and rely solely on the police ask people to disregard some unpleasant realities about both the nature of criminal assaults and the responsibilities of the police. Even assuming that the victim can "see it coming" and has the time and ability to call the police, Department of Justice statistics reveal that they can get to the scene within five minutes about 28% of the time. The idea that police protection is a service that people can summon in a timely fashion is a notion that often is mocked by gun owners, who love to recite the challenge: "Call for a cop, call for an ambulance, and call for a pizza. See who shows up first."

Criminals choose the time and place of their assaults and take pains to ensure that their crimes occur when the police are not around. Criminals choose their victims and take pains to select those over whom they believe they have an advantage, be it in the possession of a weapon, youth, strength, or number. Therefore, the victim almost certainly will be alone and at a disadvantage relative to his assailant. The encounter will not be on equal terms; the fight will not be "fair." Without a weapon, an "equalizer" to overcome those natural disadvantages, it is unlikely that the victim will have an effective means of self-defense. Without a weapon, it is very likely that whether the victim lives or is maimed or injured will depend largely or entirely on the mercy of his or her assailant.

To make matters worse, while laws deprive citizens of the ability to defend themselves effectively outside the home, thereby placing them in the position of having to rely on the police for their protection in extremis, it is a settled principle of law throughout the U.S. that the police have no legal duty to protect any individual from crime. This holds true even in cases where the police have been grossly negligent in failing to protect a crime victim.

The function and responsibility of the police is to serve solely as a general deterrent, for the benefit of the community as a whole; they are not personal bodyguards. Those who would prohibit the carrying of arms for self-defense thus bear a burden of establishing on what basis and moral authority the government, having no obligation to protect any particular individual, deprives particular individuals of the ability—and means—to protect themselves.

FAILED PREDICTIONS

Opponents of the new licensing laws argue that:

- More guns on city streets will lead to more violence and deaths.
- The laws will transform the streets of America into "Dodge City," as previously law-abiding citizens take to settling hotheaded arguments over fender benders and slights to their dignity with guns.
- The carrying of weapons by ordinary citizens jeopardizes the safety of the police.
- Citizens' lack of training will lead to false confidence in or unrealistic expectations about the usefulness of firearms, with the possible result that license holders will take foolish risks.
- Due to insufficient training, license holders will lack good judgment in determining when it is appropriate to use their weapons, resulting in wrongful shootings and wrongful brandishing of firearms.
- Insufficient proficiency with their weapons will result in the shooting of innocent bystanders or loved ones.

While opponents of licensing laws are not wrong to point out that those adverse results are potential consequences of the widespread carrying of weapons, it is no longer necessary to speculate about what the effects of such laws might be. There now is evidence from 25 different states with diverse rural and metropolitan populations—including the cities of Miami, Houston, Dallas, Pittsburgh, Philadelphia, Richmond, Atlanta, New Orleans, Seattle, and Portland—regarding perhaps as many as 1,000,000 permit holders carrying their weapons for hundreds of millions of man-hours. The results are in, and they show unequivocally that the number of persons currently in possession of permits to carry firearms ranges from one to five percent of the state's population; almost no criminals apply for permits; permit holders do not take to settling their traffic disputes or arguments with guns, or "take the law into their own hands"; shall-issue licensing states have almost no problems with violent criminality or inappropriate brandishing of firearms by permit holders; and some permit holders have used their guns to defend themselves and others.

There appears to be no reported case of any permit holder adjudged to have wrongfully killed another in connection with carrying and using his weapon in public. As of this writing, shall-issue licensing laws are creating no reported law enforcement problem in any of the 25 states that have enacted them. Dodge City has not returned, and blood is not running in the streets.

The New Laws Save Lives

A 1997 study by John Lott and David Mustard, "Crime, Deterrence and Right-to-Carry Concealed Handguns," provides significant criminological support for the claim that, far from increasing bloodshed, shall-issue systems save lives, prevent rapes and robberies, and confer benefits that extend well beyond those garnered by the people who are issued the permits. Analyzing crime data from all 3,054 counties in the U.S. throughout the period 1977–92, Lott and Mustard found that, when shall-issue licensing laws went into effect in a county, murders fell on average by 7.65%, rapes by 5.2%, robberies by 2.2%, and aggravated assaults by 7.0%. Had all the counties in the nation had such laws, the researchers suggest that there would have been 1,414 fewer murders, 4,177 fewer rapes, 11,898 fewer robberies, and 60,363 fewer aggravated assaults. On the other hand, property crime rates increased 2.7% after the passage of shall-issue laws. Lott and Mustard conclude that criminals appear to respond to the threat of being shot by victims by substituting less risky, non-confrontational crimes.

For most violent crimes like murder, rape, and aggravated assault, the new concealed-weapon laws had the greatest deterrent effect in counties with high crime rates. Significantly, Lott and Mustard also found that "concealed handguns are the most cost-effective method of reducing crime thus far analyzed by economists, providing a higher return than increased law enforcement or incarceration, other private security devices, or social programs like early educational intervention."

The study has been the subject of strong criticism by a number of other criminologists who, in performing their own analyses of the data, find reason to question some of Lott and Mustard's conclusions. Lott, however, has produced strong rebuttals of critics' arguments. What is most notable about this debate is that, despite fears of opponents that the licensing laws will lead to increased crime and violence, the criminologists finding fault with the Lott-Mustard study are arguing only that shall-issue licensing laws have no demonstrable effect on violent crime rates—that is, they neither decrease violent crime rates (as Lott maintains) nor increase them.

Thus, even if one believes the critics of Lott-Mustard, the reality is that, after up to 10 years of intense scrutiny of national data, there is no comprehensive economic analysis supporting the view that shall-issue licensing laws are a danger to public safety; the debate is over how much they benefit society. In a free society, the burden of proof is borne by those who would restrict the liberty of others. Opponents of shall-issue licensing laws are lacking in hard criminological data and analyses condemning those laws and justifying opponents' desire to prevent persons who satisfy the licensing standards from carrying handguns for self-defense.

Shall-issue licensing systems are not, as sometimes is asserted by their opponents, another example of America's free-wheeling, hands-off approach to guns. The licensing systems are gun control. On the basis of years of experience in 25 states, it is possible to conclude that shall-issue licensing systems work. They accomplish the twin goals of providing a mechanism by which law-abiding citizens can carry the means with which to defend themselves from a violent criminal assault that imminently threatens life or grievous bodily harm and provide the public with reasonable assurance that those who receive permits are persons who will act responsibly.

"Contrary to the gun lobby's claim,
no evidence exists to suggest that 'an
armed society is a polite society.'"

ALLOWING PEOPLE TO CARRY CONCEALED HANDGUNS WILL INCREASE VIOLENT CRIME

Part I: Douglas Weil, Part II: Bill Kolender

A growing number of states have passed laws making it easier for people to carry handguns and other concealed weapons. The authors of the following two-part viewpoint criticize these "carrying concealed weapons" (CCW) laws. Part I is by Douglas Weil, the research director for the Center to Prevent Handgun Violence, a gun control research and advocacy group. Weil argues that lax background checks result in the arming of unqualified and dangerous people. Studies that claim that loosened gun restrictions result in lower violent crime rates are flawed, he asserts. In Part II, Bill Kolender argues against a proposed California law making it easier for people to carry concealed weapons. He contends that such a measure will not increase public safety and may result in more gun homicides. Kolender is sheriff of San Diego County.

As you read, consider the following questions:

1. What examples of the wrong sort of people carrying guns does Weil describe?
2. What position do law enforcement officers take on the issue of gun permits, according to the authors?
3. What sort of message do concealed weapons laws send to young people, according to Kolender?

Part I: Reprinted from Douglas Weil, "Carrying Concealed Weapons Is Not the Solution," at http://www.intellectualcapital.com/issues/98/0326/iccon.asp, March 26, 1998, by permission of the author. Part II: Reprinted from Bill Kolender, "Look for Trouble If Guns Law Is Eased," San Diego Union-Tribune, June 28, 1996, by permission of the author.

I

Why should you worry about more people carrying concealed handguns?

On Sept. 10, 1997, five men licensed to carry concealed handguns got into a fight outside a Pittsburgh saloon after exchanging "hostile looks." All of the men fired their weapons and ended up in the hospital.

[In November 1997] in Indianapolis, two women were unintentionally shot when a concealed handgun fell out of a man's pocket at a crowded Planet Hollywood restaurant.

In February 1997, two Tulsa men were arguing over who would take their four-year-old granddaughter home from day care. One of the men, who had a permit to carry a concealed weapon, shot the other man in front of 250 school children.

LIMITED BACKGROUND CHECKS

Why were these dangerous and poorly-trained people allowed to carry concealed handguns? They live in states that recently weakened "carrying concealed weapons" (CCW) laws.

This legislation—a favorite of the gun lobby—takes discretion away from law enforcement in determining who receives a concealed weapons license and requires the state to allow virtually anyone who is not a convicted felon to carry a loaded handgun. Under this system, the background check required of applicants for CCW licenses is supposed to screen out people with violent criminal histories, but it cannot screen out all criminals or people with bad tempers or bad judgment—and no one should think otherwise.

Daniel Blackman is one example of a dangerous man who was allowed to carry a concealed weapon despite prior criminal behavior. In February 1996, the former candidate for judge in Broward County, Florida, threatened to put three bullets in the head of a meter maid who had written him a ticket—behavior that should have prevented him from carrying a concealed handgun but did not. Though he was arrested, Blackman was not convicted of a crime because he agreed to seek psychological treatment. A year later, Blackman was arrested again, this time for pulling a gun on an emergency-room doctor who refused to write him a prescription. Only then was his CCW license revoked.

In states with lax CCW laws, hundreds of licensees have committed crimes both before and after their licensure. For example, in Texas, which weakened its CCW law in 1996, the Department of Public Safety reported that felony and misdemeanor cases involving CCW permit holders rose 54.4% between 1996 and 1997. Charges filed against Texas CCW holders included kidnapping, sexual assault, aggravated assault with a deadly weapon, illegal drug possession and sales, drunken driving and impersonating a police officer. Clearly, the Texas background check does not ensure that everyone who receives a CCW license is a responsible or upstanding citizen.

From Texas to Illinois and California to Delaware, law-enforcement officials have led the charge against this dangerous liberalization because they know that more guns will only lead to more violence. Thanks to the efforts of our men and women in blue and concerned citizens, the gun lobby has not passed any new concealed-weapons legislation in more than a year. Despite the opposition of most voters, the gun lobby currently is trying to pass these senseless laws in Michigan and Nebraska, and also has set its sights on Kansas, Ohio and Missouri.

FLAWED STUDIES

The gun lobby attempts to justify this dangerous political agenda by citing research conducted by Dr. John Lott. Lott's study concludes that making it easier for citizens to carry concealed weapons reduces violent crime rates. What the gun lobby and Lott do not say is that this study has been totally discredited by many well-respected, independent researchers.

In fact, in a nationally-televised symposium at which Lott's work was critiqued, Dr. Daniel Nagin of Carnegie Mellon University, Dr. Daniel Black of the University of Kentucky, and Dr. Jens Ludwig of Georgetown University agreed that Lott's study is so flawed that "nothing can be learned of it" and that it "cannot be used responsibly to formulate policy." Since then, no credible evidence has been produced to rebut the conclusions of Black, Nagin and Ludwig, or other researchers who have identified additional flaws with Lott's work.

Contrary to the gun lobby's claim, no evidence exists to suggest that "an armed society is a polite society." In reality, the United States already has more guns in civilian hands than any other industrialized nation, and not surprisingly, we also have one of the world's highest rates of gun crime. As the casualties of weak concealed-weapons laws begin to mount, it is unconscionable that Lott and the gun lobby continue to use this flawed data to put more guns on the street.

Fortunately, the American people and law enforcement know better. They deserve primary consideration from their state representatives, not the special-interest gun lobby. It is truly a matter of life and death.

II

When I hear about the efforts of the gun lobby to make it easier to get permits to carry concealed weapons in California, I immediately picture a Chargers-Raiders game at the [football stadium]—its stands packed with gun-toting fans.

Proponents of this shocking scenario insist this would be the best and safest of all worlds. You couldn't pay me enough to be sitting in those stands. A football game or any public event teaming with armed individuals is a potential powder keg. An argument or a fist fight could escalate into a gun battle, and someone could get killed.

Law enforcement organizations throughout California vehemently oppose the weakening of requirements for carrying a concealed weapon. And recent polls show that nearly 75 percent of California voters are opposed as well.

But, apparently not all California lawmakers are interested in what law enforcement or private citizens think. In January 1996, the Assembly passed AB 638, which would apply minimum standards to concealed weapons permits.

If AB 638 becomes law, nearly every California resident over the age of 21 will qualify to carry a concealed weapon as long as he or she has no record of a felony conviction or recorded history of mental illness. This bill removes the current requirement that an applicant show good and sufficient cause to be issued a permit. [Editor's note: AB 638 failed to become law.]

The bill also eliminates the discretion of the issuing official. As the issuing agency for San Diego County, the Sheriff's Office would be forced to parcel out permits to anyone meeting the minimum standards, including individuals convicted of assault, prowling or drunk driving. Felons who have plea bargained down to misdemeanor charges also would qualify for permits.

CONCEALED WEAPONS AND CRIME

Don't get me wrong. I am not against the ownership of firearms. I recognize and understand the fear that drives some people to purchase guns. But I don't buy the argument that allowing average citizens to carry concealed handguns will cut down on crime and increase public safety.

In March 1995, a study by criminologists at the University of Maryland examined the effects of weakened concealed-weapons laws in Florida, Mississippi and Oregon, finding that gun homicides increased an average of 26 percent while other types of homicides stayed the same.

In most cases, a concealed weapon is useless as a means of protection. It tends to give carriers a false sense of security. Even police officers aren't entirely immune to gunshot wounds in confrontations with criminals. A 1993 FBI study shows that among 54 officers killed in 54 shooting incidents, 85 percent did not have a chance to fire their weapons. And 25 percent were shot with their own guns. Imagine, if these well-trained professionals cannot always protect themselves with their guns, how would the average citizen fare against an experienced criminal?

What few people realize is that the nation's 24,000 gun homicides each year don't rest on the shoulders of the violent criminal alone. Nearly 50 percent of murder victims are killed by people without criminal intent. The shouting match over a parking space, the fist fight on the playground or a lovers' quarrel can result in a death when guns are accessible.

AB 638 also has the potential of raising the stakes for law enforcement officers—men and women on the front lines in the fight against violent crime. Our officers and deputies are already at risk due to the proliferation of handguns. AB 638 would increase the potential hazard that police face in every traffic stop or any other encounter with a citizen.

A HARMFUL MESSAGE

And what message are we sending to our children when Mom or Dad comes home and tosses a gun on the kitchen table? Guns soon would come to represent the ultimate means of protection and even a status symbol for young people. Can we afford to send this message, particularly at a time when violent crime among juveniles is escalating?

5

"Gun-free school zones can make it
clear . . . society no longer tolerates
guns in or near our schools."

GUNS SHOULD BE BANNED FROM SCHOOLS

Jay Nixon

A wave of schoolplace shootings in 1997 and 1998 prompted much debate on how to prevent violence in schools. In the following viewpoint, Jay Nixon, attorney general for the state of Missouri, defends legislation he proposed that would ban all guns within one thousand feet of public schools (existing state law already prohibited guns within schools). Nixon argues that creating gun-free school zones would make schools safer and send a strong message that guns are not to be tolerated in places of learning.

As you read, consider the following questions:

1. How many Missouri students were discovered with guns in 1996, according to Nixon?
2. According to the author, what other safety precautions and laws have been passed governing zones around schools?
3. What does Nixon believe should be done with students who carry guns or are otherwise considered to be at-risk?

Reprinted from Jay Nixon, "Guns and Schools Don't Mix," St. Louis Post-Dispatch, December 29, 1997, by permission of the St. Louis Post-Dispatch. Copyright 1997.

I am greatly concerned with the stance taken by the Second Amendment Coalition and others to oppose gun-free school zones. The legislation I have proposed attempts to protect our children, as well as the rights of gun owners, and includes appropriate exceptions for those who live within 1,000 feet of a school zone, for those who own businesses or work within 1,000 feet of a school zone and for law enforcement officials. Yet, some still oppose the proposals, for fear their rights are being trampled.

As a hunter and an avid sportsman, I respect the concerns many have over efforts to regulate gun use. I appreciate the right we have as citizens to own guns, but with that right comes responsibility. In this case, we have a responsibility to use common sense and recognize that guns in and near schools are a threat to schoolchildren.

GUNS DO NOT BELONG NEAR SCHOOLS

In 1996, Missouri school officials discovered 341 students with guns at school—in their lockers, in their backpacks or hidden in their clothing. No doubt others were not discovered and even more students, gang members, dropouts and others had guns in the school parking lot, in cars and near the school property.

Obviously, laws do not prevent acts of violence, or those in West Paducah [Kentucky] would not have suffered the great loss they incurred when three young women were shot to death in the school hallway. [A 14-year-old student was arrested following the December 1, 1997, incident.] Obviously laws do not prevent all crimes, or we would have no one in our prisons. But laws do make clear the standards of society and provide consequences for those who abuse those standards.

Gun-free school zones can make it clear to children and adults society no longer tolerates guns in or near our schools. It is apparent that this message is not getting through when a 10-year-old brings a 9mm handgun for show and tell, as was reported in southwest Missouri. Gun-free school zones can also provide increased penalties for those who cross this line just as drug-free school zones have done.

Society has supported and demanded that increased precautions be taken to protect children in and near schools. We have reduced speed limits and provided crossing guards, and we have adopted drug-free zones.

These zones have increased the amount of prison time for drug dealers selling near a school. They also send a strong message to young people and those who would prey on young people that society considers drug abuse on or near school property one of the most offensive of crimes. To those who say that gun-free school zones do not work, I would point out that 758 offenders have been convicted of distributing drugs near schools and have been subject to increased prison time.

INTERVENING WITH AT-RISK STUDENTS

Increased school safety is not just about punishment for those who cross the line. We must also make every effort to intervene with at-risk juveniles and to maintain order and discipline in our schools, so that students have every opportunity to learn.

One current effort that is proving successful in some Missouri schools is the creation of alternative schools. More than 40 alternative schools are already operating around the state and have been funded in part with money from the Safe Schools Act [a 1996 Missouri state law]. I have visited many of these schools, and I know this is an effort worthy of our support.

Alternative schools provide separate education and counseling opportunities for disruptive students away from the regular classroom. This system provides appropriate intervention for at-risk students; and, equally important, the system allows the regular classroom teacher to give full attention to students who are trying to learn. Disruptive students are no longer allowed to slow the progress of the entire class or threaten the discipline and safety of our public schools.

Our students have a right to study in an atmosphere that is disciplined and conducive to learning. Gun-free school zones and alternative schools are two important steps to guaranteeing that right for all students.

"Attempts to outlaw guns from
schools, no matter how well
meaning, have backfired."

ADULTS SHOULD BE PERMITTED TO
CARRY GUNS IN SCHOOLS

John R. Lott Jr.

Many people have called for increased gun control measures for
the nation's schools in the wake of several school shootings in
1997 and 1998—including a March 1998 incident in Arkansas
in which two boys opened fire and killed four students and one
teacher. In the following viewpoint, John R. Lott Jr. argues many
of these shootings, including the Arkansas tragedy, occurred in
schools in which firearms were totally banned. He proposes instead that teachers and other law-abiding adults should be allowed to carry guns in schools. Armed teachers not only may be
able to stop shootings in progress, he contends, but may also
deter people from instigating such actions in the first place. Lott
cites research he conducted which he says shows that laws en-
abling citizens to carry concealed handguns reduces the number
of deaths and injuries caused by public shootings. Lott is a research fellow at the University of Chicago School of Law and
author of More Guns, Less Crime.

As you read, consider the following questions:

1. What incident in Pearl, Mississippi, does Lott describe to
   support his argument that guns can save lives?
2. What lessons does the author draw from the actions of
   terrorists in Israel?
3. How has media coverage of gun use affected the debate over
   gun control, according to Lott?

[The] horrific shootings in Arkansas have, predictably, spurred calls for more gun control. [On March 24, 1998, two boys (ages thirteen and eleven) shot and killed four students and one teacher outside a middle school.] But it's worth noting that the shootings occurred in one of the few places in Arkansas where possessing a gun is illegal. Arkansas, Kentucky and Mississippi— the three states that have had deadly shootings in public schools over the past half-year prior to April 1998—all allow law-abiding adults to carry concealed handguns for self-protection, *except* in public schools. Indeed, federal law generally prohibits guns within 1,000 feet of a school.

Gun prohibitionists concede that banning guns around schools has not quite worked as intended—but their response has been to call for more regulations of guns. Yet what might appear to be the most obvious policy may actually cost lives. When gun-control laws are passed, it is law-abiding citizens, not would-be criminals, who adhere to them. Obviously the police cannot be everywhere, so these laws risk creating situations in which the good guys cannot defend themselves from the bad ones.

Consider a fact hardly mentioned during the massive news coverage of the October 1997 shooting spree at a high school in Pearl, Mississippi: An assistant principal retrieved a gun from his car and physically immobilized the gunman for a full 4½ minutes while waiting for the police to arrive. The gunman had already fatally shot two students (after earlier stabbing his mother to death). Who knows how many lives the assistant principal saved by his prompt response?

GUNS CAN DETER SHOOTINGS

Allowing teachers and other law-abiding adults to carry concealed handguns in schools would not only make it easier to stop shootings in progress, it could also help deter shootings from ever occurring. Twenty-five or more years ago in Israel, terrorists would pull out machine guns in malls and fire away at civilians. However, with expanded concealed-handgun use by Israeli citizens, terrorists soon found the ordinary people around them pulling pistols on them. Suffice it to say, terrorists in Israel no longer engage in such public shootings—they have switched to bombing, a tactic that doesn't allow the intended victims to respond.

The one recent shooting of schoolchildren in Israel further illustrates these points. On March 13, 1997, seven seventh- and eighth-grade Israeli girls were shot to death by a Jordanian soldier while they visited Jordan's so-called Island of Peace. The *Los Angeles Times* reports that the Israelis had "complied with Jordanian requests to leave their weapons behind when they entered the border enclave. Otherwise, they might have been able to stop the shooting, several parents said."

Together with my colleague William Landes, I have studied multiple-victim public shootings in the U.S. from 1977 to 1995. These were incidents in which at least two people were killed or injured in a public place; to focus on the type of shooting seen in Arkansas we excluded shootings that were the byproduct of another crime, such as robbery. The U.S. averaged 21 such shootings per year, with an average of 1.8 people killed and 2.7 wounded in each one.

CONCEALED WEAPONS LAWS

We examined a whole range of different gun laws as well as other methods of deterrence, such as the death penalty. However, only one policy succeeded in reducing deaths and injuries from these shootings—allowing law-abiding citizens to carry concealed handguns.

The effect of "shall-issue" concealed handgun laws—which give adults the right to carry concealed handguns if they do not have a criminal record or a history of significant mental illness—has been dramatic. Thirty-one states now have such laws. When states passed them during the 19 years we studied, the number of multiple-victim public shootings declined by 84%. Deaths from these shootings plummeted on average by 90%, injuries by 82%. Higher arrest rates and increased use of the death penalty slightly reduced the incidence of these events, but the effects were never statistically significant.

With over 19,600 people murdered in 1996, those killed in multiple victim public shootings account for fewer than 0.2% of the total. Yet these are surely the murders that attract national as well as international attention, often for days after the attack. Victims recount their feelings of utter helplessness as a gunman methodically shoots his cowering prey.

LOPSIDED MEDIA COVERAGE

Unfortunately, much of the public policy debate is driven by lopsided coverage of gun use. Tragic events like those in Arkansas receive massive news coverage, as they should, but discussions of the 2.5 million times each year that people use guns defensively—including cases in which public shootings are stopped before they happen—are ignored. Dramatic stories of mothers who prevented their children from being kidnapped by carjackers seldom even make the local news.

Attempts to outlaw guns from schools, no matter how well meaning, have backfired. Instead of making schools safe for children, we have made them safe for those intent on harming our children. Current school policies fire teachers who even accidentally bring otherwise legal concealed handguns to school. We might consider reversing this policy and begin rewarding teachers who take on the responsibility to help protect children.

IS ABORTION JUSTIFIABLE?

CHAPTER PREFACE

Induced abortion is a common medical procedure in the United States and the world. The Alan Guttmacher Institute, a private organization that researches reproductive health issues, estimates that about 46 million women—35 out of every thousand women of childbearing age—have an abortion each year. In the United States, where abortion rates have been declining since 1990, approximately 1.4 million women have an abortion each year. According to the institute, 43 percent of American women will have an abortion at some point in their lifetimes.

Although it has become commonplace, abortion has been a polarizing social policy issue in the United States since at least 1973, when the Supreme Court in the case of Roe v. Wade overturned state laws prohibiting or restricting the procedure. On one side of the debate are those who call themselves pro-choice and who believe that women have a fundamental right to make decisions about their bodies—such as whether to terminate a pregnancy—without government interference. They contend that the Roe case marked an important advance in personal freedom and saved women from the risks of illegal abortions. "Without the protections of Roe, all other legal and civil rights are meaningless," argues Gloria Feldt, president of the Planned Parenthood Federation of America. "If you can't determine the fate of your body, all other rights pale."

On the other side of the issue, those who call themselves pro-life believe that human life begins at conception and that a woman's right to control her body should not override the right of the fetus to live. "Abortion is the willful destruction of a potential life, and that's wrong," asserts Heather King, a lawyer who has had (and regretted having) three abortions. In addition, abortion opponents assert that, far from being a panacea to women's liberation, having an abortion can inflict lasting physical and emotional harm to women. "The violence implicit in the act of abortion is directed not only against our children but against ourselves," argues King.

The main goal of the political pro-life movement for many years after 1973 was to get the Supreme Court to overturn its decision in Roe v. Wade. Abortion opponents helped to elect two pro-life presidents, Ronald Reagan and George Bush, who appointed five Supreme Court justices between them. In cases since Roe the Supreme Court has upheld some state laws passed to discourage abortion, such as mandatory waiting periods and parental consent for minors. But it has refused to overturn *Roe*, most notably in the 1992 case of *Pennsylvania v. Casey*, in which the Court asserted that the right to terminate pregnancy was a "component of liberty we cannot renounce." Most observers now believe that to go back to the situation as it existed before *Roe* would require a constitutional amendment, a development many agree is unlikely in the foreseeable future.

With its legalized status in the United States relatively secure, abortion is now more than ever an issue of conscience for women with an unplanned or unwanted pregnancy. Their decisions are often complicated by the fact that many of the purveyors of abortion information and counseling in the United States have underlying pro-life or pro-choice agendas. The viewpoints in this chapter examine some of the basic moral and health questions surrounding abortion.

| *"Abortion is a violent killing of the most innocent of humans."*

ABORTION IS MURDER

Benjamin J. Stein

Benjamin J. Stein is an economist, writer, and television actor. In the following viewpoint, he argues that abortion is murder—the taking of a human life. Abortion supporters willfully ignore this unpleasant aspect of abortion. The millions of abortions that have occurred in America since *Roe v. Wade* in 1973 constitute a national tragedy, he concludes.

As you read, consider the following questions:

1. How many abortions have taken place in America since 1973, according to Stein?
2. Why do abortion supporters oppose the showing of television advertisements depicting abortion, according to the author?
3. Why does the author refuse to consider the current era to be "A Golden Age" for America?

Here I am cleaning up my son's room watching a talk show and they are talking about our time—to the effect that we are now living in "The Golden Age" or at least "A Golden Age" in the history of America. This talk is based on the performance of the United States economy since about the end of 1991 until now [1998], when we have had an uninterrupted economic expansion accompanied by rates of inflation that are low by the standards of the Vietnam and post-Vietnam era.

A GOLDEN AGE?

The Golden Age metaphor seems to apply especially to corporate earnings, which have risen very fast since 1987, more than doubling in that time period. This rise, combined with low interest rates, has powered a breathtaking rise in prices on the nation's stock markets, which I like a lot. . . .

More Americans than ever are millionaires, and while precise numbers are hard to come by, estimates from the Northern Trust Company are that more than one in every hundred Americans is a millionaire, and families with more than $5 million in assets are no longer rare.

I keep thinking of numbers like this and the idea of the Golden Age.

Then I think about some other numbers. Since 1973, when the United States Supreme Court, with no precedent before it at all, decided that it was not constitutionally permissible for states to restrict abortions for most women, there have been an estimated 37 million or more abortions performed on United States women and their babies.

Every single one of these abortions violently ended the life of an American baby, as I see it. Last year, the Golden Age year of 1997, saw abortion "clinics" and hospitals end the lives of about 1.4 million American babies.

PERSPECTIVES ON ABORTION

Now, I want to be the first to admit that not everyone sees abortion as the ending of a life. There are probably some people who still see a baby in the womb as unfeeling tissue, like a mole or subcutaneous fat. They see the baby in the sonogram looking like a baby and they don't believe it's a baby. They see the baby reacting to a needle and moving away from it and they don't think it's a life. They know that a baby in the womb relaxes when she or he hears soothing music and they don't think there's a baby there. There are people who know that babies look just like postpartum babies very soon after conception, when they are still in the womb, and have a strong sense of pain, but those people can still call an abortion something other than the violent killing of a baby. None so blind as those who will not see, goes the adage.

Of course, there are also people who realize very well that a baby is a life in being, but honestly say that these lives are silent, have no votes, and are entitled to less legal and moral protection than the lives of grownups. If these pre-born lives are inconvenient, goes the reasoning of this group, then it is the right of the mother to kill her child. This is a brutal, but honest, approach.

And, of course, there are those who believe that the killing of about a million and a half babies per year is worthwhile if it saves a handful of women from being killed or maimed in illegal abortions. Never mind that every one of those babies is maimed and killed in an abortion, so that you really have a calculus in which the lives of about a hundred thousand babies are traded for the lives of one grown woman. But this quantum of people who see abortion as something other than gruesome, who believe it is justified for the convenience of adults and adolescents, and who will kill any number to save a tiny number, are in an interesting position: they cannot look at their handiwork or the handiwork they defend.

Across the country, they shrink from photos of the babies killed in abortions. Through their mighty political groups, the pro-abortionists compel TV stations to refuse advertisements showing partial birth and other abortion artifacts. They will not even allow viewers (or themselves, I suspect) to see what their policies have wrought. They are, at least to my mind, like the Germans who refused to think about what was happening at Dachau and then vomited when they saw—and never wanted to see again.

Abortion Takes Innocent Lives

For the rest of us, who see abortion as the violent taking of innocent life, it is hard indeed to see our era as a Golden Age. How would we feel if a disease claimed a million and a half unborn lives every year? Would we think we were in a Golden Age? How would we feel if an enemy invader killed a million and a half of our unborn every year?

I know that there are intelligent people who disagree strongly with what I say here. I used to disagree strongly myself—before we had our own adopted son, before we saw what might have been sucked out and ground up in a "clinic" or "women's health centers" (most absurd terms for killing rooms for little girls and boys), before we learned what everyone now knows about just how alive a baby in the womb is. But I think any intelligent man or woman who thinks about just the possibility that abortion is murder will have a hard time stopping before the terminus of the notion that it is murder. And for those who don't care to make the trip down that road, perhaps you can imagine the feelings of the tens of millions of us who see clearly that abortion is a violent killing of the most innocent of humans. Perhaps you can see why some of us don't see this as "A Golden Age"—and why we won't see it that way as long as the killing goes on, no matter how high the market goes. I love the high market, but it's dirt compared with life.

"It is time to recognize the murder case against abortion for what it is: a stupendous vaudeville of moral folly."

ABORTION IS NOT MURDER

Paul Savoy

People who support abortion rights have failed to convincingly argue for abortion in moral terms, argues Paul Savoy in the following viewpoint. He questions the inference—held by many on both sides of the abortion question—that if the fetus is a person, abortion must therefore be murder. Abortion, he asserts, is best seen as the refusal to let one's body be used as a life support system. Refusing to perform such a nine-month act of self-sacrifice may be a selfish decision, but it is not equivalent to murder. Savoy is an attorney and former law professor at Southwestern University in Los Angeles and the University of California at Davis.

As you read, consider the following questions:

1. What argument of Judith Jarvis Thomson does Savoy utilize?
2. Why is the moral status of an unborn child irrelevant to the abortion question, according to the author?
3. What sort of ethical framework should be used to discuss the morality of abortion, according to Savoy?

Excerpted from Paul Savoy, "The Coming New Debate on Abortion," Tikkun, September/October 1993. Reprinted from Tikkun: A Bi-Monthly Jewish Critique of Politics, Culture & Society.

I s abortion murder? It is generally assumed, even by pro-choice advocates, that if the fetus is a person with an individual right to life, then abortion is murder. Justice Harry Blackmun, in his opinion for the Supreme Court in *Roe v.Wade*, had no doubt about the validity of this assumption. "If this suggestion of personhood is established," Blackmun wrote, "the [pro-choice] case collapses, for the fetus' right to life is then guaranteed specifically by the [Fourteenth] Amendment." Yet it is not exactly clear how one gets from the premise that a fetus is a person to the conclusion that abortion is murder. Perhaps the step appears so simple and obvious those on both sides of the debate assume that no explanation is required. The step is neither easy nor obvious, however. And if we subject it to closer moral scrutiny, we shall find that we are not only inclined to reject it, but that treating the unborn child as a person with an individual right to life, far from conceding victory to the pro-life lobby, actually exposes the abortion-is-murder argument as a radical failure of moral reasoning. Indeed, it is the unwillingness of abortion rights advocates to face up to the issue of abortion in the moral terms that pro-lifers have posed it that has substantially contributed to the moral vulnerability of the pro-choice position.

WITHHOLDING LIFE SUPPORT

More than twenty years ago, before the Supreme Court decided *Roe v.Wade*, Judith Jarvis Thomson, a philosophy professor at the Massachusetts Institute of Technology, offered an analogy to counter the image of woman as Terminator. In an article in *Philosophy and Public Affairs*, Thomson asked the reader to imagine waking up one morning and finding oneself in bed with a famous and unconscious violinist suffering from a fatal kidney ailment.

You discover, to your dismay, that the circulatory system of the unconscious violinist has been connected to your healthy kidneys by means of a tube, a feat accomplished while you slept so that you had in no way consented to the procedure. You had simply been selected by the Society of Music Lovers, because of your blood type and other favorable conditions, to serve as a kind of human dialysis machine. If you were then to demand that you be immediately disconnected from the violinist, the attending physician might reply with an argument that is familiar to participants in the abortion debate: The violinist is a *person*, and since disconnecting his circulatory system from your kidneys would result in his death, it cannot be permitted. Moreover, you cannot plead self-defense since the violinist is unconscious and not personally guilty of any aggression against you.

Unplugging him would therefore constitute murder.

Such an argument, Professor Thomson suggested, would strike most readers as ridiculous. Yet it is, in principle, indistinguishable from the abortion-is-murder argument. Whatever the imperfections in Thomson's lucid analogy—some might argue that a woman who voluntarily engages in intercourse is responsible for the life she conceives—the metaphor of pregnant woman as human dialysis machine succeeds in making one point perfectly clear: An abortion is closer to the refusal to allow one's body to be used as a life support system than it is to an ax murder by the local butcher.

THE ALIEN METAPHOR

Another metaphor that counters the devaluation of women by anti-abortion forces can be found in *Alien*, that ultimate sci-fi horror story of the reproductive cycle. In the film, the offspring of an unwanted pregnancy is portrayed as an intruder into the last frontier of inner space, resembling a penis with teeth bursting out of the chest cavity in a kind of equal-opportunity Caesarean. Has there ever been a more graphic statement of the unspoken facts of fertility? "Many women, good mothers, who become unwillingly pregnant, speak of the fetus they carry as an invader, a tumor, a thing to be removed," Sallie Tisdale wrote in a sobering meditation in *Vogue* on the reproductive experience as an act of invasion as much as love. Whatever moral status may be ascribed to an unborn child—alien invader, innocent human being, or a person with a right to life—no one has the right to use another's body as a life support system without her consent. It is time to recognize the murder case against abortion for what it is: a stupendous vaudeville of moral folly.

But are pro-choice advocates, in their strenuous defense of the right not to sustain unborn life, committing another kind of moral folly? Those of us who oppose legal restrictions on abortion but wish to address the issue as a moral question, as a decision made in the context of a morally lived life, must ask ourselves whether failing to nurture the life of an unborn child simply perpetuates the pervasive ethos of selfishness in our society. How can communities of care and mutual aid treat the refusal of aid to unborn life as a choice worthy of moral respect?

A DIFFERENT ETHICAL FRAMEWORK

One answer is that the question mistakenly assumes that acting selfishly is always immoral. To deny the ailing violinist the benefit of my kidneys is no doubt a selfish act. It would be a marvelous act of caring, if not saintliness, were I to spend the next nine months keeping the violinist alive by letting him remain hooked up to my body. But should I decide to unplug the violinist, my decision could hardly be characterized as immoral, even though disconnecting him resulted in his death.

This is not to deny the value of nurturing human life. It is merely to say that the debate about the morality of abortion must undergo a change of venue: from the ethical framework that governs the duty to refrain from killing, to the community of values that informs the duty of self-sacrifice. If the kind of self-sacrifice that pro-life ethics would impose on a pregnant woman were enforced in a nondiscriminatory manner by a Uniform Code of Altruism, we would have to construct a barbed-wire fence around the United States and declare it a federal penitentiary.

| "[*Abortion*] is certainly the best solution in a case of rape."

RAPE JUSTIFIES ABORTION

Barbara Hernandez

Barbara Hernandez is the pseudonym of a woman who was raped, became pregnant, and subsequently decided to have an abortion. Now a teacher, she recounts in the following viewpoint the events that led to her decision to abort her pregnancy and to change her opinion on abortion. Abortion is a personal decision that is the best option in some circumstances and should remain legal, she concludes.

As you read, consider the following questions:

1. How did Hernandez respond emotionally to her experiences of rape and abortion?
2. According to the author, why did her doctor recommend that she get an abortion?
3. Why should abortion remain legal, according to Hernandez?

Excerpted from Barbara Hernandez, "That Terrible Night," in *Abortion: My Choice, God's Grace: Christian Women Tell Their Stories*, edited by Anne Eggebroten, published by New Paradigm Books, PO Box 60008, Pasadena, CA 91116; Tel: (626) 792-6123; fax: (626) 792-2121; e-mail: hopepub@loop.com; web site: http://www.hope-pub.com. Copyright ©1994 Anne Eggebroten. Reprinted with permission.

That terrible night will haunt me for the rest of my life. On March 19, 1989, I went to San Antonio, Texas, on a business trip for a child development workshop. At the time I was a student at the University of Texas at Austin.

My married sister lived in San Antonio, so I decided to stay with her for the weekend. Arriving at her house, however, I found she had suddenly gone to my parents' home for the weekend. Only my brother-in-law was there, so I changed my mind. I would only stay overnight. I knew the workshop would finish late, and I didn't want to drive back to Austin alone at night.

When I got to my sister's after the child development meetings I was tired, but I decided to prepare dinner for my brother-in-law and me. After eating, I sat in the living room for a while watching television. My brother-in-law, Joe, thought I was bored and asked if there was any place I would like to go for a drink or dancing. I was very tired and decided to stay home. He still went out.

THE RAPE

Later that night, while I was in bed asleep, I heard a noise. Someone was opening the front door. Automatically I realized it was Joe, so I didn't get up to check, and fell back to sleep. I then heard the noise again. My bedroom door was opening and someone's tall shadow was standing there. I saw it was just Joe, so I relaxed, thinking he was getting something from the closet. Then I realized that he was approaching the bed. In that instant my eyes flew open and my heart started pumping fast. I was scared and confused about what he was up to. I asked him what was wrong. He answered that he wanted to be in bed with me. I could not believe my ears, but as soon as I realized what he had said, I jumped out of the bed and went toward the bedroom door. Before I reached it, he grabbed me and pushed me harshly on the bed.

I was frightened, screaming and crying and hoping some neighbor would hear my screams and come to help me. No one heard. Meanwhile my brother-in-law was struggling to take my clothes off. Because I was fighting back so hard, I was using up all my strength. I was kicking and hitting him and trying to get away, but he was so strong that nothing was successful. Still I kept fighting him back, but it made him more ferocious; he pushed me harder on the bed and took advantage of me. Joe attacked me sexually. I felt terrible—I just wanted to die.

When he was done, with the little strength I had left, I dragged myself out of the bed and ran into the bathroom and locked myself in. I was so frightened that I didn't want to come out and ended up staying there until I heard no noise in the house.

Finally I crept out cautiously, making sure Joe was not around. In the bedroom I got dressed as fast as I could and ran out of the house so quickly I fell down the steps. I drove off and stopped at the nearest phone booth to call my brother. Because I was crying so hard, he could hardly understand me. I managed to get the story out. It took a few moments for him to absorb the shock. When he finally found his voice, I could feel his anger towards Joe as well as his sorrow for me.

The night was beginning to fade into dawn and I still had to drive back to Austin. On my way back I kept getting flashbacks to the terror of that night. A few minutes after I reached my apartment, my brother arrived. He took me to the doctor and also took care of all the legal procedures for our brother-in-law to be punished for what he had done. He also informed my parents and my sister that I had been raped and by whom. What had happened was so hard and painful for everyone in my family to believe. Everyone felt anger and hatred toward Joe and concern about me.

SHOCKING NEWS

I stayed in shock for several weeks, not only because of what had happened but also because of the doctor's later report. In the initial exam the doctor had performed a complete physical. I had been torn and bruised during the attack, but she wasn't sure whether I would have any long-term problems. When I returned to her office a few weeks later, she did another physical exam. This time the results were terrifying: I was pregnant. My heart stopped when she told me the news.

What a difficult position I was in. I had to make a decision on whether I was going to go through with this pregnancy. I was scared and confused because I believed that abortion was an immoral act, a sin. In fact, having been a Catholic all my life, I saw abortion as murder. I had not given the issue much thought, yet suddenly I had to decide whether I myself was to have an abortion.

Because of the circumstances of my rape, the doctor was totally against my continuing the pregnancy. She explained to me that in these circumstances I did not have to feel guilty if I chose an abortion. She presented it as a way to save my life, my sanity. It would not be murder. She was very clear that by no means should I go through with the pregnancy. She said that if I did, there would be chances of my not living a normal life because the flashbacks from my terrible experience would continue. Finally a joint decision was made by the doctor, my parents and me and an abortion was performed.

At first I felt guilty. I had ended a life that was just beginning. But gradually I realized that because of my circumstances, it was better for both the embryo and me.

A PERSONAL DECISION

I now believe that abortion is a decision that may come from a woman's unique set of circumstances. It is certainly the best solution in a case of rape or serious deformity. In my situation it was the answer. This is why the legal status of abortion must remain as it is. Because of my experience, I support the laws permitting abortion. It is up to the woman to evaluate her circumstances and determine whether she is to continue her pregnancy or terminate it. I had to make that decision.

| *"Abortion only re-victimizes women who have been raped."*

RAPE DOES NOT JUSTIFY ABORTION

American Life League

The following viewpoint is taken from a pamphlet by the American Life League in which it argues that rape does not justify abortion. Regardless of the circumstances of conception, an innocent life is still being taken. In addition, the organization asserts that abortion does nothing to heal the emotional trauma that rape victims experience, and may in fact make their situations worse. The American Life League is a national organization that opposes abortion.

As you read, consider the following questions:

1. What is the only "authentic" pro-life position, according to the American Life League?
2. What effects, according to the American Life League, does abortion have on rape victims?
3. How common is pregnancy resulting from rape, according to the American Life League?

Reprinted, with permission, from *Abortion: Not Even When the Pregnancy Is the Result of a Rape?* A 1995 *American Life League* pamphlet. (Endnotes in the original have been omitted in this reprint.)

> Opponents of abortion rights walk a fine line when they condone any abortion. Based on their own definition, they are guilty of being accessories to "murder" in certain circumstances by accepting rape and incest exceptions.

This quote from the Religious Coalition for Abortion Rights (now the Religious Coalition for Reproductive Choice) shows that even they recognize the inconsistency of making exceptions to the pro-life position!

Human life begins at conception. Pro-life people take this fact seriously, and understand it to mean—as it does mean—that the person living inside the womb is as real as you or I. Therefore, the preborn child must be treated equally, and be given the same protection you and I enjoy under our Constitution.

WHAT ABOUT RAPE?

It is wrong to discriminate against people who have been born because of the manner in which they came into the world, and it is also wrong to discriminate against preborn people by attempting to justify abortion in cases where the mother has been raped. Sadly, sometimes people who otherwise believe that the preborn child deserves the right to life fail to see a preborn child conceived through rape as fully human. An authentic pro-life position rejects abortion in any circumstances!

A CLOSER LOOK

Why do some people believe abortion can be justified in the case of rape? Some people believe in good faith that when rape results in pregnancy, abortion can remove the painful evidence of that rape. But will it?

Will abortion erase the memory of the rape or heal the emotional and physical pain of the assault? Will abortion, in effect, erase the rape of a woman? Hardly. Rape is an act of violence inflicted upon a woman. She is an innocent victim, and this knowledge may someday help her come to terms with the rape and rebuild her life. Abortion, on the other hand, is an act of violence that a mother inflicts on her own child. Through abortion, the mother becomes the aggressor, and this knowledge may haunt her long after she has dealt with the rape.

Abortion only re-victimizes women who have been raped. Anyone who thinks abortion is justified for rape victims should consider the following:

This new human being, who is uniquely the mother's child, may well be the only good—the only healing—that will come to this woman from her rape experience. The woman deserves affirmation, love and time to recover from the assault. Her baby is not a monster, and telling a woman that her best option is to get rid of her baby as soon as possible may only reinforce in her mind the idea that she is dirty, or a monster, herself.

In any pregnancy, the preborn child stimulates hormones in the mother's body to nurture the baby. These hormones often cause wide mood swings, which are especially influential to the mother who has been traumatized by rape and is aghast at the thought of being pregnant. The bonding between the mother and child that often occurs in pregnancy hasn't yet made the child seem "real" to the mother, real though the child is, and abortion seems to be a quick fix.

THE TRAUMA CAUSED BY RAPE

Counselors who work with rape victims are familiar with the emotional trauma many women undergo as a result of rape. According to authors Sandra Makhorn and William Dolan, a woman often believes "that she is somehow tainted, dirty, and dehumanized" and knows "that many will see her either as pitiful and helpless or as disgusting and defiled." It has been reported that women who have had abortions often deal with exactly the same psychological symptoms as the rape victim: depression, guilt, low self-esteem, uncontrollable sadness and withdrawal.

The "quick fix" abortion "solution" is condescending and can only serve to reaffirm the sense of helplessness and vulnerability. Makhorn asserts that "Attitudes projected by others and not the pregnancy itself pose the central problem to the pregnant victim." When the trauma of rape is compounded by the trauma of abortion, it is hardly possible that abortion will lessen the emotional impact of the assault.

Many people mistakenly believe that pregnancy resulting from rape is very common. For a number of reasons, however, only a small number of women become pregnant as a result of sexual assault. Why? Many factors affect female fertility. Not only does age affect it, but so does a woman's natural cycle, which renders her able to conceive only approximately 4 to 6 days out of the month, and severe emotional trauma, which may prevent ovulation. Factors affecting male fertility include sexual dysfunction, and drug and alcohol use. It is estimated that, on average, only 0.49 percent—or one-half of one percent—of women who are raped become pregnant as a result.

It is a cruel irony that while a father cannot receive the death penalty for the crime of rape, his preborn child conceived in that rape can be executed without trial, jury or judge. Moreover, justice to the mother will not be achieved by sending her to the local abortion clinic to solve her problem. A mother's real needs must be met. Providing life-affirming medical, financial and emotional care meets these needs, and pro-life groups around the country . . . are doing this work.

No Exceptions

Pro-lifers are hypocrites if they condemn the murder of a pre-born child in one circumstance but allow it in another. Think for a moment about your circle of friends. Can you tell just by looking at them how they were conceived? If one had been conceived in rape, would you treat him or her differently? Of course not. Regardless of how a life begins, each person is as valuable as the next. It is no different with preborn children's lives. They are valuable because they are human beings.

| "Over one hundred potential
complications have been associated
with induced abortion."

HAVING AN ABORTION CAN BE HARMFUL TO A WOMAN'S HEALTH

David C. Reardon

David C. Reardon is a medical ethicist and author of several books on abortion, including *Aborted Women, Silent No More* and *Making Abortion Rare: A Healing Strategy for a Divided Nation*. He argues that medical studies have shown that abortion causes physical and psychological harms among many of the millions of women who have undergone the procedure. Potential side effects and risks of abortion include infections, infertility, and severe emotional distress. Public health policy toward abortion must be reevaluated in light of these risks, he concludes.

As you read, consider the following questions:

1. What assumptions about the safety of abortion have guided national abortion policy, according to Reardon?
2. What are some of the physical and psychological complications of abortion, according to the author?
3. In Reardon's opinion, why do many women choose to have abortions?

Reprinted from David C. Reardon, "The Aftereffects of Abortion," 1990 brochure from the Elliot Institute, at http://www.afterabortion.org/complic.html, by permission of the author.

In 1973 the United States Supreme Court struck down every federal, state, and local law regulating or restricting the practice of abortion. This action was based on the premise that the states no longer had any need to regulate abortion because the advances of modern medicine had now made abortion "relatively safe." Therefore, the Justices concluded, it is unconstitutional to prevent physicians from providing abortions as a "health" service to women.

National abortion policy is built upon this judicial "fact" that abortion is a "safe" procedure. If this "fact" is found to be false, then national policy toward abortion must be re-evaluated. Indeed, if it is found that abortion may actually be dangerous to health of women, there is just cause for governments to regulate or prohibit abortion in order to protect their citizens. This is especially true since over 1.5 million women undergo abortions each year.

Since the Court's ruling in 1973, there have been many studies into the aftereffects of abortion. Their combined results paint a haunting picture of physical and psychological damage among millions of women who have undergone abortions.

The Physical Complications of Abortion

National statistics on abortion show that 10% of women undergoing induced abortion suffer from immediate complications, of which one-fifth (2%) were considered major.

Over one hundred potential complications have been associated with induced abortion. "Minor" complications include: minor infections, bleeding, fevers, chronic abdominal pain, gastrointestinal disturbances, vomiting, and Rh sensitization. The nine most common "major" complications which are infection, excessive bleeding, embolism, ripping or perforation of the uterus, anesthesia complications, convulsions, hemorrhage, cervical injury, and endotoxic shock.

In a series of 1,182 abortions which occurred under closely regulated hospital conditions, 27 percent of the patients acquired post-abortion infection lasting 3 days or longer.

While the immediate complications of abortion are usually treatable, these complications frequently lead to long-term reproductive damage of much more serious nature.

For example, one possible outcome of abortion related infections is sterility. Researchers have reported that 3 to 5 percent of aborted women are left inadvertently sterile as a result of the operation's latent morbidity. The risk of sterility is even greater for women who are infected with a venereal disease at the time of the abortion.

In addition to the risk of sterility, women who acquire post-abortal infections are five to eight times more likely to experience ectopic pregnancies. Between 1970–1983, the rate of ectopic pregnancies in USA has risen 4 fold. Twelve percent of all maternal deaths are due to ectopic pregnancy. Other countries which have legalized abortion have seen the same dramatic increase in ectopic pregnancies.

Cervical damage is another leading cause of long-term complications following abortion. Normally the cervix is rigid and tightly closed. In order to perform an abortion, the cervix must be stretched open with a great deal of force. During this forced dilation there is almost always microscopic tearing of the cervix muscles and occasionally severe ripping of the uterine wall, as well.

According to one hospital study, 12.5% of first trimester abortions required stitching for cervical lacerations. Such attention to detail is not normally provided at an outpatient abortion clinic. Another study found that lacerations occurred in 22 percent of aborted women. Women under 17 have been found to face twice the normal risk of suffering cervical damage due to the fact that their cervixes are still "green" and developing.

Whether microscopic or macroscopic in nature, the cervical damage which results during abortion frequently results in a permanent weakening of the cervix. This weakening may result in an "incompetent cervix" which, unable to carry the weight of a later "wanted" pregnancy, opens prematurely, resulting in miscarriage or premature birth. According to one study, symptoms related to cervical incompetence were found among 75% of women who undergo forced dilation for abortion.

Cervical damage from previously induced abortions increases the risks of miscarriage, premature birth, and complications of labor during later pregnancies by 300–500 percent. The reproductive risks of abortion are especially acute for women who abort their first pregnancies. A major study of first pregnancy abortions found that 48% of women experienced abortion-related complications in later pregnancies. Women in this group experienced 2.3 miscarriages for every one live birth. Yet another researcher found that among teenagers who aborted their first pregnancies, 66% subsequently experienced miscarriages or premature birth of their second, "wanted" pregnancies.

When the risks of increased pregnancy loss are projected on the population as a whole, it is estimated that aborted women lose 100,000 "wanted" pregnancies each year because of latent abortion morbidity. In addition, premature births, complications

72

of labor, and abnormal development of the placenta, all of which can result from latent abortion morbidity, are leading causes of handicaps among newborns. Looking at premature deliveries alone, it is estimated that latent abortion morbidity results in 3000 cases of acquired cerebral palsy among newborns each year. Finally, since these pregnancy problems pose a threat to the health of the mothers too, women who have had abortions face a 58 percent greater risk of dying during a later pregnancy.

THE PSYCHOLOGICAL EFFECTS OF ABORTION

Researchers investigating post-abortion reactions report only one positive emotion: relief. This emotion is understandable, especially in light of the fact that the majority of aborting women report feeling under intense pressure to "get it over with."

Temporary feelings of relief are frequently followed by a period psychiatrists identify as emotional "paralysis," or post-abortion "numbness." Like shell-shocked soldiers, these aborted women are unable to express or even feel their own emotions. Their focus is primarily on having survived the ordeal, and they are at least temporarily out of touch with their feelings.

Studies within the first few weeks after the abortion have found that between 40 and 60 percent of women questioned report negative reactions. Within 8 weeks after their abortions, 55% expressed guilt, 44% complained of nervous disorders, 36% had experienced sleep disturbances, 31% had regrets about their decision, and 11% had been prescribed psychotropic medicine by their family doctor.

In one study of 500 aborted women, researchers found that 50 percent expressed negative feelings, and up to 10 percent were classified as having developed "serious psychiatric complications."

Thirty to fifty percent of aborted women report experiencing sexual dysfunctions, of both short and long duration, beginning immediately after their abortions. These problems may include one or more of the following: loss of pleasure from intercourse, increased pain, an aversion to sex and/or males in general, or the development of a promiscuous life-style.

Up to 33 percent of aborted women develop an intense longing to become pregnant again in order to "make up" for the lost pregnancy, with 18 percent succeeding within one year of the abortion. Unfortunately, many women who succeed at obtaining their "wanted" replacement pregnancies discover that the same problems which pressured them into having their first abortion still exist, and so they end up feeling "forced" into yet another abortion.

In a study of teenage abortion patients, half suffered a worsening of psychosocial functioning within 7 months after the abortion. The immediate impact appeared to be greatest on the patients who were under 17 years of age and for those with previous psychosocial problems. Symptoms included: self-reproach, depression, social regression, withdrawal, obsession with need to become pregnant again, and hasty marriages.

The best available data indicates that on average there is a five to ten year period of denial during which a woman who was traumatized by her abortion will repress her feelings. During this time, the woman may go to great lengths to avoid people, situations, or events which she associates with her abortion and she may even become vocally defensive of abortion in order to convince others, and herself, that she made the right choice and is satisfied with the outcome. In reality, these women who are subsequently identified as having been severely traumatized, have failed to reach a true state of "closure" with regard to their experiences.

Repressed feelings of any sort can result in psychological and behavioral difficulties which exhibit themselves in other areas of one's life. An increasing number of counselors are reporting that unacknowledged post-abortion distress is the causative factor in many of their female patients, even though their patients have come to them seeking therapy for seemingly unrelated problems.

Other women who would otherwise appear to have been satisfied with their abortion experience, are reported to enter into emotional crisis decades later with the onset of menopause or after their youngest child leaves home.

Numerous researchers have reported that postabortion crises are often precipitated by the anniversary date of the abortion or the unachieved "due date." These emotional crises may appear to be inexplicable and short-lived, occurring for many years until a connection is finally established during counseling sessions.

A 5 year retrospective study in two Canadian provinces found that 25% of aborted women made visits to psychiatrists as compared to 3% of the control group.

Women who have undergone post-abortion counseling report over 100 major reactions to abortion. Among the most frequently reported are: depression, loss of self-esteem, self-destructive behavior, sleep disorders, memory loss, sexual dysfunction, chronic problems with relationships, dramatic personality changes, anxiety attacks, guilt and remorse, difficulty grieving, increased tendency toward violence, chronic crying, difficulty concentrating, flashbacks, loss of interest in previously enjoyed activities and people, and difficulty bonding with later children.

Among the most worrisome of these reactions is the increase of self-destructive behavior among aborted women. In a survey of over 100 women who had suffered from post-abortion trauma, fully 80 percent expressed feelings of "self-hatred." In the same study, 49 percent reported drug abuse and 39 percent began to use or increased their use of alcohol. Approximately 14 percent described themselves as having become "addicted" or "alcoholic" after their abortions. In addition, 60 percent reported suicidal ideation, with 28 percent actually attempting suicide, of which half attempted suicide two or more times.

| "Despite the statistical safety of abortion ... health issues are now part of the debate over the procedure."

THE HARMS OF HAVING AN ABORTION HAVE BEEN EXAGGERATED

Sharon Lerner

Abortion opponents have exaggerated the health risks of abortion in order to discourage pregnant women from having the procedure, argues Sharon Lerner in the following viewpoint. Claims that abortion causes breast cancer, fertility problems, and psychological trauma are not supported by the best medical evidence, she maintains, asserting that abortion providers are competent medical professionals who have an excellent safety record. Lerner is a freelance writer specializing in health issues.

As you read, consider the following questions:

1. What, according to Lerner, are the goals and methods of "crisis pregnancy centers"?
2. What have studies indicated about the link between abortion and breast cancer, according to the author?
3. What is the most important influence of a woman's emotional state following an abortion, according to Lerner?

Reprinted from Sharon Lerner, "The Truth About Abortion and a Woman's Health," *Glamour*, November 1997, by permission of the author.

"The medical field doesn't want you to know how dangerous abortion really is." Karen McCubbin, director of the Susan B. Anthony Women's Centre in Denton, Texas, is trying to talk me out of having an abortion. I have come to this new "crisis pregnancy center" to find out what pro-life counselors are telling pregnant women these days. McCubbin has gently asked if I think having an abortion is right for me. Then, with very little prompting, she urges me to consider these "facts": "The procedure is done completely blind. The doctor is on the outside and all the instruments are on the inside, and many girls have punctured uteruses and hemorrhaging." My cervix might be torn or lacerated, she continues. I might never be able to have children afterward. I could suffer any number of other serious complications while on the operating table. The chances that my intestines could be pulled out are "good," for instance. "I don't have the numbers right here in front of me," McCubbin says, "but that's a real common one."

Or I might end up "like a drooling vegetable," she warns, handing me a copy of *Christi's Choice*, a video that describes an 18-year-old who suffered cardiac and respiratory arrest during an abortion and is now blind and brain-damaged, unable to walk, talk or care for herself. "No abortionists have to be trained in anesthesia," McCubbin explains. "I know as much about it as they do."

Like many of the 3,500 loosely allied crisis pregnancy centers in the United States, the Susan B. Anthony Women's Centre is situated right next door to a real abortion provider, Denton Women's Health Services, and advertises under "abortion alternatives" in the Yellow Pages. By offering counseling, free car seats and other maternity gear, it aims to give women an incentive to carry their pregnancies to term. But the Susan B. Anthony Centre goes far beyond simply hoping its driveway will be mistaken for that of its next door neighbor.

ALLEGED RISKS

Through its parent organization, Life Dynamics, it also funds and distributes research on the alleged risks of abortion to women's health. It offers free legal help to any woman who feels she's been physically or psychologically damaged by abortion. Lawyers who agree to prosecute abortion-malpractice cases—Life Dynamics claims that 87 cases are pending—have access to office space at the center, as well as to dossiers on individual doctors, lists of expert witnesses and animated videos of botched abortions to present in court.

Mark Crutcher, Life Dynamics' founder and president, has said he hopes to force abortion doctors out of business by driving up their malpractice insurance rates. So far, he hasn't succeeded—rates for providers haven't budged. But by styling himself as a women's-health advocate, Crutcher has already achieved one goal: He has successfully opened a new front in the legislative war on abortion.

Despite the statistical safety of abortion—"It's about as dangerous as having a shot of penicillin and more than 10 times safer than childbirth." says Stanley Henshaw, deputy director of research at the Alan Guttmacher Institute, a reproductive health think tank—health issues are now part of the debate over the procedure. Bills requiring doctors to warn patients about a purported link between abortion and breast cancer have been introduced in at least eight states since January 1997. And at least seven state legislatures have considered laws to require warnings about abortion-related psychological harm. The upshot: Pro-choice activists must now fend off health-related legislative actions as well as protect abortion providers and patients from violence and harassment. . . .

With seemingly all abortion-related health information filtered through a political lens, it's hard to know what—or whom—to believe. Here, a hard look at the evidence.

ABORTION AND BREAST CANCER

True or false? Abortion causes breast cancer.

"Women who choose abortion suffer more and deadlier breast cancer." That's what Christ's Bride Ministries, a pro-life group based in Virginia, announced in 1996 on billboards and buses from Massachusetts to Florida. A widely distributed pamphlet, "Before You Choose: The Link Between Abortion and Breast Cancer," makes a similar case. "Millions of induced abortions around the world," it reads, can account for "the mysterious jump in the breast cancer rate."

The question of whether an induced or spontaneous abortion might contribute to a woman's chances of developing breast cancer intrigued scientists long before abortion opponents seized upon it. In general, the more estrogen a woman is exposed to, the greater her breast cancer risk—that's why women who enter puberty early and menopause late have higher rates of the disease. During pregnancy, estrogen production increases sharply. Later in pregnancy, however, breast tissue "matures" in a cellular process called differentiation, which both readies the breasts for nursing and seems to offer protection against cancerous changes. Women who have carried a pregnancy to term at a young age tend to have lower rates of breast cancer than those who have never been pregnant or who delayed pregnancy until their thirties.

Some scientists theorized that women who miscarried or aborted would experience a surge of estrogen without the benefit of differentiation. But years of research failed to prove that this translated into an increased risk of breast cancer.

In 1996, Karin Michels, an epidemiologist at Harvard Medical School, analyzed more than 40 studies, spanning some 40 years, of the link between abortion and breast cancer. The studies were so inconsistent—some showed double the rate of breast cancer in women who had had abortions, others showed an opposite effect or no association at all—that Michels and her coauthors concluded that the research was probably contaminated with "reporting bias." Women with breast cancer, they noted, are concerned with discovering its cause, and are thus more likely than women without a disease to accurately report their medical histories—including a history of abortion. Since numerous other studies have shown that healthy women often fail to disclose abortions—especially if they took place before the procedure was legal—this alone could account for the different breast cancer rates in the two groups.

Most recently, a groundbreaking Danish study, published in 1997 in the *New England Journal of Medicine*, managed to eliminate the problem of reporting bias by analyzing the actual medical records of more than one million women. It found that abortion had no overall effect on breast cancer. Says Boston University epidemiologist Lynn Rosenberg, "This is really strong evidence."

The Danish study did pique interest in a tiny subset of women —less than one percent of the million women studied—who had abortions after the first 18 weeks of pregnancy and who did have slightly higher rates of the disease. While future studies will probe the phenomenon, Michels says, "I don't give much credence to that result; it pertains to too small a group." It is also possible that women who had late abortions may have had other health problems predisposing them to breast cancer.

So little is known about the causes of breast cancer that epidemiologists are reluctant to call the issue completely settled. But the National Cancer Institute, the American Cancer Society, the American College of Obstetricians and Gynecologists (ACOG) and the National Breast Cancer Coalition have all agreed that, as ACOG notes, "Evidence is insufficient to support claims that induced abortion has an effect on the later development of breast cancer."...

DILATION AND EXTRACTION ABORTIONS

True or false? D and X abortions pose more risks to women than other methods.

In what may be the bitterest—and most confusing—abortion battle yet, pro-life groups have lobbied hard to ban one particular method, which they call "partial-birth abortion" and which doctors refer to as intact dilation and extraction or D and X. Done between the sixteenth and twenty-sixth weeks of pregnancy, the procedure—which most doctors say is rarely performed—involves dilating the cervix, collapsing and emptying the fetal skull, and removing the fetus intact.

Opponents focus primarily on the admittedly gruesome technical details of the surgery, but the notion that it poses a risk to the woman has also crept into the debate. Nancy Romer, M.D., chair of the obstetrics and gynecology department at Miami Valley Hospital in Dayton, Ohio, and a member of Physicians' Ad Hoc Coalition for Truth, opposes the procedure primarily on philosophical grounds. Yet she also has "serious medical concerns" that D and X might injure the cervix and make it difficult for a woman to carry future pregnancies to term.

In May 1997 the American Medical Association (AMA) broke with its tradition of opposing legislation that interferes with a doctor's autonomy by announcing its support for a federal ban, passed by both houses of Congress in the same month. AMA spokesman John C. Nelson, M.D., called D and X a "crummy procedure" that could be easily replaced with equally appropriate, possibly safer methods for the very small percentage of abortions performed past 18 weeks.

But prominent experts in the field disagree. ACOG, among others, says that D and X is sometimes "the best or most appropriate method to save the life or preserve the health of a woman." Physicians for Reproductive Choice and Health says the contested technique is a "safer, less risky medical option during health- and life-threatening events that can occur during pregnancy," such as cancer, severe high blood pressure and respiratory, kidney, heart or liver failure.

The alternatives to D and X entail risks of their own, including those posed by induced labor and surgery. Phillip Stubblefield, M.D., chairman of obstetrics and gynecology at Boston Medical Center, believes that D and X may be the safest method of abortion in most pregnancies past 20 weeks. "Compared with other procedures, D and X decreases the fair risk you'll tear the uterine wall and injure the mother," he says.

Some women who have undergone more than one late-term abortion for a fetus with severe birth defects say there's another reason to preserve the D and X option. "It's terrible to say it was better," says a woman who had a previous second-trimester abortion by induction (in which labor is induced with injections of saline solution), "but D and X was much easier to endure. There was minimal pain.". . .

RU 486

True or false? RU 486 is dangerous for women.

At the Susan B. Anthony Centre, McCubbin refers to the abortion drug RU 486 (which recently completed U.S. clinical trials but is not yet on the market) as a "human pesticide." "That's what it's actually called in the field," she told me, shaking her head. "Usually you abort the baby at home and you have to carry it to the doctor. And girls die regularly from hemorrhaging."

Life Dynamics literature makes similar use of unsubstantiated health claims. In a memo mailed to 100,000 health professionals, Mark Crutcher claimed that RU 486 has a questionable safety record in other countries and was rushed through the Food and Drug Administration's (FDA's) preliminary approval process.

It's true that RU 486 has drawbacks: The drug is used only very early in pregnancy (up to seven or eight weeks) and it has a higher failure rate than surgical abortions—just under 5 percent versus under one percent. An abortion with RU 486 routinely involves heavy bleeding, cramps, nausea and vomiting, although the FDA knows of no deaths attributed to the procedure. And although a woman would never have to carry the tiny amount of tissue passed to her doctor, a medical abortion could take place in a woman's home.

In the French studies, only about two thirds of patients aborted in the first four hours after taking the contraction-inducing drug. The overwhelming majority of women who have used the method would choose it again, but the side effects contribute to slightly higher levels of dissatisfaction when compared with surgery.

The FDA announced September 1997 that RU 486 was a safe and effective method of abortion, based on its review of evidence from well over 200,000 medical abortions in France, Great Britain and Sweden, where it is already approved, and an additional 2,121 in trials in the United States. The review process was not rushed. "It took six months, so it was typical for a priority drug," says FDA spokesman Lawrence Bachorik. . . .

PSYCHOLOGICAL HARM

True or false? Abortion causes long-term psychological trauma.

Those bent on stopping abortions have focused especially on

its psychological after-effects, which are arguably murkier and harder to disprove. Psychotherapist Vincent Rue, Ph.D., codirector of the Institute for Pregnancy Loss in Portsmouth, New Hampshire, argues that some girls and women who have abortions suffer from a form of post-traumatic stress disorder he calls post-abortion syndrome, symptoms of which include depression, impulsive behavior, feelings of helplessness, low self-esteem, hostility and sexual dysfunction. Those who don't report such feelings, Rue has written, may be experiencing "psychic numbing."

The vast majority of psychological and psychiatric professionals disagree with Rue's assessment. "Postabortion syndrome" is not listed in the profession's bible of symptoms and diagnoses, *The Diagnostic and Statistical Manual–IV.* The largest study to dispute abortion's negative effects on mental health was published in the February 1997 issue of *Professional Psychology: Research and Practices.* Researchers looked at nearly 4,500 young women's responses to questionnaires before and after abortion. The most important influences on a woman's postabortion emotional state, they found, was her psychological state before abortion. Low income and lack of employment were related to low self-esteem. The more children a woman had, the more likely she was to suffer from depression. But having had an abortion did not appear to exacerbate preexisting psychological problems or cause new symptoms.

Nancy Felipe Russo, Ph.D., a psychology professor at Arizona State University in Tempe and one of the study's coauthors, acknowledges that an abortion—as well as an unwanted pregnancy—can be very stressful. "It's normal to feel sadness and regret as well as relief after an abortion," she says. But, Russo emphasizes, this is not the same as permanent psychological damage. "If a woman freely chooses an abortion and has friends, family members or counselors for support, she'll usually get through it just fine.". . .

ABORTION AND FERTILITY

True or false? Abortion can compromise fertility.

The Life Action Advocates Web site lists an increased risk of miscarriage in its section on physical complications of abortion. What it doesn't say: Because the study cited is 17 years old, it included many women who had illegal—and thus much riskier—abortions. More recent studies of women who have had legal abortions showed they had no higher rate of miscarriage than expected among women generally.

Women who terminate pregnancies in their teens or twenties

and then have trouble conceiving in their thirties may wrongly attribute their problems to past abortions. "Women often think that's the reason they're infertile. It's as if they think they're being punished," says Cecilia Schmidt-Sarosie, M.D., an infertility specialist at New York University School of Medicine. But experts say there's absolutely no evidence that an abortion without complications compromises fertility. Instead, the greatest threats to a woman's ability to have children are sexually transmitted diseases—now at epidemic levels—and advanced age.

Nevertheless, several states require doctors performing abortions to list these purported fertility dangers on informed consent forms. Such a law exists in Mississippi, where Joseph Booker Jr., M.D., is one of a handful of abortion providers. "I say the portion of the warning that's medically accurate," Dr. Booker reports, "but I really shouldn't have to say anything because it's a bunch of malarkey."

ABORTION PROVIDERS

True or false? Abortion providers are poorly trained medical outcasts.

Like many pro-life activists, Life Dynamics' Crutcher attacks abortion's safety by claiming that doctors who do them are outcasts from "legitimate" medical specialties. "Abortion is kind of like the last outpost," he told me. "That's where you go when your career is in shambles because of malpractice actions or just because you're a bad doctor and you can't get a practice going. Even [abortion supporters] say, 'All we get are the dregs and the washouts of the medical profession to work in an abortion clinic.'"

It's undeniable that the occupational hazards of providing abortions include violence and harassment, and that there is a nationwide shortage of providers as a result. "Many doctors who are pro-choice have been turned away from abortion practice," says Carole Joffe, Ph.D, a sociologist and author of *Doctors of Conscience: The Struggle to Provide Abortion Before and After Roe v. Wade.* "And a tiny proportion of people who enter to fill the void are inept. But the overwhelming majority of providers are extremely competent."

In fact, antiabortion hostility may even be contributing to abortion's safety. "It's precisely because of this cultural climate that abortion is now one of the most scrutinized—and safest—procedures in medicine," says Joffe.

CHAPTER 3

IS AFFIRMATIVE ACTION NECESSARY?

CHAPTER PREFACE

Affirmative action is one of the most controversial social policy issues to emerge in America in recent years. Ironically, both proponents and detractors of affirmative action generally profess agreement on the same overall goal: The United States should ensure equal opportunity for all its citizens in employment, education, and business opportunities. Supporters argue that, because of past and present discrimination against women and minorities, affirmative action programs in government, businesses, and schools are necessary to secure equal opportunity for these social groups. Opponents, however, contend that affirmative action in practice has evolved into a system of racial and gender preferences that exacerbate racial divisions and result in "reverse discrimination" against white males. Both sides accuse the other of misleading the public over the actual workings of affirmative action programs and of failing to uphold the equal opportunity ideal.

The term "affirmative action" was first used by the federal government in President John F. Kennedy's Executive Order 10925. That directive ordered federal contractors to "take affirmative action to ensure that applicants are employed, and employees are treated during their employment, without regard to their race, creed, color, or national origin." Since then, the term has come to encompass a wide array of social policies that have evolved through federal legislation, presidential actions, state and local laws, and the actions of private colleges and businesses—all aimed at proactively eliminating discriminatory barriers against women and minorities. Title VII of the 1964 Civil Rights Act established broad prohibitions against discrimination by race and gender in private employment and created the Equal Employment Opportunity Commission (EEOC) to receive and respond to complaints of discrimination. A series of executive orders and initiatives by Presidents Lyndon Johnson and Richard Nixon expanded affirmative action programs in the late 1960s and early 1970s. In 1970, for instance, Nixon directed that businesses who contracted with the federal government should set "specific goals and timetables" for minority employment. The Equal Employment Opportunity Act of 1972 extended Title VII protections to educational institutions, leading many colleges and universities to take measures to admit minorities in greater numbers.

By 1998 the federal government had no less then 160 affirmative action programs overseeing the hiring of government workers as well as the employment practices of companies contracted to do business with the federal government. In addition, affirmative action programs are embodied in state and local laws, are used extensively in college admissions, and have been embraced by corporations seeking to ensure a diverse workforce. Many civil rights leaders claim that affirmative action programs have been very successful in providing opportunities for minorities and women. "Extensive discrimination continues to permeate American society depriving women and people of color equal opportunity," according to a position paper of the Leadership Conference on Civil Rights. "Affirmative action programs in education, employment, and business help to even the playing field for women and people of color."

However, in the 1980s and 1990s a growing number of academics and political leaders have criticized affirmative action. They contend that such programs in practice give undue preferences and advantages to minorities and women in ways that run counter to American ideals of fairness and individual rights. Steven Yates, author of *Civil Wrongs: What Went Wrong with Affirmative Action*, asserts that in an effort to fight unjust discrimination against minorities and women, affirmative action programs have resorted to "equally unjust, equally harmful, and probably unconstitutional practices that give preference to some [minorities and women] at the expense of others [white men]." Critics of affirmative action also claim that such programs unfairly cast doubt on the achievements of those who benefit from them.

Opponents have succeeded in abolishing some affirmative action programs in recent years. In 1996 the University of California system did away with all racial preferences in its admissions policies, while the public colleges in the state of Texas were ordered to do so by a federal court. The numbers of blacks and Hispanics admitted and enrolled in universities in both states dropped precipitously. Some observers seized on these developments as evidence of the continued necessity of affirmative action programs, while others concluded that they demonstrate how much affirmative action had previously skewed the college admissions process. The viewpoints in this chapter discuss whether race should play a role in the college admissions process as well as other key questions in the course of debating the past and future of affirmative action.

| "Affirmative action has indeed proved helpful in leveling the playing field so that all Americans can pursue the American dream."

AFFIRMATIVE ACTION COUNTERS DISCRIMINATION

Hilary O. Shelton

Hilary O. Shelton is deputy director of the Washington Bureau of the National Association for the Advancement of Colored People (NAACP), America's oldest civil rights organization. In the following viewpoint, she argues that discrimination against women and minorities remains a significant social problem. Affirmative action programs—which she defines as efforts to integrate society by expanding educational and employment opportunities—have promoted equality of opportunity in employment, housing, and education for minorities and women. Opponents of affirmative action, Shelton asserts, have used misleading and deceptive arguments that associate affirmative action with racial quotas and reverse discrimination against whites.

As you read, consider the following questions:

1. What presidential executive orders created and expanded affirmative action, according to Shelton?
2. What examples of successful affirmative action programs does the author describe?
3. What response does Shelton make to the claims that affirmative action results in quotas and reverse discrimination?

From Hilary O. Shelton, "Affirmative Action: It's Still Needed." This article appeared in the June 1998 issue of, and is reprinted with permission from, The World & I, a publication of The Washington Times Corporation, copyright ©1998.

Do we still need affirmative action programs today? Absolutely, YES! If we are still committed, as a nation, to equal opportunity for all Americans regardless of race, gender, nationality, or handicap, we must have time-proven programs in place, providing a structured approach to full inclusion by all members of our vastly diverse population.

Affirmative action is necessary because discrimination is still very much a part of our country and our institutions. Some believe that equal opportunity programs such as affirmative action are no longer needed because discrimination no longer exists or because Title VII of the Civil Rights Act provides the necessary protections against discrimination.

Unfortunately, there are many misperceptions about exactly what affirmative action programs are set up to do, how they work, how successful they have been over the years, how fair they are, and how misrepresented these programs have been, both intentionally and unintentionally. Let me help address many of the myths, misunderstandings, distortions, and, in some cases, intentionally disingenuous interpretations of what affirmative action actually is and does.

What Is Affirmative Action

Affirmative action can be defined, in short, as any effort taken to fully integrate our society by expanding educational, employment, and contracting opportunities to the multitude of gender, ethnic, national origin, and handicapped-condition groups that have been and remain locked out of full economic, social, and/or political participation in our country. Present-day affirmative action programs were born out of President John F. Kennedy's 1961 Executive Order 10925, which created the President's Commission on Equal Employment Opportunity.

There are scholars in the civil rights community who argue that affirmative action's roots can be traced back to the Civil War amendments. In either case, modern-day affirmative action programs based on flexible "goals and timetables" were established at a White House conference convened by President Lyndon B. Johnson shortly after the signing of the Civil Rights Act of 1964 and the Voting Rights Act of 1965.

President Johnson convened this conference of over 300 CEOs of major U.S. corporations to pose the question, "Now that we have signed antidiscrimination provisions into our nation's laws and created safeguards to prevent voter discrimination, how do we integrate our nation's workplaces, schools, and economic institutions?" The CEOs responded in corporate business terms by recommending to the president that the nation employ common corporate practices of flexible "goals and timetables," the same effective way the business community approaches everything from "merger acquisitions" to "market takeovers."

The CEOs noted that this approach allows companies to plan ways of more fully integrating our society. In 1965, President Johnson issued Executive Order 11246 to see that this same approach was expanded to our educational institutions and our federal, state, and local contracting practices. Unfortunately, detractors of affirmative action have also distorted its meaning and principle.

REWRITING HISTORY

Opponents of affirmative action have rewritten history and clearly ignored present realities in their eagerness to eliminate present programs. They argue that affirmative action programs are no longer needed in education. They claim that the vestiges of racial and gender discrimination are dead and buried, yet the same discriminatory practices in college admissions are locking out promising young people from professional careers and productive lives.

In the late 1960s and early '70s, the NAACP and other civil rights and education organizations argued that many of our national standardized tests were "culturally discriminatory." As a result, adjustments were made to address our nation's commitment to cultural diversity based on principles of inclusion and full participation rather than segregation.

Proposition 209, the antiaffirmative action initiative that passed in California in 1996, using misleading language, abolished these advances by eliminating even the consideration of such diversity. As a result of this nouveau-segregationist, antiaffirmative action proposition, when classes began at Boalt Law School at the University of California, Berkeley, in the Fall of 1997, the 270-member entering class had the same number of African Americans that the University of Mississippi had in 1962: one. A step backward to the old ways of the segregated South.

Present-day zealots focusing on eliminating affirmative action seem to flirt on the brink of a very wise man's definition of insanity. In this case, "insanity" is defined as doing the same thing over and over again yet expecting a different result. We need only compare what happens when affirmative action is eliminated, as in the aforementioned example, and how affirmative action has affected access to higher education.

In 1955, only 4.9 percent of college students ages 18–24

were African American. This figure rose to 6.5 percent during the next five years but by 1965 had slumped back to 4.9 percent. Only in the wake of affirmative action measures in the late 1960s and early '70s did the percentage of black college students begin to climb steadily: In 1970, 7.8 percent of college students were African American, in 1980, 9.1 percent, and in 1990, 11.3 percent.

DRAMATIC VICTORIES

The civil rights movement has clearly had its share of dramatic victories, among them, Brown v. Board of Education and the other cases striking down segregation. Legislation such as the Civil Rights Act and the Voting Rights Act helped to advance the Constitution's promise of equal opportunity for all, including ethnic minorities, women, and others.

These judicial and legislative victories were not enough to overcome long-entrenched discrimination. One problem was that these measures frequently focused on issues of formal rights (such as the rights to vote, eat in public facilities, and sleep in public accommodations) that were particularly susceptible to judicial or statutory resolution.

In July 1970, a federal district court enjoined the state of Alabama from continuing to discriminate against African Americans in the hiring of state troopers. The court found that "in the 37-year history of the patrol, there has never been a black trooper." The order included detailed, nonnumerical provisions for assuring an end to discrimination, such as stringent controls on the civil-service certification procedure and an extensive program of recruitment of minority job applicants.

Eighteen months later, not a single African American had been hired as a state trooper, or for a civilian position connected with the state troopers. Through assertive strategies by the time the case reached the court of appeals in 1974, 25 African-American troopers and 80 African-American support personnel had been hired. Due to well-crafted affirmative action programs, the U.S. Supreme Court ultimately affirmed the orders.

In 1979, women represented only 4 percent of entry-level officers in the San Francisco Police Department. By 1985, under an affirmative action program ordered in a case in which the Department of Justice sued the city for discrimination, the number of women in the entry class had risen to 175, or 14.5 percent of the overall class.

A federal district court review of the San Francisco Fire Department in 1987 led to a consent decree that increased the number of African Americans in officer positions from 7 to 31; Hispanic officers increased from 12 to 55 and Asians from 0 to 10. Women were admitted as firefighters for the first time in the department's history.

MAKING A DIFFERENCE

Affirmative action is making sure that we have competent, educated leaders from and for all communities in America. Research shows that women's advancement in medical science has been accompanied by increased attention to women's health issues, such as breast and ovarian cancer, as well as expanded research in other areas.

Affirmative action programs do indeed make a fundamental difference. A government study showed that women made greater gains at private companies doing business with the federal government (and therefore subject to federal affirmative action requirements) than at other companies. Female employment, in fact, rose 15.2 percent among federal contractors and only 2.2 percent elsewhere.

Affirmative action programs impel people in power to seek "merit" in untraditional places, rather than continue to make choices based on old habits, which have created a "tradition" of excluding members of certain groups. . . .

OPPONENTS' DECEPTIVE ARGUMENTS

Many deceptions are being promoted about affirmative action.

It is often said that ethnic minorities and women receive "preferences," yet affirmative action does not require any. In matters such as college admissions, for example, women and minorities do not assume they will be treated any differently than, for example, the children of alumni or of politicians.

It is often argued that affirmative action is actually a system of hard-and-fast quotas. This is illogical. The use of quotas in hiring, contracting, and educational admissions is illegal and has been cited as such since the 1977 Supreme Court decision in *Bakke v. University of California*.

The Supreme Court went further. Programs that claim to be affirmative action are also illegal if an unqualified person receives benefits over a qualified one; numerical goals are so strict that the plan lacks reasonable flexibility; the numerical goals bear no relationship to the available pool of qualified candidates and could therefore become quotas; the plan is not fixed in length; or innocent bystanders are harmed through its implementation.

Accusations of reverse discrimination are often made by those who hope to eliminate affirmative action, though evidence demonstrates that reverse discrimination is quite rare. For example, of the 91,000 employment discrimination cases before the Equal Employment Opportunity Commission, less than 2 percent are reverse discrimination cases.

Furthermore, a study conducted by Rutgers University and commissioned by the U.S. Department of Labor found that reverse discrimination is not a significant problem in employment and that a "high proportion" of claims brought by white men were "without merit." In essence, affirmative action provides employers with the largest, most diverse pool of qualified applicants from which to choose.

AMERICA'S CHOICE

We have a fundamental choice about what kind of communities we want to work, earn, and live in. It is up to us to make our communities reflect our deepest American values of inclusiveness and equal opportunity for all who make up the diversity which is America. People really don't want to turn back the clock.

Affirmative action has indeed proved helpful in leveling the playing field so that all Americans can pursue the American dream. Thanks in large part to affirmative action, millions of women and men have been given an equal opportunity in education, employment, and housing.

While many private and public studies corroborate the effectiveness of affirmative action for women and minorities, numerous studies and congressional studies also show, regrettably, that serious discrimination persists in our society. Thus, we still need affirmative action. As long as there is discrimination based on race or gender, race- and gender-conscious remedies must be legally available.

"Affirmative action is institutionalized racism."

AFFIRMATIVE ACTION IS AN INEFFECTIVE REMEDY FOR DISCRIMINATION

John O'Sullivan

Affirmative action in practice has become a system of institutionalized racism that practices the discrimination it is supposed to combat, argues John O'Sullivan in the following viewpoint. Its victims include whites and Asians who are denied jobs and college placements, women and minorities whose education and work achievements are viewed with suspicion and resentment, and minority college students who, having been admitted under a system of racial preferences, find themselves unable to complete their studies. Affirmative action has conferred no benefits to individuals or to American society, and should be abolished outright, he concludes. O'Sullivan is editor-at-large of *National Review*, a conservative magazine.

As you read, consider the following questions:

1. How has the reach of affirmative action been expanded since its inception, according to O'Sullivan?
2. What does the author argue to be three social costs of affirmative action?
3. What policies does O'Sullivan suggest for improving the prospects of people in poor and minority communities?

A ffirmative action has never been simply a "hand up" to "people who have had a hard time." It originally meant preferential treatment for people belonging to the racial group that had had a hard time, namely, American blacks under slavery and Jim Crow, or to the sex that feminists falsely claimed to have had a hard time, namely, American women under motherhood. Many of its supposed beneficiaries, however, had not themselves had a hard time, having been born into rich or successful middle-class families, or having married rich or successful men, or even having married poor and unsuccessful men who accepted a duty to support wives and children out of a bread-winner's income. And, of course, many people who had had a hard time, for instance, poor white males, were not eligible for affirmative-action preferences.

As time went by, affirmative action was expanded to cover people who had not only missed hardship personally but who came from racial or ethnic groups (Hispanics, non-Japanese Asians, and Pacific Islanders) that had missed above-average hardship collectively, if only because they were not present in American history in substantial numbers. And the number of beneficiaries was further swelled by adding in newly arrived immigrants of the same race, ethnicity, or linguistic affinity as the so-called "protected classes," even though they could not have suffered more (or less) hardship in America than other new immigrants who happened to be non-Hispanic white males.

The result today is a large, incoherent system of racial and gender spoils—the only remaining example of institutionalized racism in America—that has by now entirely lost touch with its original justification of compensation for hard times. Even its advocates—as shameless a bunch of casuists as you will find outside the public-relations department of Hell—concede this by implication when they shift the argument from hardship and past discrimination to the current justification of "diversity." And that last covers a further multitude of lies.

No Benefits

It would be rhetorically shrewd to put on a mantle of reason-ableness and . . . concede a few modest benefits to affirmative action. But it would be wrong. There are no good effects that can be traced to it—none, nil, *nada*, zero.

Affirmative action has victims of varying degrees of obvious-ness. Most obvious are those outside the "protected classes," mainly non-Hispanic whites but also some Asians, who have been told that they failed examinations which they had in fact passed, who have been denied places at colleges for which they in fact qualified, who have been kept out of jobs for which they were eligible, and who have lost promotions that they had earned by their performance at work. They are plainly victims of racial and gender discrimination, and all attempts to claim otherwise are either lies or self-delusion.

Next in line are those members of the "protected classes" who would have succeeded in work or college without the benefit of affirmative action. Their credentials were honestly won, but they labor under the suspicion of favoritism. And that suspicion is inevitable until some social scientist invents a method of discriminating between real and "assisted" qualifications (which would, however, nullify affirmative action's purpose). Indeed, it is a revealing paradox that supporters of racial preferences alternate between claiming as their beneficiary any successful black American (for example, Colin Powell) and denouncing as racist those who cast doubt on any successful black American as "an affirmative-action hire."

How Beneficiaries Become Victims

Least obvious, but victims nonetheless, are the beneficiaries themselves. For instance, as Thomas Sowell has noted, racial preferences in college admission systematically mismatch talent and opportunity. The top 10 percent of minority students find themselves competing at Ivy League colleges with the top 1 percent of white and Asian students; the top 50 percent compete with the top 10 percent; and so on down the scale.

As a result, many beneficiaries of preferences have no hope of excelling against their supposed peers, struggle hard merely to keep up, get discouraged, perform poorly by their own standards, and even drop out of school altogether. The modestly successful middle-class career they would have enjoyed if they had attended a first-rate second-class school is lost to them, perhaps forever.

Those who do just well enough at school either fall at a later occupational hurdle—or require a succession of preferences to maintain the elite career that they have been told is their birthright. And because they are clever people (rather than absolutely brilliant), they will sense that their success is bogus and is therefore occasionally resented by their colleagues. Unless they are also of superhuman honesty, they will seek refuge from this uncomfortable self-knowledge and join the dropouts in embracing the theory that white racism is pervasive and explains their various plights. In terms of personal achievement and happiness, everyone is worse off.

HARMFUL EFFECTS

If everyone is worse off, that means society is worse off, too. But society also suffers some general ill-effects from affirmative action in addition to the damaged life-chances of its victims. I will briefly mention three of these, of which the first is a loss of efficiency owing to the mismatch of talent and opportunity discussed above.

Estimating the cost of this mismatch is a fairly simple exercise in regulatory economics. The Environmental Protection Agency, for example, regularly estimates the cost to the economy of its various regulations. But there has been a strange reluctance among economists to estimate the costs of affirmative action. Indeed, the only such estimate dates from February 1993. Peter Brimelow and Leslie Spencer, writing in *Forbes* magazine, estimated that the direct and indirect compliance costs of racial preferences amounted to about $120 billion annually, and that the opportunity costs equaled about 4 percent of gross domestic product annually. They are certainly not lower now.

Why are economists reluctant to repeat this discovery? Here the second effect of affirmative action comes in. It has created for its support a vast necessary engine of lies, dissimulation, and coercion. For many years, university administrators have consistently lied about how they have introduced racial bias into admission procedures. When whistleblowers (like, for instance, a young student at the Georgetown University law school) revealed that minority students needed lower test scores than whites for admission, they were themselves denounced as liars, and sometimes threatened with disciplinary action. And that continued until the courts in recent cases forced colleges to make their admission standards public, and the allegations turned out to be true.

Nor has the lying ceased even now. Administrators seek to salvage "diversity" in admissions from court prohibitions against rigging test scores by arguing that such scores must be supplemented by other indicators of a student's ability—involvement in community work, artistic endeavors, and so forth. Well and good, except that such considerations will not salvage "diversity" unless minority students systematically outperform whites and Asians when it comes to community and artistic involvement. There is, needless to say, no evidence that they do.

And what is true of college admissions is equally true of corporations, small businesses, the states, and the federal government; racial preferences are simultaneously enforced and denied. Of course, both those telling the lies and those believing them have in reality always known the truth. But that is worrying rather than reassuring, because until recently demanding assent to the lie (and stigmatizing those who cling to the truth) has been a feature of totalitarian rather than democratic societies. But when a *New York Times* editorial can declare that to use the word "quota" to describe affirmative action (that is, to speak the plain truth) is "racist," perhaps we have created a totalitarian enclave in our politics where affirmative action survives because it cannot be honestly described.

The third general effect is the spread of racism. Of a multitude of potential examples, I will cite just one: racial and ethnic segregation in the universities and its acceptance by the college authorities. We are shocked at this, but why? Race-conscious policies make people conscious of race.

ABOLISH AFFIRMATIVE ACTION

It follows from what I have said so far that I cannot see how affirmative action could be mended. It is rotten at the root, and the only thing to be done is to abolish it outright.

Of course, there are many policies that we could pursue to better the prospects of people in poor and minority communities—improving public education, making vouchers available so that parents can remove their children from unimproved schools, restoring law and order where it has broken down, assisting church charities. We should, indeed, pursue such policies irrespective of our attitude to affirmative action. What we should not do is to suggest that such reforms are compensation for removing racial and sexual preferences, since that would wrongly suggest that preferences are a benefit.

Common sense suggests that in a few (rare) instances, race or ethnicity is a real qualification for a particular job. Appointing a black policeman to patrol an area where most people are black and there has been a history of bad relations between police and the community might well be reasonable. But that would not justify demanding that test scores in police examinations be faked, or that hiring and promotion be done not on merit but on the basis of racial proportionalism. The problem that needs remedying here is not old-fashioned racism; it is that in recent years federal agencies have set such unreasonable standards for what legitimately constitutes a "job-related" test.

INSTITUTIONALIZED RACISM

Affirmative action is entrenched in almost every area of American life. It is supported by a New Class whose general political interests it reflects and advances, by a Democratic coalition whose constituent groups it favors, and by countless bureaucrats in the public and private sectors who administer its complexities.

Racial preferences in the public sector have suffered a few significant reverses in the courts, and in some state referenda. But those reverses have yet to be translated into action on the ground; figures like Mayor Willie Brown of San Francisco have announced their intention not to enforce the law and have suffered neither rebuke nor consequences; and the federal government continues to enforce compliance with preferences and set-asides that the courts have disallowed.

Needless to say, there is little stomach in the GOP for a fight on issues tinged with race; a modest bill outlawing public-sector preferences has been tabled; and there is no indication that the Republicans intend to tackle racial preferences in the private sector any time soon. Indeed, corporate America is now largely in favor of affirmative action as a talisman against discrimination lawsuits. Conservatives are celebrating a liberal pause as if it were a retreat.

What should replace affirmative action? Let me repeat: affirmative action is institutionalized racism. Why do we need to do anything other than abolish it? Any "replacement" must be worthwhile on its own merits. If it is, it need not be justified as a replacement for something that should not be there in the first place.

> "An insistence on color-blindness
> means the effective exclusion today
> of African Americans from positions
> of influence, wealth, and power."

RACIAL PREFERENCES IN HIGHER EDUCATION ARE NECESSARY

Nathan Glazer

Nathan Glazer is a Harvard University sociologist whose books include *Affirmative Discrimination* and *We Are All Multiculturalists Now*. Although he criticized affirmative action policies in many of his earlier writings, he defends them in the following viewpoint that focuses on college admissions. Glazer argues that while the principle that merit alone should govern entry into colleges is a sound one, applying it would mean that African-American enrollment in prestigious universities such as Harvard would drop precipitously. Such a development, he contends, given the long history of black Americans' struggle for equality, would be harmful for American society. Universities should be free to use racial preference in their admissions policies to ensure black participation, he concludes.

As you read, consider the following questions:

1. Who are the major supporters of affirmative action, according to Glazer?
2. What distinctions does the author draw between African Americans and other American minority groups that were given affirmative action?
3. What observations and judgments does Glazer make about Proposition 209, the 1996 California state ballot measure that banned racial preference policies for all state universities?

Reprinted from Nathan Glazer, "In Defense of Preference," *The New Republic*, April 6, 1998, by permission of *The New Republic*. Copyright 1998, The New Republic, Inc.

The battle over affirmative action today is a contest between a clear principle on the one hand and a clear reality on the other. The principle is that ability, qualifications, and merit, independent of race, national origin, or sex should prevail when one applies for a job or promotion, or for entry into selective institutions for higher education, or when one bids for contracts. The reality is that strict adherence to this principle would result in few African Americans getting jobs, admissions, and contracts. What makes the debate so confused is that the facts that make a compelling case for affirmative action are often obscured by the defenders of affirmative action themselves. They have resisted acknowledging how serious the gaps are between African Americans and others, how deep the preferences reach, how systematic they have become. Considerably more than a mild bent in the direction of diversity now exists, but it exists because painful facts make it necessary if blacks are to participate in more than token numbers in some key institutions of our society. The opponents of affirmative action can also be faulted: they have not fully confronted the consequences that must follow from the implementation of the principle that measured ability, qualification, merit, applied without regard to color, should be our only guide.

A CHANGE OF MIND

I argued for that principle in a 1975 book titled, provocatively, *Affirmative Discrimination*. It seemed obvious that that was what all of us, black and white, were aiming to achieve through the revolutionary civil rights legislation of the 1960s. That book dealt with affirmative action in employment, and with two other kinds of governmentally or judicially imposed "affirmative action," the equalization of the racial proportions in public schools and the integration of residential neighborhoods. I continued to argue and write regularly against governmentally required affirmative action, that is, racial preference, for the next two decades or more: it was against the spirit of the Constitution, the clear language of the civil rights acts, and the interests of all of us in the United States in achieving an integrated and just society.

It is not the unpopularity of this position in the world in which I live, liberal academia, that has led me to change my mind but, rather, developments that were unforeseen and unexpected in the wake of the successful civil rights movement. What was unforeseen and unexpected was that the gap between the educational performance of blacks and whites would persist and, in some respects, deepen despite the civil rights revolution and hugely expanded social and educational programs, that inner-city schools would continue to decline, and that the black family would unravel to a remarkable degree, contributing to social conditions for large numbers of black children far worse than those in the 1960s. In the presence of those conditions, an insistence on color-blindness means the effective exclusion today of African Americans from positions of influence, wealth, and power. It is not a prospect that any of us can contemplate with equanimity. We have to rethink affirmative action.

In a sense, it is a surprise that a fierce national debate over affirmative action has not only persisted but intensified during the Clinton years. After twelve years (1981–1993) under two Republican presidents, Ronald Reagan and George Bush, who said they opposed affirmative action but did nothing to scale it back, the programs seemed secure. After all, affirmative action rests primarily on a presidential executive order dating back to the presidencies of Lyndon Johnson and Richard Nixon which requires "affirmative action" in employment practices from federal contractors—who include almost every large employer, university, and hospital. The legal basis for most of affirmative action could thus have been swept away, as so many noted at the time, with a "stroke of the pen" by the president. Yet two presidents who claimed to oppose affirmative action never wielded the pen.

Public Discontent and Elite Support

Despite the popular majority that grumbles against affirmative action, there was (and is) no major elite constituency strongly opposed to it: neither business nor organized labor, religious leaders nor university presidents, local officials nor serious presidential candidates are to be found in opposition. Big business used to fear that affirmative action would undermine the principle of employment and promotion on the basis of qualifications. It has since become a supporter. Along with mayors and other local officials (and of course the civil rights movement), it played a key role in stopping the Reagan administration from moving against affirmative action. Most city administrations have also made their peace with affirmative action.

Two developments outside the arena of presidential politics galvanized both opponents and defenders of affirmative action. The Supreme Court changed glacially after successive Republican appointments—each of which, however, had been vetted by a Democratic Senate—and a number of circuit courts began to chip away at the edifice of affirmative action. But playing the largest role was the politically unsophisticated effort of two California professors to place on the California ballot a proposition that would insert in the California Constitution the simple and clear words, taken from the Civil Rights Act of 1964, which ban discrimination on the basis of race, national origin, or sex. The decision to launch a state constitutional proposition, Proposition 209, suddenly gave opponents the political instrument they needed to tap the majority sentiment that has always existed against preferences. [Proposition 209 passed in 1996.]

While supporters of affirmative action do not have public opinion on their side, they do have the still-powerful civil rights movement, the major elites in education, religion, philanthropy, government, and the mass media. And their position is bolstered by a key fact: how far behind African Americans are when judged by the tests and measures that have become the common coin of American meritocracy.

THE EDUCATION SKILLS GAP

The reality of this enormous gap is clearest where the tests in use are the most objective, the most reliable, and the best validated, as in the case of the various tests used for admission to selective institutions of higher education, for entry into elite occupations such as law and medicine, or for civil service jobs. These tests have been developed over many years specifically for the purpose of eliminating biases in admissions and appointments. As defenders of affirmative action often point out, paper-and-pencil tests of information, reading comprehension, vocabulary, reasoning, and the like are not perfect indicators of individual ability. But they are the best measures we have for success in college and professional schools, which, after all, require just the skills the tests measure. And the tests can clearly differentiate the literate teacher from the illiterate one or the policeman who can make out a coherent arrest report from one who cannot.

To concentrate on the most hotly contested area of affirmative action—admission to selective institutions of higher education—and on the group in the center of the storm—African Americans: If the Scholastic Assessment Test (SAT) were used for selection in a color-blind fashion, African Americans, who in 1998 make up about six percent of the student bodies in selective colleges and universities, would drop to less than two percent, according to a 1994 study by the editor of the *Journal of Blacks in Higher Education*.

Why is this so? According to studies summarized in Stephan and Abigail Thernstrom's book, *America in Black and White*, the average combined SAT score for entering freshmen in the nation's top 25 institutions is about 1300. White applicants generally need to score a minimum of 600 on the verbal portion of the test—a score obtained by eight percent of the test-takers in 1995—and at least 650 on the mathematics section—a score obtained by seven percent of the test-takers in 1995. In contrast, only 1.7 percent of black students scored over 600 on the verbal section in 1995, and only two percent scored over 650 on the math. This represents considerable progress over the last 15 years, but black students still lag distressingly far behind their white counterparts.

There is no way of getting around this reality. Perhaps the tests are irrelevant to success in college? That cannot be sustained. They have been improved and revised over decades and predict achievement in college better than any alternative. Some of the revisions have been carried out in a near-desperate effort to exclude items which would discriminate against blacks. Some institutions have decided they will not use the tests, not because they are invalid per se, but because they pose a barrier to the increased admission of black students. Nor would emphasizing other admissions criteria, such as high school grades, make a radical difference. In any case, there is considerable value to a uniform national standard, given the enormous differences among high schools.

Do qualifications at the time of admission matter? Isn't the important thing what the institutions manage to do with those they admit? If they graduate, are they not qualified? Yes, but many do not graduate. Two or three times as many African American students as white students drop out before graduation. And the tests for admission to graduate schools show the same radical disparities between blacks and others. Are there not also preferences for athletes, children of alumni, students gifted in some particular respect? Yes, but except for athletes, the disparities in academic aptitude that result from such preferences are not nearly as substantial as those which must be elided in order to reach target figures for black students. Can we not substitute for the tests other factors—such as the poverty and other hardships students have overcome to reach the point of applying to college? This might keep up the number of African Americans, but not by much, if the studies are to be believed. A good number of white and Asian applicants would also benefit from such "class-based" affirmative action.

(I have focused on the effect of affirmative action—and its possible abolition—on African Americans. But, of course, there are other beneficiaries. Through bureaucratic mindlessness, Asian Americans and Hispanics were also given affirmative action. But Asian Americans scarcely need it. Major groups—not all—of Hispanic Americans trail behind whites but mostly for reasons we understand: problems with the English language and the effect on immigrant children of the poor educational and economic status of their parents. We expect these to improve in time as they always have with immigrants to the United States. And, when it comes to women, there is simply no issue today when it comes to qualifying in equal numbers for selective institutions of higher and professional education.)

RAMIFICATIONS FOR AMERICAN DEMOCRACY

How, then, should we respond to this undeniable reality? The opponents of affirmative action say, "Let standards prevail whatever the result." So what if black students are reduced to two percent of our selective and elite student bodies? Those who gain entry will know that they are properly qualified for entry, that they have been selected without discrimination, and their classmates will know it too. The result will actually be improved race relations and a continuance of the improvements we have seen in black performance in recent decades. Fifteen years from now, perhaps three or four percent of students in the top schools will be black. Until then, blacks can go to less competitive institutions of higher education, perhaps gaining greater advantage from their education in so doing. And, meanwhile, let us improve elementary and high school education—as we have been trying to do for the last 15 years or more.

Yet we cannot be quite so cavalier about the impact on public opinion—black and white—of a radical reduction in the number of black students at the Harvards, the Berkeleys, and the Amhersts. These institutions have become, for better or worse, the gateways to prominence, privilege, wealth, and power in American society. To admit blacks under affirmative action no doubt undermines the American meritocracy, but to exclude blacks from them by abolishing affirmative action would undermine the legitimacy of American democracy.

My argument is rooted in history. African Americans—and the struggle for their full and fair inclusion in U.S. society—have been a part of American history from the beginning. Our Constitution took special—but grossly unfair—account of their status, our greatest war was fought over their status, and our most important constitutional amendments were adopted because of the need to right past wrongs done to them. And, amid the civil rights revolution of the 1960s, affirmative action was instituted to compensate for the damage done to black achievement and life chances by almost 400 years of slavery, followed by state-sanctioned discrimination and massive prejudice.

Yet, today, a vast gulf of difference persists between the educational and occupational status of blacks and whites, a gulf that encompasses statistical measures of wealth, residential segregation, and social relationships with other Americans. Thirty years ago, with the passage of the great civil rights laws, one could have reasonably expected—as I did—that all would be set right by now. But today, even after taking account of substantial progress and change, it is borne upon us how continuous, rooted, and substantial the differences between African Americans and other Americans remain.

The judgment of the elites who support affirmative action—the college presidents and trustees, the religious leaders, the corporate executives—and the judgment even of many of those who oppose it but hesitate to act against it—the Republican leaders in Congress, for example—is that the banning of preference would be bad for the country. I agree. Not that everyone's motives are entirely admirable; many conservative congressmen, for example, are simply afraid of being portrayed as racists even if their opposition to affirmative action is based on a sincere desire to support meritocratic principle. The college presidents who support affirmative action, under the fashionable mantra of diversity, also undoubtedly fear the student demonstrations that would occur if they were to speak out against preferences.

But there are also good-faith motives in this stand, and there is something behind the argument for diversity. What kind of institutions of higher education would we have if blacks suddenly dropped from six or seven percent of enrollment to one or two percent? The presence of blacks, in classes in social studies and the humanities, immediately introduces another tone, another range of questions (often to the discomfort of black students who do not want this representational burden placed upon them). The tone may be one of embarrassment and hesitation and self-censorship among whites (students and faculty). But must we not all learn how to face these questions together with our fellow citizens? We should not be able to escape from this embarrassment by the reduction of black students to minuscule numbers.

The weakness in the "diversity" defense is that college presidents are not much worried about the diversity that white working-class kids, or students of Italian or Slavic background, have to offer. Still, there is a reputable reason for that apparent discrepancy. It is that the varied ethnic and racial groups in the United States do not, to the same extent as African Americans, pose a test of the fairness of American institutions. These other groups have not been subjected to the same degree of persecution or exclusion. Their status is not, as the social status of African Americans is, the most enduring reproach to the egalitarian ideals of American society. And these other groups have made progress historically, and make progress today, at a rate that incorporates them into American society quickly compared to blacks.

Excluding Blacks from Elite Institutions

This is the principal flaw in the critique of affirmative action. The critics are defending a vitally important principle, indeed, the one that should be the governing principle of institutions of higher education: academic competence as the sole test for distinguishing among applicants and students. This principle, which was fought for so energetically during the 1940s and 1950s through laws banning discrimination in admission on the basis of race, national origin, or religion, should not be put aside lightly. But, at present, it would mean the near exclusion from our best educational institutions of a group that makes up twelve percent of the population. In time, I am convinced, this preference will not be needed. Our laws and customs and our primary and secondary educational systems will fully incorporate black Americans into American society, as other disadvantaged groups have been incorporated. The positive trends of recent decades will continue. But we are still, though less than in the past, "two nations," and one of the nations cannot be excluded so thoroughly from institutions that confer access to the positions of greatest prestige and power.

On what basis can we justify violating the principle that measured criteria of merit should govern admission to selective institutions of higher education today? It is of some significance to begin with that we in the United States have always been looser in this respect than more examination-bound systems of higher education in, say, Western Europe: we have always left room for a large degree of freedom for institutions of higher education, public as well as private, to admit students based on nonacademic criteria. But I believe the main reasons we have to continue racial preferences for blacks are, first, because this country has a special obligation to blacks that has not been fully discharged, and second, because strict application of the principle of qualification would send a message of despair to many blacks, a message that the nation is indifferent to their difficulties and problems.

Many, including leading black advocates of eliminating preference, say no: the message would be, "Work harder and you can do it." Well, now that affirmative action is becoming a thing of the past in the public colleges and universities of California and Texas, we will have a chance to find out. Yet I wonder whether the message of affirmative action to black students today really ever has been, "Don't work hard; it doesn't matter for you because you're black; you will make it into college anyway." Colleges are indeed looking for black students, but they are also looking for some minimal degree of academic effort and accomplishment, and it is a rare ambitious African American student seeking college entry who relaxes because he believes his grades won't matter at all.

One of the chief arguments against racial preference in college and professional school admissions is that more blacks will drop out, the quality of blacks who complete the courses of instruction will be inferior, and they will make poorer lawyers, doctors, or businessmen. Dropping out is common in American higher education and does not necessarily mean that one's attendance was a total loss. Still, the average lower degree of academic performance has, and will continue to have, effects even for the successful: fewer graduating black doctors will go into research; more will go into practice and administration. More blacks in business corporations will be in personnel. Fewer graduating black lawyers will go into corporate law firms; more will work for government.

And more will become judges, because of another and less disputed form of affirmative action, politics. Few protest at the high number of black magistrates in cities with large black populations—we do not appoint judges by examination. Nor do we find it odd or objectionable that Democratic presidents will appoint more black lawyers as judges, or that even a Republican president will be sure to appoint one black Supreme Court justice. What is at work here is the principle of participation. It is a more legitimate principle in politics and government than it is for admission to selective institutions of higher education. But these are also gateways to power, and the principle of participation cannot be flatly ruled out for them.

Whatever the case one may make in general for affirmative action, many difficult issues remain: What kind, to what extent, how long, imposed by whom, by what decision-making process? It is important to bear in mind that affirmative action in higher education admissions is, for the most part, a policy that has been chosen (albeit sometimes under political pressure) by the institutions themselves. There are racial goals and targets for employment and promotion for all government contractors, including colleges and universities, set by government fiat, but targets on student admissions are not imposed by government, except for a few traditionally black or white institutions in the South.

Let us preserve this institutional autonomy. Just as I would resist governmentally imposed requirements that these institutions meet quotas of black admissions, so would I also oppose a judicial or legislative ban on the use of race in making decisions on admission. Ballot measures like Proposition 209 are more understandable given the abuses so common in systems of racial preference. But it is revealing that so many other states appear to have had second thoughts and that the California vote is therefore not likely to be repeated. (A recent report in *The Chronicle of Higher Education* was headlined "LEGISLATURES SHOW LITTLE ENTHUSIASM FOR MEASURES TO END RACIAL PREFERENCES"; in this respect, the states are not unlike Congress.)

We should retain the freedom of institutions of higher and professional education to make these determinations for themselves. As we know, they would almost all make room for a larger percentage of black students than would otherwise qualify. This is what these institutions do today. They defend what they do with the argument that diversity is a good thing. I think what they really mean is that a large segment of the American population, significant not only demographically but historically and politically and morally, cannot be so thoroughly excluded. I agree with them.

TWO NATIONS

I have discussed affirmative action only in the context of academic admissions policy. Other areas raise other questions, other problems. And, even in this one area of college and university admissions, affirmative action is not a simple and clear and uncomplicated solution. It can be implemented wisely or foolishly, and it is often done foolishly, as when college presidents make promises to protesting students that they cannot fulfill, or when institutions reach too far below their minimal standards with deleterious results for the academic success of the students they admit, for their grading practices, and for the legitimacy of the degrees they offer. No matter how affirmative action in admissions is dealt with, other issues remain or will emerge. More black students, for example, mean demands for more black faculty and administrators and for more black-oriented courses. Preference is no final answer (just as the elimination of preference is no final answer). It is rather what is necessary to respond to the reality that, for some years to come, yes, we are still two nations, and both nations must participate in the society to some reasonable degree.

Fortunately, those two nations, by and large, want to become more united. The United States is not Canada or Bosnia, Lebanon or Malaysia. But, for the foreseeable future, the strict use of certain generally reasonable tests as a benchmark criterion for admissions would mean the de facto exclusion of one of the two nations from a key institutional system of the society, higher education. Higher education's governing principle is qualification—merit. Should it make room for another and quite different principle, equal participation? The latter should never become dominant. Racial proportional representation would be a disaster. But basically the answer is yes—the principle of equal participation can and should be given some role. This decision has costs. But the alternative is too grim to contemplate.

| "Preference ostensibly given to overcome the legacy of racism takes the form of racism, engenders racism, nurtures racism, [and] embitters the national community."

RACIAL PREFERENCES IN HIGHER EDUCATION MUST BE ABOLISHED

Carl Cohen

Carl Cohen is a professor of philosophy at the University of Michigan and the author of *Naked Racial Preference: The Case Against Affirmative Action*. In the following viewpoint, he criticizes colleges for admissions policies that give systematic preferences to members of minority groups in order to ensure a racially diverse student body. Such racial preferences, he contends, are fundamentally unfair, counterproductive, and in many instances unconstitutional. Universities should instead rely on the principle of tolerating no discrimination—either positive or negative—by race, color, or sex in the admission and teaching of students.

As you read, consider the following questions:

1. What are some of the divergent meanings of the term "affirmative action," according to Cohen?
2. What four groups of people bear the burdens of racial preferences, in the author's view?
3. In what ways may race *not* be used in college admissions policy, according to Cohen?

Reprinted from Carl Cohen, "Race Preference in College Admissions," *Heritage Lectures*, no. 611, April 29, 1998, by permission of The Heritage Foundation.

"Affirmative action" has long had many meanings. The Civil Rights Act of 1964 authorized courts to take "affirmative action" to uproot racially discriminatory practices. That objective was, and remains, morally right. But that same statute forbade race preference; it is morally wrong. Affirmative action and race preference are thus plainly distinguishable; the former (in its original sense) is right and lawful, the latter is neither.

Preference and affirmative action are widely confounded in the public mind because race preferences were introduced (beginning about 1970) in the honorable name of affirmative action. What was to have been eliminated was given the name of what had been designed to eliminate it. Most folks today, with unintended irony, mean by "affirmative action" that very preference by skin color that affirmative action was devised to eradicate.

The result is doubly unfortunate: Wrongful practices fly the flag of justice, and morally right policies are smeared by association with what everyone sees intuitively to be unfair. Remedy for identifiable injuries inflicted by a given institution is a demand of justice; but that is redress for damage from that institution, not preference by color. Henceforth, let us be clear: It is not affirmative action but generalized race preference that is at issue. That our universities do give systematic preference by skin color—often blatantly—is indisputable. I will present overwhelming evidence of this later; but we all know that it is so.

RACE PREFERENCE IS WRONG

Here is the fundamental principle: Giving preference by race, by skin color, is wrong, unjust; when done by an agency of the state it is unlawful, a violation of federal statutes and of our Constitution. The motives are often good; we understand that. But the conduct is wrong and not tolerable in a good society.

I begin with this historical note: In his Brief in the case of *Brown v. Board of Education*, Thurgood Marshall, then executive director of the Legal Defense Fund of the National Association for the Advancement of Colored People, wrote in 1954:

> Distinctions by race are so evil, so arbitrary and invidious that a state, bound to defend the equal protection of the laws must not invoke them in any public sphere.

I cheered when I read that then, as I cheer today when I re-read it. The truth of this principle does not change with the times. Let us seek to respond justly to injury, giving appropriate remedy where remedy is due, and credit where credit is due, without regard to race. But if ever we are to heal our racial wounds it will be through a national determination, morally resolute and backed by law where that is appropriate, never again to give preference by race or color or sex. The long-term success of a democratic polity requires a deep and widespread commitment to the principle that the laws protect all equally.

Racial discrimination is wrong, no matter the color preferred. We begin to transcend racism when we stop the practice of every form of it, by every public body, now. To give favor to males or to females, or to whites or to blacks or to persons of any color, is morally wrong because doing so is intrinsically unfair. Color, nationality, and sex are not attributes that entitle anyone to more (or less) of the good things in life, or to any special favor (or disfavor). When, in the past, whites or males did receive such preference that was deeply wrong; it is no less wrong now when the colors or sexes are reversed. Justice Thurgood Marshall long ago made it clear that the plain words of federal law

> proscribe racial discrimination . . . against whites on the same terms as racial discrimination against non-whites.

Equality applies to all.

REDRESSING PAST DISCRIMINATION

But what of those who have been badly hurt by earlier racial discrimination? Do they not deserve to be compensated? Yes, of course; persons may indeed be entitled to remedy for unlawful injury done to them because they were black or brown or female. We give such remedy, rightly—but it is the injury for which remedy is given, not the skin color or sex. There is all the difference in the world between compensation for injury and preference by race.

When preference is given flatly by skin color or by national origin, the inevitable result is the award of advantages to some who deserve no advantage, and the imposition of burdens upon some who deserve no burden. Most often, those who benefit did not suffer the wrong for which compensation is supposedly being given; those who are disadvantaged by the preference most often did not do any wrong whatsoever, and certainly not that earlier wrong to a minority group for which the preference is alleged redress.

The oppression of blacks and some other minorities in our country has been grievous, a stain on our history; no honest person will deny that. But the notion that we can redress that historical grievance by giving preference now to persons in the same racial or sexual group as those earlier wronged is a mistake, a blunder. It supposes that rights are possessed by groups, and that therefore advantages given to some minority group now can be payment for earlier injuries to other members of that minority. But moral entitlements are not held by groups. Whites as a group do not have rights, and blacks as a group do not have rights; rights are possessed by persons, individual human persons. And when persons are entitled to be made whole for some injury earlier done to them, the duty owed is not to members of their race or sex or nationality, not to their group, but to them as individuals. The effort to defend preference as group compensation fails because it fundamentally misconceives the relation between wrongs and remedies.

This does not mean that affirmative action must be abandoned. In its original sense, affirmative action was intended to insure the elimination of racially discriminatory practices, and no reasonable person would want to oppose that. But if by affirmative action one means (as many Americans now do mean) preferential devices designed to bring about redistribution of the good things in life to match ethnic proportions in the population, affirmative action in that sense must be rejected because the preferences it employs are inconsistent with the equal treatment of all persons.

UNIVERSITIES AND STUDENT DIVERSITY

The argument applies to our public universities with special force, because here the habits of democracy are molded. But many universities now give very marked preference by race and seek to justify what they do by the quest for diversity. A diverse student body is an appropriate goal for a university—but that goal, as Justice Lewis F. Powell said explicitly in his opinion in *University of California v. Bakke*, is intellectual diversity, diversity of judgment and viewpoint. [Editor's note: The Supreme Court ruled in 1978 that Allan Bakke was wrongfully denied admission to the University of California at Davis Medical School when he had higher test scores than several black students admitted under the school's affirmative action program.] When our universities announce that they are striving for diversity, we know that what they are really seeking to achieve is racial proportionality; they profess an intellectual objective, but their real goal is racial balance. This passion for racial balance "misconceives"—that is Justice Powell's word—the diversity that might serve educative ends. And however meritorious those educative ends, it is worth noting that they cannot possibly serve as the "compelling" objective that is required for the constitutional use of racial classifications by the state.

Justice Powell, in *Bakke*, very specifically addressed this "racial balance" defense of admissions preference; he wrote that such a purpose is "facially invalid," invalid on its face! He concludes:

> Preferring members of any one group for no reason other than race or ethnic origin is discrimination for its own sake. This the Constitution forbids.

This principle of equal treatment is the moral foundation upon which the Equal Protection Clause of the 14th Amendment ultimately rests; our Supreme Court has repeatedly emphasized that the rights guaranteed by that clause are individual rights, the rights of persons ["No state shall...deny to any person the equal protection of the laws"] and not the rights of groups. Race preferences in admission fly in the face of the Civil Rights Act of 1964, whose Section 603 reads, in full:

> No person in the United States shall, on the ground of race, color, or national origin, be excluded from participation in, be denied the benefits of, or be subjected to discrimination under any program or activity receiving Federal financial assistance.

And race preferences fly in the face of the Equal Protection Clause. Justice Powell, in *Bakke*, put this eloquently:

> The guarantee of equal protection cannot mean one thing when applied to one individual and something else when applied to a person of another color. If both are not accorded the same protection, then it is not equal.

That is why every program relying upon naked preference by race or sex, whether in the form of set-asides in the award of contracts or bonuses for hiring persons of certain colors, or additional consideration in competitive employment, or college admissions—all such preferences, whether defended as compensatory or as redistributive, or for the sake of racial diversity—must be unjust.

RACE PREFERENCE IS BAD

Beyond its unfairness, racial preference is injurious and counterproductive. Ask yourself: Who reaps the benefits and who bears the burdens of race preference?

The beneficiaries of race preference are a few members of the preferred group (if, in fact, they succeed in graduating from the college to which they have been preferentially admitted), and the newly emerged corps of administrators whose livelihood is derived from the oversight and enforcement of preferences. The vast majority of the members of the minority groups in question—in whose interests preferences had purportedly been designed—receive no benefits whatever.

The burdens of preference, on the other hand, are borne by four large groups, for each of which the costs are greater by far than the alleged returns.

1. *The cruelest burdens, the most damaging and the longest-lasting, are those borne by the members of the preferred minority group as a whole, who are inescapably undermined by racial preferences.* When persons are appointed, admitted, or promoted because of their racial group, it is inevitable that the members of that group will, in the institution giving such preference, perform less well on average. Membership in the minority group most certainly does not imply inferiority; that is a canard—but that stereotype is reinforced by the preferences given.

Since the standards for the selection of minorities are, by hypothesis, lower, because they were diluted by considerations of color, sex, or nationality, it is a certainty that, overall, the average performance of those in that group will be weaker—not because of their ethnicity, of course, but because many among them were selected on grounds having no bearing on the work or study to be pursued. Preference thus creates a link between the minority preferred and inferior performance.

This burden is borne not only by those individuals preferred, but by every member of the minority group, including all those who genuinely excel. The general knowledge that persons with black or brown skins are given preference insures lower expectations from all whose skins are like that. Every minority member is painted with the same brush. No one—not even the minorities themselves—can know for sure that any member of a preferred group has not been given special favor; skin color, the most prominent of personal characteristics, thus becomes an inescapable onus. If some demon had sought to concoct a scheme aimed at undermining the credentials of minority businessmen, professionals, and students, to stigmatize them permanently and to humiliate them publicly, there could have been no more ingenious plan devised than the preferences now so widely given in the name of affirmative action.

2. *Unfair burdens are imposed upon individuals—deserving applicants and employees—who do not win the places they would otherwise have won because of their pale skin.* One often hears the claim that the burdens of preference can be readily borne because they are so widely shared by very many among the great white majority. That is false. Most among the white majority suffer no direct loss. Those who do suffer directly are a small subset, but a subset whose members are rarely identifiable by name. If a university gives admission

preference to blacks, some whites who would have been admitted but for that racial favoritism will not be admitted. We cannot learn who those persons are, but the unfairness to unidentifiable individuals who lose because of their race is nevertheless very great. Moreover, every applicant with a pale skin not admitted or appointed may rightly wonder whether it were he from whom the penalty had been exacted.

3. *Institutions that give preference pay a heavy price.* Inferior performance (a consequence not of skin color but of stupid selection criteria) results in the many inefficiencies and the many hidden costs. In academic institutions, intellectual standards are lowered, explicitly or in secret; student performance is unavoidably lower, on average, than it would have been without the preferences, as is faculty productivity and satisfaction. The political need to profess equal treatment for all, while knowingly treating applicants and faculty members unequally because of their race, produces pervasive hypocrisy. Even great public institutions hide their policies, describe them deceptively, and sometimes even lie about them. This loss of integrity and public respect has been a fearful cost of race preference, from which recovery will require a generation.

4. *Society at large suffers grievously from the distrust and hostility that race preference engenders.* Members of ethnic groups tussling for a larger slice of the preferential pie come to distrust and despise their opposite numbers in competing minorities who (as will always appear to be the case) seem to get more than their "share" of the spoils. And fights develop over who is a member of what group, and who is entitled to its benefits. Indian tribes coming into great petroleum wealth have to develop rules for deciding what makes one a member of the tribe; is it one drop of blood? In the end we will need new Nuremberg laws and official boards to apply the rules of race membership. Ugly business.

In schools, playgrounds, and parks, in commerce and sports, in industrial employment, even in legislatures and courts, the outcome of preference is increasing racial tension and increasing self-segregation. More and more we come even to abandon the ideal of an America in which persons and not groups are the focus of praise and blame, of penalty and reward. I have been teaching at the University of Michigan since 1955; I report to you what all the talk about diversity and multiculturalism cannot hide: Preferential affirmative action on our campus (as on many campuses around the nation) has driven race relations among us to a point lower than it has ever been. The story is long and complicated and has many variants, but the short of it is this: Give preference by race and you create hostility by race. And for that we Americans are paying, and we will pay, a dreadful price.

Preference ostensibly given to overcome the legacy of racism takes the form of racism, engenders racism, nurtures racism, embitters the national community, and infects every facet of public life with racial criteria whose counterproductivity is matched only by their immorality. . . .

THE UNIVERSITY IS NO EXCEPTION

Unable to deny the facts of preference revealed, universities now take the tack that, even though they do discriminate, they do so in ways that are justifiable. On what grounds?

The racial balance argument has been rejected by the Supreme Court, that we know. When the University of California argued that its preferences were justified by the need to "reduc[e] the historic deficit of traditionally disfavored minorities" in the academic world—to promote racial balance—Justice Powell dispatched that argument in one crisp paragraph:

> If petitioner's [the University of California's] purpose is to assure within its student body some specified percentage of a particular group merely because of its race or ethnic origin, such a preferential purpose must be rejected not as insubstantial but as facially invalid. Preferring members of any one group for no reason other than race or ethnic origin is discrimination for its own sake. This the Constitution forbids. [Editor's note: This passage and all subsequent quotations in this viewpoint are taken from Lewis F. Powell's majority opinion in *University of California v. Bakke* (1978) 438 U.S. 265.]

The second argument commonly heard is some variety of the argument for compensation: "Let's level the playing field," or "Are we not obliged to compensate for earlier shackles on the racers' ankles?" and so on. I have explained why this does not justify preference by skin color. But even beyond this, the Supreme Court has rejected compensation as a justification of the university because giving racial remedies is not within the competence of universities: Preference may never be given, Justice Powell points out,

> in the absence of judicial, legislative, or administrative findings of constitutional or statutory violations. . . . Without such findings . . . the government has no greater interest in helping one individual than in refraining from harming another,

and thus no compelling justification for the preference.

But the university (then and now)

does not purport to have made, and is in no position to make, such findings. Its broad mission is education, not the formulation of any legislative policy or the adjudication of particular claims of illegality. Hence, the purpose of helping certain groups whom the faculty . . . perceive[s] as victims of "societal discrimination" does not justify a classification that imposes disadvantages upon persons like respondent [Allan Bakke] who bear no responsibility for whatever harm the beneficiaries of the special admissions program are thought to have suffered. To hold otherwise would be to convert a remedy heretofore reserved for violations of legal rights into a privilege that all institutions throughout the Nation could grant at their pleasure to whatever groups are perceived as victims of societal discrimination. This is a step we have never approved.

Generalized admission preferences by race are, in sum, not justifiable. Compensation to individuals who have been damaged is sometimes a demand of justice, but that is redress for injury, not entitlement by color. Skin-color groups have no right to redress because groups do not possess rights.

What possible defense remains? Only the alleged value of intellectual diversity in education. California's Supreme Court, in *Bakke*, had barred all uses of race in admissions. Justice Powell found that too preclusive; his was a thoughtful, nuanced response. In some cases, race may be taken into account. Justice Powell wrote,

The file of a particular black applicant may be examined for his potential contribution to diversity without the factor of race being decisive.

In weighing the "qualifications of each applicant," "treated as an individual in the admissions process," ethnic background may serve as a "plus." But note well: Only in dealing with particular individuals, as individuals, is such consideration condoned. Race may be taken into account in some ways in some cases—but there are many ways in which, as Justice Powell makes exceedingly clear in this same judgment, race may not be taken into account.

HOW RACE CANNOT BE USED IN ADMISSIONS POLICY

University spokespersons often argue that since the courts permit race to be used as one factor among many, and since they do (of course) consider race as one factor among many, they are doing no more than what the law permits. This argument is embarrassing, an egregious example of the fallacy of affirming the consequent: P implies Q; Q is true; therefore, P is true.

We could argue as well that good health requires a balanced

diet, and that since I do eat a balanced diet I must be healthy. Considering race as but one factor among many is a necessary use, but it is certainly not a sufficient condition of its legitimate use. There are many ways, explicitly noted in *Bakke*, in which race may not be used:

- Item: An admissions system is unconstitutional if it employs any means, overt or covert, "of according racial preference."
- Item: A special admissions program is to be condemned not only when places are saved for minorities, but when the system is (as that at the University of California was) "undeniably a classification based on race and ethnic background."
- Item: "The fatal flaw in petitioner's [the University of California's] preferential program is its disregard of individual rights as guaranteed by the Fourteenth Amendment." And how does the Equal Protection Clause of that amendment bear on university admissions? Recall Justice Powell's explicit invocation of that clause: "The guarantee of equal protection cannot mean one thing when applied to one individual and something else when applied to a person of another color. If both are not accorded the same protection, then it is not equal."

All these forbidden practices using race are precisely the practices of our universities today. Without a doubt we do "accord racial preference." Without a doubt our admissions system is a "classification based on race and ethnic background." Even the president of the University of Michigan has publicly admitted that we do discriminate systematically on the basis of race and ethnic background. To applicants with credentials identical in every significant way we give sharply different responses—rejecting some while admitting others—with those different responses based only upon race! Is that, or is that not, treating one person one way and another in a different way because of color? Is that, or is that not, the manifest denial of the equal protection of the laws?

- Item: However you describe an admission system, whether as a quota or as a goal, it is incontrovertibly an unconstitutional system, said Justice Powell, if it employs a "line drawn on the basis of race and ethnic status."

Lines drawn on the basis of race and ethnic status pervade our admissions systems today, and do so explicitly. No reasonable person can doubt, after examining our actual practices honestly, that what we do is in plain and certain violation of the principles of *Bakke*. . . .

No appeal to the diversity argument, as expressed in *Bakke*, can possibly rescue admissions systems that are hopelessly saturated with systematic racial discrimination. Such systems are very likely to be quashed soon by our courts. . . .

A final thought: Citizens of the United States, black and white, in preponderant majority support affirmative action but find skin-color preference morally objectionable. Ours is a reasonably healthy democracy; I conclude that our bodies politic will tolerate public discrimination not much longer. Race preference will go. . . . We are well-advised to begin to think hard, now, about the ways we can heal our social wounds without resorting to preference by race.

"Affirmative action seeks to prevent
... discrimination ... before it
happens by urging institutions to
scrutinize their decision-making
practices for sex-based stereotyping
and other discriminatory actions."

WOMEN NEED AFFIRMATIVE ACTION PROGRAMS TO FIGHT DISCRIMINATION

Judy L. Lichtman, Jocelyn C. Frye, and Helen Norton

In the following viewpoint, Judy L. Lichtman, Jocelyn C. Frye, and Helen Norton argue that women face significant barriers in the workplace due to gender discrimination, resulting in upper-level jobs being dominated by men. Government and private affirmative action programs are necessary to remove those barriers and allow women to compete on merit. The authors conclude that retaining affirmative action is essential to ensure that women have equal opportunities in pursuing education, employment, and business opportunities. Lichtman is president of the Women's Legal Defense Fund, a feminist organization that has helped to develop federal legislation on family leave and other issues. Frye is the WLDF's policy counsel for work and family programs, while Kaplan is the organization's director of equal opportunity programs.

As you read, consider the following questions:
1. What examples of discriminatory practices against women do Lichtman, Frye, and Norton describe?
2. What examples of successful affirmative action programs do the authors illustrate?
3. What impact has affirmative action had on businesses' profitability, according to the authors?

Throughout our nation's history, qualified women have been shut out of employment, education, and business opportunities solely because of their sex. Affirmative action has countered this discrimination by opening doors for women previously denied opportunities regardless of their merit. Despite significant progress in recent years, however, women remain far short of reaching equality. Without affirmative action, discrimination will continue to thwart efforts to make our national dream of equal opportunity a reality.

Unfortunately, some opponents of affirmative action have deliberately distorted the public policy debate into a series of false choices, seeking to pit blacks against whites, men against women, Americans against immigrants. These opponents have often purposefully centered their attacks on race-based affirmative action programs to capitalize on racial fears and divisions. Their failure to address women's stake in this debate demonstrates their ignorance of or indifference to women's ongoing quest for equality.

SEX DISCRIMINATION

Recognizing our long national history of sex discrimination—and our nation's comparatively short commitment to antidiscrimination efforts—is key to understanding affirmative action's continuing relevance to the lives of American women.

Sex discrimination has long limited women's choices. Women have too often been cut off from educational opportunities and tracked into lower-paying, sex-segregated jobs—discouraged, for example, from pursuing fields like medicine, business, or the skilled trades. As late as 1968, for instance, newspapers and employers segregated help-wanted ads by gender, with one section advertising the better-paying jobs only for men and a separate section listing "women's jobs"—thus systematically excluding women from choice opportunities without regard to their qualifications.

Though some of the most blatant forms of discrimination have grown rare with time and aggressive law enforcement, sex discrimination remains all too prevalent. Indeed, it's important to note that, despite centuries of discrimination, Title VII of the Civil Rights Act, the [1964] federal law barring job discrimination, is barely thirty years old. Federal laws banning sex discrimination in education date only to 1972, and less than twenty-five years have passed since the Supreme Court first recognized in 1971 that governmental sex discrimination was indeed unconstitutional.

Given this short history of efforts to realize equal opportunity in our society, the ongoing force of sex discrimination should surprise no one. A few examples make clear how discrimination continues to limit women's opportunities. For instance, a federal judge in California found that Lucky's Stores, a major grocery chain, routinely segregated women in low-wage, dead-end jobs while hiring men for jobs that led to management opportunities. Women were denied access to critical training programs and were steered, against their wishes, into part-time rather than full-time jobs.

In yet another example, a District of Columbia federal court found that Price Waterhouse, the major accounting firm, refused to promote a woman to partnership because she wasn't considered sufficiently "feminine"—even though she had generated millions of dollars more revenue than any other candidate.

Social science studies further document the continued vitality of sex discrimination. A National Bureau of Economic Research project sent equally qualified pairs of male and female applicants to seek jobs at a range of Philadelphia restaurants. This "audit" found that high-priced restaurants offering good pay and tips were twice as likely to offer jobs to the male applicants over their equally qualified female counterparts.

MEN DOMINATE TOP JOBS

The not-so-surprising result of ongoing discrimination is that white men still dominate most upper-level, managerial jobs. For example, women and people of color make up fewer than 5% of senior managers (vice president and above) in Fortune 1000 companies, even though women constitute 46% and people of color 21 % of the overall workforce. Women also continue to face significant barriers when seeking the higher-paying nontraditional jobs offered in the skilled and construction trades. In 1993, fewer than 1% of American auto mechanics, carpenters, and plumbers were women; only 1.1% of electricians and 3.5% of welders were women.

Not surprisingly, men are much more likely to be high wage earners than women. For example, 16.4% of white men were high wage earners (earning $52,364 or more annually) in 1992, compared to only 3.8% of white women, 1.6% of black women, and 1.8% of Hispanic women. In contrast, only 11.6% of white men were low wage earners (earning $13,091 or less a year), compared to 21.1% of white women, 26.9% of black women, and 36.6% of Hispanic women.

Women are painfully aware that merit still too often takes a back seat to discrimination. Qualified women consistently earn less than their male counterparts. For example:

- College-educated Hispanic women annually earn $1,600 less than white male high school graduates and nearly $16,000 less than college-educated white men.
- College-educated black women annually earn only $1,500 more than white male high school graduates and almost $13,000 less than college-educated white men.
- College-educated white women earn only $3,000 more a year than white male high school graduates and $11,500 less than white men with college degrees.

How Affirmative Action Corrects Discrimination

Affirmative action seeks to prevent the sort of discrimination described above *before* it happens by urging institutions to scrutinize their decision-making practices for sex-based stereotyping and other discriminatory actions. Affirmative action also enables institutions to correct discrimination once it is identified. Here are examples of the sorts of programs that have greatly improved women's access to key opportunities:

- Procter & Gamble's affirmative action program includes aggressive outreach of women and people of color to ensure a substantial and diverse pool of candidates for promotion to leadership positions. Over the last five years, 40% of new management hires have been women and 26% people of color.
- In the aftermath of the Lucky's Stores case discussed above, Lucky's created an affirmative action program to identify and groom women candidates for promotion that has doubled the percentage of women managers.
- A number of universities and employers have developed initiatives to provide specialized counseling and training to encourage women to enter engineering and other technical programs.
- The Department of Labor's Office of Federal Contract Compliance Programs (OFCCP), which enforces federal contractors' affirmative action responsibilities, has opened doors for women through targeted enforcement. It created thousands of new opportunities for women in the coal mining industry in the 1970s and in the banking industry in the 1980s. In the 1990s, the OFCCP's Glass Ceiling Initiative, which reviews contractors' efforts to create leadership opportunities for women and people of color, has generated promising changes in corporate attitudes and actions.

These programs counter the sex discrimination that too often taints decisions about education, business, and job opportunities. Largely because of programs like these, women have made significant progress in recent years:

- Women earn more—in 1963, women earned fifty-nine cents for every dollar earned by men; today, women earn on average seventy-one cents for every dollar earned by men.
- More women are in the pipeline for top jobs—in 1980, white women were 27.1% of all managers (middle and upper level) and women of color 3.2%; by 1990, white women were 35.3% of managers and women of color 6.9%.
- Women have moved into professional jobs previously occupied almost entirely by men—in 1993, 18.6% of architects were women compared to only 4.3% in 1975, 47.6% of economists were women compared to only 13.1% in 1975, and 22.8% of lawyers and judges were women compared to only 7.1% in 1975.

Affirmative action has proven successful in opening doors for qualified women. Rolling back these programs would prematurely abandon our long-standing national commitment to women's equality.

AFFIRMATIVE ACTION AND MERIT

Indeed, affirmative action is critically important to women because it strives to create an environment where merit can thrive and succeed, allowing qualified women to compete fairly on a level playing field, free from sex and race discrimination. To paraphrase Professor Roger Wilkins of George Mason University, affirmative action encourages institutions to develop fair and realistic criteria for assessing merit, and then to recruit a diverse mix of individuals qualified to take advantage of the available opportunities.

However, affirmative action's opponents too often mischaracterize such programs as the enemy of merit. Yet in a string of cases spanning nearly two decades and most recently reaffirmed in June 1995 in *Adarand Constructors, Inc. v. Pena*, the Supreme Court has made clear that lawful affirmative action in no way permits or requires quotas, reverse discrimination, or favorable treatment of unqualified women and minorities. The Supreme Court thus developed principles to ensure that affirmative action expands opportunities in a way that is fair to all Americans; it and other courts have consistently struck down programs that abuse or disregard these safeguards. In this manner, affirmative action creates a climate where qualified women—and men—can compete and excel.

Indeed, affirmative action programs have opened doors for qualified white men, too. For example, women-owned businesses currently create more jobs than all of the *Fortune* 500 companies combined, employing millions of women, people of color—and white men. Similarly, the affirmative action programs developed to respond to severe underrepresentation of minorities often create new training slots for black and white workers, thus generating opportunities for white workers that would not have existed without a commitment to affirmative action.

THE BOTTOM LINE

Affirmative action also improves businesses' bottom line—again, creating an environment where excellence can prevail. A growing number of businesses recognize that affirmative action policies boost productivity and increase profits by creating a diverse workforce drawn from a larger talent pool, generating new ideas, targeting new markets, and improving workplace morale.

Recent studies document how diversity boosts a company's performance. For example, a 1993 University of North Texas study pitted ethnically diverse teams of business students against all-white teams in solving business-related problems. The researchers found that the ethnically diverse teams viewed business situations from a broader range of perspectives and produced more innovative solutions to problems. Moreover, a study of stock market leaders by Covenant Investment Management found that the market performance of companies with good records of hiring and promoting women and people of color was 2.4 times higher than the performance of companies with poor records. Indeed, the one hundred companies with the best records of hiring women and people of color earned an 18.3% average return of investment, while the one hundred lowest ranked companies earned an average return of only 7.9%.

Tools like affirmative action have enabled women to make significant progress. Women today are professors, corporate executives, police officers, road dispatchers, and pilots. Yet they are still far, far short of reaching equality. As discussed above, women with college degrees earn only slightly more than men with high school diplomas—and substantially less than their male counterparts with college degrees.

The need for affirmative action remains. Because the law establishes clear safeguards against abuses, thus allowing affirmative action to create a climate where excellence can prevail, any concerns about unfairness can be answered simply by enforcing the law rather than scuttling it and its promise of equal opportunity for all. Unfortunately, however, too many opponents of affirmative action prefer to blame such programs for continuing racial and gender divisions, instead of confronting the root problems of sexism and racism. The sad truth is that our country's long history of discrimination lingers today in sex- and race-based stereotyping and other stigmatizing assumptions. Affirmative action seeks to help break down these barriers by bringing together diverse individuals at school and on the job.

"Is affirmative action the chief cause
of women's gains in the workplace?
My answer is: No."

WOMEN DO NOT NEED AFFIRMATIVE ACTION PROGRAMS

Susan Au Allen

Susan Au Allen is an attorney and president of the U.S. Pan Asian American Chamber of Commerce, a nonprofit organization representing Asian American business professionals. The following viewpoint is taken from a 1996 address in Las Vegas, Nevada, to a convention gathering of female legislators. Allen argues that affirmative action has two distinct meanings: programs that promote opportunities for both genders and all racial groups, and programs that give preferential treatment to select groups based on race or sex. She argues that most affirmative action programs fall within the second group, and criticizes them on the grounds that they unfairly discriminate against white men. She also questions whether existing income gaps between men and women are truly the result of gender discrimination.

As you read, consider the following questions:

1. How many government-sanctioned affirmative action programs exist, according to Allen?
2. What negative side effects do affirmative action programs create, according to the author?
3. How does Allen compare affirmative action with "family feuds"?

Excerpted from Susan Au Allen's speech to the annual conference of the National Order of Women Legislators, Las Vegas, Nevada, November 11, 1996. Reprinted by permission of the author.

I come to Las Vegas . . . [t]o tell you about the quiet revolution in Americans' view on fairness in education, at work, in business and in public life. I especially want to share my ideas about women and affirmative action.

Do I really mean an affirmative action revolution? Indeed, I do and I mean it exactly how a good dictionary defines it:

"A revolution is a sudden change, an upheaval in how people in a society relate to one another, and share power together."

The quiet but steady revolution in affirmative action puts individual rights over group rights. And it's a powerful one. . . .

CHANGING MINDS

Americans have changed their minds about affirmative action. The United States Supreme Court has changed its mind. There is a global shift in Americans' view on fairness. The view is that America offers opportunity for individuals, not groups. That is the great secret of American democracy, and it is one that dozens of singular foreign visitors to this country—like Alexis de Tocqueville, have pointed out to us in their books and comments. . . .

The biggest impetus for this revolution is an American Great Awakening. They have lived with the effects of affirmative action for more than a generation, they have felt its power and sting, and they are reevaluating it.

Now, I am not talking about the diversity which American corporations talk about. Diversity is a fact of life in most large corporations because the market controls much of the hiring. No one quarrels with the idea of a diverse workforce or student population. What I have trouble with is how diversity is achieved. Usually, it is through rigid rules that set numeric diversity goals. Typically, the government writes the rules for the public sector and through government contracts and grants, the private sector must also comply. So regulations establish goals, timetables, set-asides and quotas; and they give birth to arbitrary diversity levels.

By one count, there are 169 government-sanctioned affirmative action policies over which one can sue. When there are as many as 14 dozen—14 dozen—regulations promulgated to pick or exclude people based on their color, race, ethnic origin or sex, for employment, education and contracts, you have to agree that we have problems.

One other force at work in this new thinking . . . is the courts and the U.S. Supreme Court. With *Croson* (Richmond v. Croson, 1989) and *Adarand* (*Adarand Constructors v. Pena*, 1995), both government contracting cases, and *Hopwood* (Hopwood v. Texas, 1996), a law school admissions case, the courts are weaving together a tapestry of decisions rich in the new idea. The picture in the tapestry suggests a sun setting on the affirmative action empire.

These prominent cases carved out an important legal principle. That is, preferential treatment affirmative action is justified only in strict scrutiny situations—where there is clear evidence of past discrimination—and not simply where there is a shadowy (or more often, no) connection to past wrongs. These cases prohibited quotas, set-asides, goals and timetables—as they have been used in the past 30 years.

This is, however, the court's view of affirmative action. But people in your own legislative regions may have different views. . . . [Many] may have an incomplete picture of affirmative action in America.

DEFINING AFFIRMATIVE ACTION

Consider something many Americans may not know, that affirmative action has two definitions:

1. Equal opportunity affirmative action, programs which open opportunities to both genders and all racial groups.

2. Preferential treatment affirmative action, programs which pick only some groups according to their race or sex for favored treatment. This second, very much omnipresent feature of affirmative action is usually there, though its supporters deny that it exists.

You see the equal opportunity definition in the help-wanted ads. And you the preferential treatment definition in actual hiring.

It is the preferential treatment affirmative action that most Americans have trouble with. It affects the men in our lives, men who constitute one-third of America's population. They are excluded from equal opportunity, to make room for the blacks, the Hispanics, the Native Americans, the Asians, the disabled and women, two-thirds of the population.

Every woman in this room has a father, brother, husband, male friend or son. The new affirmative action court decisions offer a true sense of fairness to the men in our lives—the fathers, husbands, brothers, sons and male friends.

Each man needs and wants the opportunity in today's economy to keep his job, put food on the table for his family and, above all, provide for his kids' future.

Has the revolutionary attitude to affirmative action done good? You bet it has. It is now easier for your brother or husband to see a level playing field in employment.

GRADING AFFIRMATIVE ACTION

And it's about time. Even affirmative action's proponents see the chinks in its walls, the growing cracks in its foundation and in its overall architecture. Richard Kahlenberg is a friend of affirmative action. He has written a good book on it called *The Remedy*, but he is no friend of its current programs and effects.

Kahlenberg carefully assessed and summed up affirmative action's impact. . . . He graded the four roles affirmative action should play:

Provide equality of opportunity—for this he gave it a B

Offer some compensation for historical wrongs, C

Create long-term color and gender-blindness, F

Reduce prejudice and build more social harmony, F

TROUBLESOME SIDE EFFECTS

As he sees it, affirmative action has been an effort to create a panacea, but it winds up, a generation later, being a remedy with troublesome side effects.

There are two side effects people experience or hear about:

Affirmative action makes most people more, not less, race and gender conscious.

By raising the value of prejudice, especially through the preferences it depends on, affirmative action alienates entire groups of people.

To be fair, it has done some good for its beneficiaries, precisely by its equal opportunity programs:

It provided equal opportunity to people who had previously been left out, and it has had some success in compensating for historical wrongs.

But on the whole, and definitely through its side-effects, affirmative action has indeed become a bad remedy, a bad drug. Fortunately, it's a bad remedy that is being recalled from the marketplace of ideas. This is what we do with ideas whose time has passed. We let them recede, and like vines in sunlight, they start to wither away.

FAIRNESS TO MEN

The new thinking in affirmative action is a refreshing fairness to men. Many of them have lost a job to someone because of preferences. Take one prominent example: Richard Cohen, liberal columnist for *The Washington Post*, lost a major promotion because, he was told, *The Washington Post* needed a woman. That this particular woman came from a very old and still-affluent American family did not matter to the Post's management. Cohen said,

"Look, I'm the first one in my family to go to college. I went to school at night, and worked in the daytime. I have to make way for Theodore Roosevelt's granddaughter? She is a victim?"

Cohen's example brings in that third force that has spurred the quiet revolution in thinking about affirmative action. It's the government, especially the Glass Ceiling Commission [a bipartisan federal panel created in 1991 to study the progress of women and minorities in the workplace], that's had an impact. The Commission's role, in my opinion, has been more provocative than positive.

It believes women deserve treatment as "disadvantaged," regardless of their actual circumstances, so all sorts of hiring and promotion decisions are justified, as in Cohen's case.

But let's look closely at the Commission's argument:

There is a major wage gap and status gap between men and women.

The wage and status gaps are due to systematic discrimination against women. Women's workplace gains in the last three decades, just when the wage and status gap narrowed, are therefore the result of affirmative action. So the Commission says, affirmative action should be expanded for women.

GENDER GAPS EXPLAINED

Unfortunately, this is circular thinking. Correlations do not establish cause, though they appear to have causal connections. In the winter, the number of frozen pipes and heavy coat sales go up, but they are coincidences, not connected. Similarly, affirmative action and women's workplace gains are coincident; but are they causally connected? Put differently—Is affirmative action the chief cause of women's gains in the workplace?

My answer is: No. It is personal choices in education and career that explain largely the gaps and changes in women's wages and work status. So as I will show in a moment, we don't need to expand affirmative action for women.

First, let's agree that as a group and on average, women do earn less than men at all educational achievement levels. But let's also look at the fields the majority of women choose to study.

Arguments like these are fuzzy without numbers, so consider an example. In 1992, 75% of masters and Ph.D.'s conferred in education went to women. In that year, 86% of masters and Ph.D.'s earned in engineering went to men. Now the average monthly wage for an advanced education degree holder is $3,048, while for an advanced engineering degree holder is $4,049. Compare the two and, as they say here in Las Vegas:

Bingo. You get a wage gap of $1,001. However, the actual wage difference is because of personal choices. On average, education jobs pay less than engineering jobs and that explains the gap.

Hard thinking also explains the status gap. The Commission found few women hold high level jobs in Fortune 1000 (3%) and even Fortune 2000 (5%) corporations. Again, personal choices explain much of the average difference in work status between men and women. Women spend less time at work, have less seniority and therefore lower status jobs. Earlier Census studies show that while a man spends 1.6% of his work year away from work, a woman spends 14.7% work year, eight times as much as men. That is, one in every six years in a woman's career, on average are spent away from work. So the U.S. Department of Labor concluded, "Women spend significantly more time away from work and are apparently unable to build the seniority that men achieve."

What does this imply? Simply that, with less seniority, women get less pay and lower ranks than men. So women's personal choices play a role in creating the disparity in time on the job, the work they do, and the status they enjoy.

This is not to say that there is no discrimination. There is, but affirmative action is not the way to correct it.

Where we can't explain the disparities, let's be frank, we find the thing called "corporate culture," where men prefer men around them. As a result, some women are passed over by men. But we still have to allow for freedom of association. We still believe in it, don't we?

HARD TO SUPPORT PREFERENTIAL TREATMENT

So I think the rationale supporting preferential treatment affirmative action for women is very tough to defend. The major claims over the cause of wage and status gaps are difficult to support.

Let me make one last point. The argument for any preferential affirmative action is that historically, some group was under-represented in some area of life, so it demands "justice" today by subverting the merits of one individual to benefit a group; women in our case. The decision to give a job, a seat in school or a contract was not made based on individual qualifications, but on membership in a group, group qualifications.

The message is: If A discriminates against B, it is fair game for B's daughter to discriminate against A's son. If we agree with that, we believe that family feuds and multi-generational feuds are a good thing.

What's left to do? I think we must join the quiet revolutionaries ushering in the new affirmative action thinking. America's many opportunities, as the Constitution made abundantly evident, are by design for individuals—not for groups. And affirmative action as we know it has turned that principle on its head.

CHAPTER 4

IS ALCOHOL BENEFICIAL FOR HUMAN HEALTH?

CHAPTER PREFACE

Americans historically have "had an uneven relationship with alcohol," argues writer Dave Shiflett. "Sometimes they love it. Other times they can't pour it down the gutters quickly enough." Alcohol consumption has been a mainstay of American life since colonial times. Social movements urging the avoidance of alcohol as a solution for immorality, crime, and sickness have been prominent in the United States since the early nineteenth century. Organizations such as the Woman's Christian Temperance Union and the Anti-Saloon League of America succeeded in persuading lawmakers to ban the sale of alcoholic beverages in several states and, from 1920 to 1933, in the entire United States. However, although alcohol consumption rates did decline during the thirteen years of Prohibition, the so-called "Noble Experiment" was ultimately deemed a failure marked by widespread illicit alcohol consumption, lax law enforcement, and the rise of organized crime gangs that supplied the public's demand for alcohol.

Virtually no one advocates a return to Prohibition, but debates remain over alcohol-related public policies and issues. One significant controversy revolves around alcohol's net health effects. On the one hand, alcohol consumption is linked to cirrhosis of the liver, stroke, breast cancer, ulcers, and other health problems. Alcohol is also a potentially addictive substance, leading to out-of-control abuse in an estimated 10 percent of its users. In addition, alcohol is blamed for eight hundred annual deaths due to overdose, according to the Centers for Disease Control and Prevention, and seventeen thousand deaths due to alcohol-related accidents, according to the National Highway Traffic Safety Administration. For these and other reasons, governments at the federal, state, and local levels have enacted a variety of public policies, many of which are designed to discourage alcohol consumption. These include banning the selling of alcohol to people under twenty-one, drug abuse education programs that equate alcohol with other drugs, and laws requiring that alcoholic beverages contain warning labels stating that alcohol causes health problems and birth defects.

However, some people have argued that these public health policies have dwelled too much on alcohol's dangers while ignoring its benefits. Many medical studies in the United States and other nations have found that moderate alcohol consumption is associated with lower rates of heart disease and reductions in overall mortality. French researchers, for instance, reported at a 1997 international nutrition conference that a person who has two to six drinks a week could have up to a 79 percent less chance of dying because of a sudden heart attack than a person who abstains from alcohol. A 1994 article in the *British Medical Journal* concluded that deaths were lower for men between ages 50 and 90 who consumed about two drinks a day.

In 1995 the U.S. government acknowledged alcohol's benefits in the official dietary guidelines the U.S. Department of Agriculture and Department of Health and Human Services publish every five years. The guidelines state that "alcoholic beverages have been used to enhance the enjoyment of meals by many societies throughout human history" and that "current evidence suggests that moderate drinking is associated with a lower risk for coronary heart disease in some individuals." This represented a reversal from the 1990 nutrition guidelines that stated that "drinking has no net health benefit."

Some observers have praised this change as an overdue recognition of alcohol's beneficial effects and assert that such information should be more widely publicized by the government. They suggest, for instance, that winemakers and other alcohol beverage manufacturers should be able to attach product labels that inform consumers about the positive studies on alcohol. "Alcohol has been around forever," argues John Hinman, an attorney representing U.S. wineries, "and to suggest that manufacturers can't openly advertise its benefits as well as its risks is ludicrous." Others, however, question the wisdom of promoting alcohol's health claims. Michael Criqui, a professor of family and preventative medicine at the University of California at San Diego, contends that "if you made broad generalizations about the benefits of drinking, you're going to raise the average consumption of society and get more people abusing alcohol." Such concerns led the World Health Organization to conclude in 1991 that "any attempt to put across a message which encourages drinking on the basis of hoped-for gains in coronary heart disease prevention would be likely to result in more harm than benefit to the population." The viewpoints in this chapter provide an array of arguments on the health benefits and risks of alcohol, and on how this information should be communicated to the American public.

"Government bodies and health
organizations . . . acknowledge
moderate alcohol consumption's
role in reducing the risk of heart
disease."

MODERATE ALCOHOL CONSUMPTION
REDUCES THE RISK OF HEART DISEASE

Wine Institute

The Wine Institute is a policy advocacy association that represents 450 wineries in the United States. In the following viewpoint, the organization argues that medical studies have conclusively demonstrated that moderate alcohol consumption can
reduce a person's risk of heart disease, and that moderate
drinkers live longer on average than both nondrinkers and heavy
drinkers. Governments and health organizations in the United
States and Europe have acknowledged these findings in their official public health advisories.

As you read, consider the following questions:

1. What studies does the Wine Institute cite in claiming that
   alcohol consumption reduces heart disease?
2. What differences exist between U.S. and British guidelines on
   drinking, according to the Wine Institute?
3. What does the American Heart Association recommend about
   alcohol, according to the authors?

Reprinted from "More Favorable Alcohol Messages Throughout U.S. and Europe," *Wine
Institute Research News Bulletin*, February 1996, by permission of the Wine Institute.
(References in the original have been omitted in this reprint.)

Throughout the United States and Europe, more government bodies and health organizations than ever before now acknowledge moderate alcohol consumption's role in reducing the risk of heart disease. While continuing to warn against the dangers of excessive consumption, more favorable public policy messages, described on the following pages, are beginning to take into account results of large-scale studies showing that light-to-moderate drinkers live longer and have lower rates of heart disease than nondrinkers.

RECENT STUDIES

Influential studies from the U.S. in 1995 include data from Harvard University's Nurses' Health Study, which examined the alcohol consumption of over 85,000 women. "As compared with abstinence," the researchers wrote in the *New England Journal of Medicine*, "light-to-moderate alcohol consumption was associated with a significantly reduced risk of death due largely to a lower risk of fatal cardiovascular disease." A National Health and Nutrition Examination Survey (NHANES) follow-up study of more than 8000 American subjects, published in the *Journal of the American College of Nutrition*, also found that "significant, independent negative risk factors for coronary heart disease morbidity and mortality included alcohol intake." Twenty-year findings from the Honolulu Heart Program also found that alcohol intake was inversely associated with "all CHD [coronary heart disease] events." This study's cohort was nearly 3000 middle-aged Japanese-American men.

Studies in Europe, too, have had impact on the alcohol policy of governments and organizations, and have provided more evidence of alcohol's potential effect on overall mortality. Published in the *British Medical Journal*, the Copenhagen City Heart Study, analyzing over 13,000 Danish subjects, found that "wine drinkers experienced a significantly lower all cause mortality than the subjects who drank no wine," which included a lower risk for both cardiovascular and cerebrovascular disease. Additionally, a study of over 12,000 middle-aged and older British male doctors, also published in the *British Medical Journal*, found that "consumption of an average of one or two units of alcohol a day is associated with significantly lower all cause mortality than is the consumption of no alcohol."

With this kind of epidemiological evidence, official advice around the world is beginning to more accurately reflect what science has been establishing about alcohol. . . . Most messages warn against risks, stating that some people should not drink at all and excessive consumption is not recommended. But most healthy adults, they also make clear, who drink moderately and preferably with meals, have consistently been found to have a lower risk for heart-related disease than both nondrinkers and heavy drinkers. The following provides a summary of official advice regarding alcohol.

United States Government. The new U.S. Department of Agriculture (USDA)-Department of Health and Human Services (DHHS) 1995 Dietary Guidelines for Americans, released in January 1996, state, "Current evidence suggests that moderate drinking is associated with a lower risk for coronary heart disease in some individuals." The new Guidelines dropped its former statements that alcohol "has no net health benefit" and "is not recommended," and concludes with its advice for today: "If you drink alcoholic beverages, do so in moderation, with meals, and when consumption does not put you or others at risk."

United Kingdom Government. The 1995 United Kingdom Department of Health report, Sensible Drinking, suggests a "maximum health advantage" of between one and two daily units (a unit is approximately one small glass of wine) for both men and women and acknowledges safe drinking levels of up to four units per day for men and three units per day for women. The report states, "It is now established that the main specific pathology which benefits from alcohol consumption is coronary heart disease," and people who drink very little or none at all, and are in the age groups where there is significant risk of heart disease, may want "to consider the possible benefits of light drinking."

European Code Against Cancer. Regarding the heart, the European Code, revised in 1994, states, "The U- or J-shaped pattern of alcohol intake in relation to risk of cardiovascular disease, cardiovascular mortality and total mortality is well-known. This classic pattern is one of decreased risk in light drinkers compared with non-drinkers and then an increasing risk as alcohol consumption increases." While factors such as age, sex, physiological conditions and diet must be considered when "providing sensible advice regarding individually recommended limits of alcohol consumption, these "limits should not exceed 20 to 30 grams of ethanol per day, i.e. about two to three drinks of beer, wine or spirits each day, and may be lower for women."

International Life Sciences Institute (ILSI). ILSI Europe's book, Health Issues Related To Alcohol Consumption, states, "Results of ecologic, case-control, and prospective studies are concordant in that moderate intake of alcohol in the form of beer, wine, or spirits apparently protects by 10–70%, according to studies of both morbidity and mortality resulting from coronary heart disease. The protective effect of alcohol seems to be present at all ages, in women as in men."

World Health Organization (WHO). A WHO technical report series chapter, "Cardiovascular Disease Risk Factors: New Areas for Research," concludes that "moderate drinking (10–30g of ethanol daily, i.e. 1–3 drinks) provides a moderate protective effect against CVD [cardiovascular disease], as compared with abstention and heavy drinking."

American Heart Association. In its *HeartStyle* publication, the American Heart Association acknowledges population studies that "have shown that people who drink light to moderate amounts of alcohol are at lower risk than non-drinkers for deaths from heart disease. Moderate alcohol consumption also appears to decrease the risk of stroke caused by clots that inhibit or halt blood flow to the brain." The advice on alcoholic beverages, published in its American Heart Association Diet pamphlet, is as follows: "If you drink them, do so in moderation. Have no more than two drinks per day of wine, beer or liquor, and only when caloric limits allow."

MESSAGE OF MODERATION

The message of moderation with alcohol—and its healthy connection with the heart, particularly when consumed with meals—continues to be acknowledged by other bodies of scientists and nutritionists throughout the United States and Europe.

VIEWPOINT

*"Alcohol is too dangerous to be
employed as a pharmacologic agent
except in highly selected situations."*

ALCOHOL SHOULD NOT BE TOUTED AS A HEART DISEASE PREVENTATIVE

Michael H. Criqui

Moderate alcohol consumption has been linked to reduced mortality from coronary heart disease in many medical studies. In the following viewpoint, Michael H. Criqui agrees that even if this is the case, promoting alcohol as a method of preventing heart disease is problematic for several reasons. Alcohol consumption is linked to increased risks of breast and colon cancer, stroke, cirrhosis, and motor vehicle accidents. In addition, it has a high potential for addiction. Recommending alcohol consumption to prevent heart disease would likely increase the number of people who become addicted to or other otherwise harmed by alcohol, he concludes. Criqui is a professor in the Departments of Medicine and Family and Preventative Medicine at the University of California, San Diego.

As you read, consider the following questions:

1. What factors does Criqui include when calculating alcohol's net effect on potential years of life lost (PYLL) before age 75?
2. Why do the media and alcoholic beverage industry emphasize alcohol's potential health benefits, according to the author?
3. What disadvantages does alcohol have as a potential "pharmacologic agent," according to Criqui?

Reprinted from Michael H. Criqui, "Alcohol and Coronary Heart Disease Risk: Implications for Public Policy," *Journal of Studies on Alcohol*, September 1997, by permission of the author. (References in the original have been omitted in this reprint.)

The enthusiasm for recommendations that the public drink alcohol apparently stems from the consistent observation that light to moderate alcohol consumption, defined as ≤ two drinks per day, is related to reduced morbidity and mortality from coronary heart disease (CHD). The biological plausibility of this association is strong, since light to moderate drinking can elevate high-density lipoprotein (HDL) cholesterol levels, which are inversely related to CHD risk, and moderate drinking can also interfere with coagulation. However, higher levels of alcohol consumption can elevate blood pressure and produce direct cardiotoxicity, including arrhythmias, left ventricular hypertrophy and cardiomyopathy. Alcohol consumption levels above two drinks per day can thus lead to an increase in total cardiovascular disease (CVD), including stroke.

CHD and CVD are not the only disease endpoints associated with alcohol consumption, and thus the overall health risks of drinking must be considered in establishing public health policy. Heavier alcohol consumption is causally related to cirrhosis of the liver, and is a causal factor in morbidity and mortality from accidental and violent causes. In addition, even moderate levels of alcohol appear related to some cancers, including breast cancer in women and colon cancer in both sexes. Such data are often considered of lesser significance than the benefit for CHD, since CHD is the single largest cause of death in developed countries. However, CHD events occur mostly at older ages.

A fairer comparison is to look at the effects of various diseases on potential years of life lost (PYLL) before age 75. Data for 1990 from Canada reveal that CHD ranks first in men, but is closely followed by motor vehicle crashes and suicide, which are linked to alcohol use and together constitute 1,600 PYLL per 100,000 person years vs only 1,150 PYLL per 100,000 person years for CHD. Several other alcohol-linked diseases, such as cirrhosis, HIV, stroke, colon cancer and homicide, make large contributions to PYLL. The data for women are even more problematic. Both breast cancer and motor vehicle accidents each account for more PYLL than CHD, and suicide, stroke, colon cancer and cirrhosis all contribute to PYLL. Overall, alcohol was estimated to have accounted for over 100,000 deaths in the U.S. in 1990.

THE AGE-DEPENDENCY OF RISK

Excess drinking is most frequent in the young. Nonetheless, lifelong patterns of drinking are formed early in adulthood. Any favorable publicity about alcohol would likely have substantial influence on drinking in the young. However, the young are at greatest risk of several of the adverse effects of alcohol, such as accidents, violence and HIV infection, and they cannot possibly enjoy much benefit since CHD is uncommon before age 35 in men and 50 in women. In addition, the correlation between mean alcohol consumption and the extent of abuse in populations has been reported to be 0.97, which should give us additional pause concerning any favorable drinking recommendation.

WHO DRINKS AND WHO DOESN'T

Should nondrinkers start drinking? In the U.S., about 80% of men and 70% of women drink alcohol, with 50% of all drinkers experiencing temporary problems with alcohol. About 12% of male drinkers (10% of all men) and 7% of female drinkers (5% of all women) are alcohol dependent. Who are the 20% of men and 30% of women who don't drink? They include persons with: (1) a family history of alcoholism. The relative risk of a person with a family history of alcoholism subsequently becoming an alcoholic is four times, with no increased risk for other psychiatric illnesses. Much of this risk is apparently mediated genetically, since the concordance in monozygotic twins is much higher than in dizygotic twins; (2) a personal history of alcohol-related problems; (3) personal experience with sequelae of alcohol abuse in relatives or friends; (4) a medical contraindication; (5) religious, ethical or moral objections; (6) a dislike of being intoxicated; (7) a dislike for the taste of alcohol. Would it be wise to recommend that anyone in any of the abstainer groups above start drinking?

Should light drinkers drink more? Although alcohol may be protective for CHD at up to 4–5 drinks per day, the optimal benefit is usually seen at approximately one drink per day. In a 1997 study, the optimal benefit actually occurred at < one drink per day. Thus, there seems little justification to encourage light drinkers to increase their intake. They will gain no additional benefit for CHD, and the potential for harm from non-CHD causes increases sharply.

THE MEDIA AND THE ALCOHOL BEVERAGE INDUSTRY

The media are looking for news. Findings in research studies have frequently been reported without the caution appropriate for an intoxicating substance with a high addiction potential, and one that is a major cause of morbidity and mortality. Medical researchers must be accurate and judicious in reporting their findings.

The alcohol beverage industry, like all profit-making enterprises, is looking for a large and expanding market for its products. Although many persons in the industry are sincerely concerned about abuse and dependence, they do not consider abuse their major responsibility, and it is not their bottom line. They are understandably more receptive to the good than to the bad news about alcohol.

Should anybody ever be told to drink more, or not to drink less? Selected patients at elevated risk of CHD who can use alcohol responsibly should discuss their drinking habits with their physician, and can be counseled based on their individual situation.

ALCOHOL AS A PHARMACOLOGIC AGENT

In essence, those who would advocate the use of alcohol for cardioprotection are suggesting use of alcohol as a pharmacologic agent. Suppose alcohol were proposed to the Food and Drug Administration (FDA) as a pharmacologic agent. Initial clinical trials would show: (1) a dose-related suppression of cognitive function and coordination in all subjects; (2) severe psychosocial dysfunction in some subjects; (3) approximately 10% of subjects would develop profound addiction with devastating consequences for themselves, their families and occasionally innocent strangers. What would be the chances for FDA approval of a pharmacologic agent with this profile?

Although it is clear that a modest intake of alcoholic beverages affords some protection against CHD, a general public health recommendation endorsing drinking is contraindicated. Alcohol is an intoxicating substance with a high addiction potential and is a leading cause of morbidity and mortality. Any recommendation is likely to increase overall consumption, and such an increase would likely be differentially greater in the young, who have little risk of CHD but high risk from alcohol-linked adverse outcomes. Alcohol is too dangerous to be employed as a pharmacologic agent except in highly selected situations.

| "It is time for the government to
acknowledge that alcohol has
benefits—social, psychological, and
physical—as well as hazards."

THE HEALTH BENEFITS OF MODERATE DRINKING SHOULD BE PROMOTED

Stanton Peele

In the following viewpoint, psychologist and researcher Stanton Peele argues that medical researchers have long understood that moderate alcohol consumption has important health advantages, such as prevention of heart disease. However, because the U.S. government has been slow to acknowledge or publicize alcohol's positive health effects, many Americans remain ignorant of them. An illustration of the government's prejudice against alcohol can be seen through its treatment of labels, Peele contends. While alcohol products are required by federal law to carry labels warning of the hazards of drinking, efforts by the wine industry to inform consumers of alcohol's potential health benefits have met with government resistance. Peele is the author of *The Truth About Addiction and Recovery: The Life Process for Outgrowing Destructive Habits* and other books on addiction.

As you read, consider the following questions:

1. How much does moderate alcohol consumption (compared with abstaining) reduce the risk of heart disease, according to Peele?
2. How, according to the author, did federal government nutrition guidelines change between 1990 and 1995 with regard to alcohol?
3. What accounts for the U.S. government's reluctance to acknowledge the benefits of alcohol, according to Peele?

Reprinted from Stanton Peele, "Alcoholic Denial," *National Review*, August 11, 1997, by permission. Copyright 1997 by National Review, Inc., www.nationalreview.com.

In 1972, Harvard epidemiologist Carl Seltzer examined data from the Framingham Heart Study and found that drinkers were less liable to heart disease than abstainers. As it turned out, the Framingham project was the first of many studies to identify moderate alcohol consumption as a prophylactic against heart disease. But the National Institutes of Health (NIH), which funded the research, refused to let Seltzer publish a paper about this result. An NIH official said, "An article which openly invites the encouragement of undertaking drinking with the implication of prevention of coronary heart disease would be scientifically misleading and socially undesirable in view of the major health problem of alcoholism that already exists in the country."

Substantial Evidence of Alcohol's Benefits

This episode, which Seltzer recounts in the May 1997 *Journal of Clinical Epidemiology*, illustrates the Federal Government's long-standing prejudice against alcohol. A quarter of a century after the NIH put the kibosh on Seltzer's paper, the connection between alcohol consumption and a reduced risk of heart disease is well established. More than fifty epidemiological studies have looked for a link, and almost all have confirmed the relationship found in the Framingham data. The research indicates that the risk of heart disease for moderate drinkers is 40 to 80 per cent the risk faced by abstainers.

About a dozen prominent sources of research data—including the American Cancer Society, Kaiser Permanente, and the Harvard Nurses Study—have established that moderate drinking significantly prolongs life. (The risk of coronary heart disease remains lower even for heavy drinkers, but other causes of death begin to weigh in at high drinking levels, causing a net increase in mortality.) The Harvard Physicians Health Study found a reduction in overall mortality of more than 20 per cent for men who had about one drink a day. The government's National Health and Nutrition Examination Survey estimated that drinking moderately (up to two drinks a day) prolongs the lives of white males by an average of 3 to 4 per cent. For women, the benefits of alcohol appear clearly only after menopause, about age fifty. But the life-prolonging benefits of light to moderate drinking persist for senior citizens, as was established by a 1992 study reported in the *Journal of the American Geriatric Society*.

With evidence like this accumulating, at some point the government had to take notice. But the process has been achingly slow. Every five years, the Federal Government releases its Nutrition and Your Health: Dietary Guidelines for Americans. In

1990, the Guidelines continued to exclude positive information about alcohol, asserting that "drinking has no net health benefit." This position had become impossible to maintain by the time the 1995 report (released in January 1996) was written. And so a slight nod was given to alcohol's benefits: "Current evidence suggests that moderate drinking is associated with a lower risk for coronary heart disease in some individuals." The Guidelines also noted, "Alcoholic beverages have been used to enhance the enjoyment of meals by many societies throughout human history." These simple statements were more than balanced by warnings about the risks associated with higher levels of alcohol intake and about the people who should not drink (adolescents, pregnant women, drivers, those taking prescription or over-the-counter medications).

The U.S. document differed in significant ways from one produced concurrently in Britain, entitled *Sensible Drinking*. The British version identified somewhat higher levels of healthy drinking (e.g., about twice as much alcohol as the one-drink daily limit for women in the U.S. Guidelines). The British guide, unlike the American one, discussed the overall impact of drinking on life expectancy as well as the likelihood that drinking by premenopausal women reduces the risk of heart disease later in life. It did not offer a blanket warning against drinking by pregnant women—a warning that is hard to justify, since there is no evidence that light to moderate drinking causes birth defects.

Even so, the niggardly acknowledgments of alcohol's benefits in the U.S. Guidelines were hard won, as interviews with the report's scientific advisors revealed. One of them, New York University nutritionist Marion Nestle, said the changes represented "a triumph of science and reason over politics." Almost immediately after the report was published, anti-alcohol interest groups such as the Marin Institute began a campaign to reverse the statement about alcohol when the pamphlet is reissued in 2000.

RAISING PUBLIC AWARENESS

Not surprisingly, the role of alcohol in preventing heart disease is still not widely known. A 1995 poll by the Competitive Enterprise Institute found that only 42 per cent of Americans were aware of medical evidence that moderate drinking reduces the risk of heart disease. Efforts by manufacturers to increase the public's awareness have been stymied by the Bureau of Alcohol, Tobacco, and Firearms (BATF). Federal regulations concerning the marketing of beer, wine, and liquor ban any statement about "curative or therapeutic effects if such statement is untrue in any particular or tends to create a misleading impression." The BATF has interpreted this rule as forbidding "all therapeutic claims, regardless of their truthfulness." It argues that such claims are inherently misleading, given the "harmful societal effects arising from the consumption of alcohol" and the danger to "those who for psychological or physical reasons are adversely affected thereby."

THE DEBATE OVER HEALTH LABELS

Since 1989, federal law has required that every container of beer, wine, and liquor sold in the United States bear warnings from the surgeon general about the hazards of drinking. For years importers and manufacturers have suggested balancing these somber statements with information about the culture, history, and possible health benefits of alcohol. The BATF has rejected every one of these requests. In May 1995, the Competitive Enterprise Institute petitioned the BATF to allow alcoholic beverages to carry health statements in addition to the mandated warnings, offering as one suggestion, "There is significant evidence that moderate consumption of alcoholic beverages may reduce the risk of heart disease."

In October 1996, having received no response, the CEI filed suit in the U.S. District Court for the District of Columbia, demanding that the BATF act on its petition. In January 1997, just before it was required to respond to the suit, the agency denied the CEI's petition. The CEI amended its complaint, seeking a declaration that the BATF's denial was invalid on First Amendment and statutory grounds. Nineteen-ninety-seven Supreme Court rulings upholding the right of liquor stores to advertise prices and the right of brewers to tell customers the alcohol content of their beer bode well for the CEI's challenge.

Meanwhile, the Wine Institute filed its own request in June 1996, seeking permission for a label saying, "To learn about the health benefits of moderate wine consumption, write for the Federal Government's Dietary Guidelines for Americans." The BATF countered by requiring that the word benefits be replaced by effects, but as of this writing it has not granted the Wine Institute's petition. [Editor's note: In February 1999 the BATF approved new labeling rules permitting wine producers to put health labels on bottles.]

The Federal Government's reluctance to admit that there might be a good side to drinking reflects a culture strongly influenced by the ideology of the temperance movement, which depicted alcohol as a demonic substance with no redeeming value. More than sixty years after the end of Prohibition, it is time for the government to acknowledge that alcohol has benefits—social, psychological, and physical—as well as hazards. Surely this is a truth with which the American people can be trusted.

"Not only is alcohol dangerous for some people, but so is the word 'moderate.'"

THE HEALTH BENEFITS OF MODERATE DRINKING SHOULD NOT BE PROMOTED

Robert Zimmerman

Robert Zimmerman, a former editor of *Prevention File*, is a writer on alcohol and drug topics. In the following viewpoint, he criticizes efforts by the wine industry to promote the health effects of moderate alcohol consumption. Not only has alcohol been linked to breast cancer and other health problems, but it is also a potentially addictive substance that many people abuse, he contends. In addition, efforts to educate people on the benefits of "moderate" drinking will fail because people have wildly different understandings of what "moderate" means.

As you read, consider the following questions:

1. How does Zimmerman describe and define the "French paradox?"
2. How do people define the term "moderate," in the author's view?
3. What warnings does federal law require on alcoholic beverage container labels, according to Zimmerman?

Reprinted from Robert Zimmerman, "Moderation and Drinking Don't Mix," *San Diego Union-Tribune*, April 22, 1998, by permission of the author.

L et's hear it for moderation! We're all for moderation, aren't we? Well, it depends.

Sen. Strom Thurmond is proposing that the warning labels on alcoholic beverages be broadened to mention that even moderate consumption of alcohol may lead to alcoholism or can cause health problems such as hypertension and breast cancer. [Editor's note: Thurmond's bill, introduced April 1, 1998, was not acted on by the 105th Congress.]

His bill sends a shudder through the Napa Valley and the rest of the wine country. The vintners have been trying to convince the government that it would be all right to put a label on their bottles associating "moderate wine consumption" with good health. We can't have it both ways.

RESEARCH ON ALCOHOL

Research on alcohol and health appears to be moving faster than federal agencies can decide what to say about it. In 1991 a "60 Minutes" feature about the so-called French paradox fell like manna from heaven for the wine people. The French, it seems, eat the kind of fatty diet that clogs arteries. Yet the French have lower rates of heart disease than such a diet would suggest. Why? Because the French drink lots of wine. Scientists have confirmed that a glass or two of wine per day—or the equivalent amount of alcohol from any other source—can lower one's risk for heart trouble.

This evidence was compelling enough for the Public Health Service in 1995 to include a mention of it in its "Dietary Guidelines for Americans," being careful to point out that the benefit comes from a "moderate" amount of alcohol—one drink a day for women or two for men. The guidelines define a drink as 12 ounces of regular beer, 5 ounces of wine, or a 1.5-ounce shot of distilled spirits.

But the *Journal of the American Medical Association* in February 1998 published new research indicating that a woman's risk of breast cancer begins to rise with one glass of wine per day and is fully 40 percent greater if she drinks from two to five glasses in a day. And the Bill Moyers Public Broadcasting Service (PBS) special on addiction summarized new research on how alcohol affects the brain in ways similar to illegal drugs and can lead to addiction. To their credit Moyers and the PBS producers did not go along with the effort by alcoholic beverage companies to keep beer, wine and whiskey from being identified with other addictive drugs.

So what should the government say about "moderate" use of alcohol? Not only is alcohol dangerous for some people, but so is the word "moderate." Health professionals who screen patients for alcohol abuse are familiar with how slippery "moderation" can be, like the guy who describes himself as a moderate drinker because he only drinks one six-pack of beer every evening.

The federal Center for Substance Abuse Prevention ran a test on how drinkers would interpret a reference to "moderate wine consumption" as it would appear on proposed wine labels. Most of the 400 people in the survey said they had read or heard news stories about the link between wine and reduced risk of heart disease, and some said they were drinking more wine as a result. But the majority said they don't usually read wine labels, and if they read one like the sample they doubt if it would change their drinking behavior.

What was most striking about the survey is what it revealed about the meaning of the term "moderate." It means whatever anyone wants it to mean. Moderate in the minds of those interviewed ranged from one or two drinks in a month, to a whole bottle of wine in an evening.

"The word 'moderate' when associated with drinking has virtually no meaning," the researchers concluded. "The more one drinks, the more drinking one thinks is moderate."

The average number of drinks per occasion that heavy drinkers thought was moderate was almost six—which is more than the generally accepted definition of "binge" drinking.

In the 1970s the National Institute on Alcohol Abuse and Alcoholism launched a campaign to encourage "responsible" drinking. The program was quietly buried when it became obvious that no one could define exactly what "responsible" drinking amounted to. Is a message about "moderate" drinking any more likely to be understood? Apparently not.

WARNING LABELS

Wine bottles and other alcoholic beverage containers since 1989 have carried a government-mandated warning that women should not drink during pregnancy because of the risk of birth defects, and that consumption of alcohol impairs one's ability to drive a car and operate machinery, and may cause health problems.

If Sen. Thurmond wants to add a specific warning about alcoholism and breast cancer, fine. There needn't be a reference to "moderate" drinking because consuming any amount of alcohol is dangerous for some people, as the research shows.

And the Bureau of Alcohol, Tobacco and Firearms, which has jurisdiction over labels, should tell the wine people to forget about trying to capitalize on the French paradox.

| "No level of alcohol use during
| pregnancy has been proven safe."

PREGNANT WOMEN SHOULD ABSTAIN FROM ALCOHOL TO PREVENT BIRTH DEFECTS

March of Dimes

The following viewpoint is taken from a public education pamphlet published by the March of Dimes, a national voluntary health agency that works to prevent birth defects and infant mortality. The foundation notes that when a pregnant woman drinks, the alcohol passes swiftly to her fetus. Babies whose mothers drink thereby run the risk of fetal alcohol syndrome (FAS), a major cause of mental retardation, or other alcohol-related birth defects that can create both physical and behavioral problems. To be safe, the foundation concludes, women who are pregnant or are trying to become pregnant should abstain from alcohol.

As you read, consider the following questions:

1. How many babies are born each year with alcohol-related damage, according to the foundation?
2. What symptoms of fetal alcohol syndrome (FAS) do the authors describe?
3. What are some of the effects of moderate and light drinking during pregnancy, according to the March of Dimes?

Reprinted, with permission, from "Drinking Alcohol During Pregnancy," a 1998 March of Dimes Birth Defects Foundation publication at www.modimes.org.

Drinking alcohol during pregnancy can cause physical and mental birth defects. Each year, more than 50,000 babies are born with some degree of alcohol-related damage. Although many women are aware that heavy drinking during pregnancy can cause birth defects, many do not realize that moderate—or even light—drinking also may harm the fetus.

In fact, no level of alcohol use during pregnancy has been proven safe. Therefore, the March of Dimes Birth Defects Foundation recommends that pregnant women do not drink any alcohol—including beer, wine, wine coolers and hard liquor—throughout their pregnancy and while nursing. In addition, since women often do not know they are pregnant for several months, women who are attempting to become pregnant should abstain from alcoholic beverages.

Women who continue to drink alcohol, even in small amounts, while attempting to become pregnant, may reduce their chances of conceiving, according to studies.

A government survey indicated that, between 1991 and 1995, there was a substantial increase in alcohol use among pregnant women. Four times more pregnant women drank frequently (defined as seven or more drinks per week, or five or more drinks on one occasion in the previous month) in 1995 than in 1991. The survey suggests that approximately 140,000 pregnant women (or about 3.5 percent) drank frequently in 1995 as compared to 32,000 (or just under 1 percent) in 1991. Women who drink frequently greatly increase the risk of alcohol-related damage to their babies. The survey also reported that 16 percent of pregnant women had at least one drink in the previous month, compared to 12 percent in 1991.

When a pregnant woman drinks, alcohol passes swiftly through the placenta to her fetus. In the unborn baby's immature body, alcohol is broken down much more slowly than in an adult's body. As a result, the alcohol level of the fetus's blood can be even higher and can remain elevated longer than in the mother's blood. This sometimes causes the baby to suffer lifelong damage.

What are the hazards of drinking during pregnancy?

According to the Institute of Medicine, each year between 2,000 and 12,000 babies in the U.S. are born with fetal alcohol syndrome (FAS), a combination of physical and mental birth defects. FAS occurs in up to 40 percent of the babies born to women who are alcoholics or chronic alcohol abusers. These women either drink excessively throughout pregnancy or have repeated episodes of binge drinking (defined as having five or more drinks on one occasion).

FAS is one of the most common known causes of mental retardation, and the only cause that is entirely preventable. Babies with classic FAS are abnormally small at birth and usually do not catch up as they get older. They may have small eyes, a short, up-turned nose and small, flat cheeks. Their organs, especially the heart, may not form properly. Many babies with FAS also have a brain that is small and abnormally formed, and most have some degree of mental disability. Many have poor coordination and a short attention span and exhibit behavioral problems.

The effects of FAS last a lifetime. Even if not mentally retarded, adolescents and adults with FAS have varying degrees of psychological and behavioral problems and often find it difficult to hold down a job and live independently.

As many as ten times the number of babies born with FAS are born with lesser degrees of alcohol-related damage. This condition is sometimes referred to as fetal alcohol effects (FAE). These children may have some of the physical or mental birth defects associated with FAS. The Institute of Medicine has proposed new, more specific diagnostic categories for FAE, referring to the physical birth defects (such as heart defects) as alcohol-related birth defects, and to the mental and behavioral abnormalities as alcohol-related neurodevelopment disorder.

During pregnancy, how much alcohol is too much?

No level of drinking has been proven safe. The full pattern of FAS usually occurs in offspring of chronic alcohol abusers, most often in women who drink four to five drinks daily or more. However, it has occurred in women who drink less. FAE can occur in babies of women who drink moderately or lightly during pregnancy.

Less is known about the long-term outlook for children with FAE than about those with FAS. March of Dimes research grantee Ronald T. Brown, Ph.D., and others at Emory University in Atlanta, followed from birth until age 10 a group of children who were exposed to alcohol before birth but did not have full-blown FAS. Dr. Brown found that, as these children reached school age, they not only scored lower on measures of intellectual ability, but also exhibited more of the behaviors that teachers traditionally label hyperactivity: aggressiveness, destructiveness, inattentiveness and nervousness. Other researchers studying alcohol-exposed school-aged children also report behavior problems, along with academic difficulties involving mathematics and memory.

Researchers are taking a closer look at the more subtle effects of moderate and light drinking during pregnancy. Studies at the

University of Washington at Seattle followed to the age of 14 a group of middle-class children whose mothers had taken three or more drinks a day in pregnancy. At age 4 years, when given intelligence tests, these children scored five points lower than the average for all children in the study. Similarly, a 1995 French study reported that 4½-year-old children of women who had approximately three drinks a day scored seven points lower on intelligence tests than children of women who drank less. The Seattle researchers also found an increased likelihood of academic problems (including difficulties with mathematics) in 7- and 14-year-old children of moderate drinkers.

ABSTAINING FROM ALCOHOL IS RECOMMENDED

If a pregnant woman had one or two drinks before she realized she was pregnant, can it harm the fetus?

It is unlikely that the occasional drink a woman took before she realized she was pregnant will harm the fetus. The fetal brain and other organs begin developing around the third week of pregnancy, however, and are vulnerable to damage in these early weeks. Because no amount of alcohol is proven safe, a woman should stop drinking immediately if she even suspects she could be pregnant and abstain from all alcohol if attempting to become pregnant.

What other problems can drinking during pregnancy cause?

Consuming alcohol during pregnancy increases the risk of miscarriage, low birthweight, stillbirth and death in early infancy. Heavy drinkers are two to four times more likely to have a miscarriage between the fourth and sixth month of pregnancy than are nondrinkers. Heavy drinkers also are two to three times more likely to lose their babies during the perinatal period, from the 28th week of pregnancy through the first week after birth.

Is it safe to drink while breastfeeding?

Small amounts of alcohol do get into breast milk and are passed on to the baby. One study found that the breastfed babies of women who had one or more drinks a day were a little slower in acquiring motor skills (such as crawling and walking) than babies who had not been exposed to alcohol. Large amounts of alcohol also may interfere with ejection of milk from the breast. For these reasons, the March of Dimes recommends that women abstain from alcohol while they are nursing.

Can heavy drinking by the father contribute to FAS?

To date, there is no proof that heavy drinking by the father can cause FAS. There is, however, increasing evidence that heavy alcohol use by the male may have some effect on pregnancy and the health of the baby. Heavy alcohol use by males can lower the level of the male hormone testosterone, leading to low sperm counts and, occasionally, to infertility.

More studies are needed to fully understand how male exposure may affect pregnancy outcome. Men who stop drinking during their partner's pregnancy also help the partner to avoid alcohol.

What is the March of Dimes doing to prevent and treat FAS and FAE?

March of Dimes–supported researchers are investigating the influence of alcohol on pregnancy. For example, one current grantee is seeking to learn how alcohol causes malformations of the head, face and heart, in order to develop ways of preventing these birth defects. Another is looking at whether drinking alcohol during pregnancy alters how the body uses vitamin A, possibly leading to birth defects.

The March of Dimes also works to prevent FAS and FAE by educating the general public, teenagers, adults of childbearing age and expectant mothers about the dangers of alcohol and other drugs to their unborn children. Because there currently is no way to predict which babies will be damaged by alcohol, the safest course is not to drink at all during pregnancy and to avoid heavy drinking during the childbearing years (because at least 50 percent of pregnancies are unplanned). All women who drink should stop as soon as they think they are pregnant. Heavy drinkers should avoid pregnancy until they believe they can abstain from alcohol throughout pregnancy.

> "The evidence is clear that there is no
> apparent risk to a child from
> exposure to one drink per day."

THE HARMS OF MODERATE DRINKING DURING PREGNANCY HAVE BEEN OVERSTATED

Ernest L. Abel

Many pregnant women are advised to give up alcohol because of the risk that the baby might develop birth defects such as fetal alcohol syndrome (FAS). In the following viewpoint, Ernest L. Abel argues that the adverse effects of heavy alcohol consumption on developing fetuses have been well documented, but there is little evidence showing occasional or moderate drinking (one drink a day) to be harmful. While he recommends that women who drink and are pregnant should take steps to reduce their alcohol consumption, he also asserts that groundless fears of alcohol have caused unnecessary stress and anxiety among pregnant women. Abel is a professor of obstetrics and gynecology at the Wayne State University School of Medicine in Detroit, Michigan. He is the author of numerous books and articles on FAS, including *Fetal Alcohol Abuse Syndrome*.

As you read, consider the following questions:

1. How frequently is fetal alcohol syndrome (FAS) found among alcoholics, according to Abel?
2. What comparisons does the author make between European and American drinking patterns?
3. What negative outcomes does Abel attribute to overly cautious warnings to pregnant women about alcohol?

Excerpted from Ernest L. Abel, "'Moderate' Drinking During Pregnancy: Cause for Concern?" *Clinica Chimica Acta*, vol. 246, March 1996. Reprinted by permission of Elsevier Science. (References in the original have been omitted in this reprint.)

About 85% of all American women 12 years of age or older drink alcohol at least once a month. The adverse effects of alcohol abuse have been well documented, including its effects on the developing embryo and fetus, which can take the form of fetal alcohol syndrome (FAS). The diagnostic characteristics of this birth defect are prenatal growth retardation, physical anomalies, and central nervous system anomalies and deficits. FAS only occurs among alcoholics, however and even in this group, occurs at a rate of only 4%. Whereas individual aspects of FAS, often called "fetal alcohol effects" or "alcohol-related birth defects", such as decreased birth weight, may occur at levels below those associated with alcoholism, many studies have found that drinking during pregnancy has no detectable effects, and in some cases is even associated with a slight increase in birth weight.

Fig. 1 depicts the relationship between consumption levels during pregnancy and mean birth weight averaged across 30 prospective studies. In this figure, drinking is stratified according to smoking status and is also shown for smokers and nonsmokers combined.

As evident from Fig. 1, there is a significant decrease of about 200 g [grams] in birth weight at alcohol consumption levels of two or more drinks per day among smokers, but no evidence of decreased birth weight below this level of consumption. This implies that the dose-response relation between maternal alcohol consumption and birth weight is not linear, and that a threshold for the decrease in birth weight occurs at alcohol consumption levels averaging two drinks a day—but even then, only for smokers. The relationship between maternal alcohol intake and preterm births is similar.

Whereas studies on animals have frequently reported decreases in birth weight following treatment of mothers with alcohol, these studies are nearly always the result of exposure to relatively large doses, producing blood alcohol levels above 1.5 g/l [grams per liter]. This level is far above the legal level of intoxication of 1 g/l and would cause most people to become stuporous. When pregnant animals are treated with much lower doses, their offspring are not impaired. . . .

DRINKING BEHAVIOR IS COMPLEX

There is much confusion and misinformation relating to drinking during pregnancy because drinking behavior is very complex. For example, women from Mediterranean backgrounds regularly drink wine with their evening meals and rarely become drunk. By contrast, women in northern European coun-

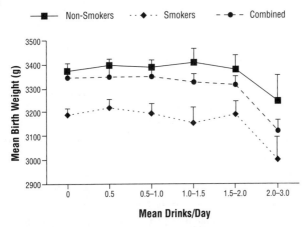

Fig. 1. Effects of alcohol on birth weight stratified by smoking status (◆ smokers; ■ non-smokers; and combined ● for both smokers and non-smokers)

tries and the United States of America are less likely to drink wine with their meals, but may drink regularly on weekends. In both cases, consumption may average one drink per day, but for the Mediterranean women this would in fact be one drink per day, whereas for the northern European or American women, it may be two drinks on Friday night and five on Saturday night. The average number of drinks is the same, but the peak blood alcohol levels would be very different. For instance, if a 70 kg [kilogram] woman consumed two drinks per hour every day, her peak blood alcohol level would be about 0.2 g/l, whereas if she drank five drinks on a Saturday night during a two-hour period, her peak blood alcohol level would be 1 g/l. Since it is the blood alcohol level, rather than the amount of alcohol consumed, that is critical for producing fetal damage, the difference in drinking patterns is a critical factor determining the potential dangers of alcohol. Studies reporting significant effects of levels of alcohol typically refer to biological effects so small as to be meaningless (e.g. a decrease in birth weight from 3500 to 3400 g). The dose-response curve for alcohol teratogenicity is not linear, and as in the case of every chemical that can affect the body, there is a "no effect" level.

Health-care professionals may recommend complete abstinence rather than "moderation" where drinking is concerned because they are "speaking a different language" than the public when it comes to terms like "moderate". For example, some alcohol researchers consider "moderate" drinking to include as many as four or five drinks per day, whereas most people would consider this level of consumption to be "heavy". Health-care providers consider "moderate" drinking a potential health hazard because they themselves have defined "moderate" operationally in quantitative terms others would call "heavy", not out of any malice, but because they are too far removed from the public they strive to protect. They mean that "heavy" drinking is a health hazard—on that issue few people would disagree. Some health-care professionals recommend abstention rather than "moderation" because they do not believe women can be trusted to follow advice. This line of reasoning assumes that if women are told that one drink per day is not harmful, they will take that as a license to drink two or three. Recommendations for abstention are based on ideology. Distrust of a woman's ability to judge for herself is patronising.

Government may have a duty to warn the public about the potential dangers of drinking, but without any guidelines as to how much alcohol constitutes a danger, such warnings are useless from a prevention standpoint. If the message of complete abstention in these warnings were heeded, every pregnant Catholic woman who took communion each Sunday would become anxious that she may have endangered her unborn child. If a sip of wine is acceptable, how about two sips, or four? Should pregnant Jewish women abstain from wine each sabbath and festival as well?

Warning signs and labels have been added to the prevention balance and have been found wanting. Women who are in no danger of harming their babies by their drinking have cut down slightly; those whose drinking constitutes a danger haven't changed their drinking habits.

MISGUIDED PATERNALISM

Misguided paternalism can also cause stress and anxiety among pregnant women. Even though their fears of alcohol-related birth defects are groundless, women alarmed by warning signs, popular magazines that present inaccurate articles that stress risks, and even physicians possibly practicing "defensive medicine" may elect to terminate healthy pregnancies "to be on the safe side".

Is there a cause for concern where moderate drinking is concerned? The evidence is clear that there is no apparent risk to a child from exposure to one drink per day—not an average, but a true single drink per day containing 13 g of alcohol. However, there is also no known benefit exposing a developing fetus to a drink per day. Abstaining women should not take up drinking alcohol during pregnancy. Women who drink alcohol should reduce its consumption as much as possible during pregnancy. Weighing the issues, the greatest danger to the life of an unborn child does not come from a drink per day but from alarmism over what might be the harm to that child, which could result in termination of an otherwise healthy pregnancy, or psychological distress that might itself lead to an unhealthy pregnancy.

CHAPTER 5

IS THE DEATH PENALTY A JUST AND EFFECTIVE PUNISHMENT?

CHAPTER PREFACE

In the 1970s, the United States appeared on the verge of abolishing the death penalty. Following a long steady decline in the number of annual executions from almost two hundred in 1935 to one in 1966, no executions were held in the United States for the next ten years. In 1972 the U.S. Supreme Court in *Furman v. Georgia* ruled that the death penalty was being applied unfairly and inconsistently by the states that utilized it and was therefore unconstitutional. The ruling nullified existing death sentences and voided all state and federal death penalty statutes then in effect.

A number of states soon enacted new death penalty statutes to address concerns raised by *Furman*. In 1976 the Supreme Court ruled in *Gregg v. Georgia* that capital punishment as such was not unconstitutional "cruel and unusual punishment" and let most of the new laws stand. In *Gregg* and several subsequent cases, the Supreme Court established some guidelines for judging the constitutionality of state capital punishment laws. The death penalty was limited to cases of criminal homicide and treason (but not rape or kidnapping). Death penalties could not be automatically mandated following a person's conviction, but instead required a jury's decision in which aggravating and mitigating circumstances of the crime were weighed. They could be carried out only after a review by a state appeals court.

Since the 1976 *Gregg* case twenty-nine states (out of the thirty-eight that have enacted death penalty statutes) have carried out executions. In South Carolina on December 18, 1998, Andrew Smith, convicted of stabbing two elderly relatives to death in 1983, was killed by lethal injection. He became the five-hundredth person to be executed in the United States in the post-*Gregg* era. Three states have been responsible for more than half of those executions: Texas, Virginia, and Florida.

The comeback of the death penalty in the United States following the 1967–1977 moratorium went against a global trend of doing away with capital punishment. More than half of the world's nations—including most Western democracies—have abolished capital punishment or have virtually abandoned it in practice. In 1997 the only three nations known to have executed more prisoners than the U.S. were China, Iran, and Saudi Arabia. The United States is also unusual among nations in that its laws and practices governing the death penalty are not nationally uniform, but instead vary from state to state and district to district.

Although public opinion in the United States has consistently supported capital punishment by a two-to-one margin, the death penalty has remained a contentious political issue. The arguments over the death penalty raise both practical issues (is the death penalty effective?) and moral ones (is it just?).

The question of the death penalty's "effectiveness" centers on whether capital punishment deters potential murderers. Proponents of the death penalty argue that it saves innocent lives because criminals refrain from murder for fear of being executed. In one noted study, Isaac Ehrlich, a statistician, examined homicide rates between 1930 and 1970 and concluded that each execution had the net effect of deterring seven to eight homicides. Death penalty opponents have strongly criticized Ehrlich's methods and conclusions; they maintain that the effectiveness of the death penalty (as opposed to life imprisonment) is either unproven or nonexistent.

The question of whether capital punishment deters crime is a side issue for many on both sides of the death penalty debate who consider the fundamental issues to be matters of justice and morality. Many death penalty opponents contend that capital punishment is immoral in all cases because it takes a human life and amounts to state-sanctioned murder. Other moral objections to the death penalty have focused on how it is administered. Supreme Court justice Harry Blackmun argued in a 1994 dissent that more than twenty years after Furman, "the death penalty remains fraught with arbitrariness, discrimination, caprice and mistake." Among the victims of the death penalty's arbitrariness, critics contend, are poor people unable to afford adequate legal representation and minorities subject to racial prejudice.

Death penalty supporters, on the other hand, reject the moral equivalency of capital punishment and murder. "Most of us," assert Alex Kozinski, a judge, and Sean Gallagher, a law clerk, "continue to believe that those who show utter contempt for human life by committing remorseless, premeditated murder justly forfeit the right to their own life." Supporters have also defended the administration of the death penalty against racial discrimination and other charges of unfairness. "While there is justification for the claim that discriminatory capital sentencing and execution occurred in the past," writes social researchers Stanley Rothman and Stephen Powers, "the charge that they persist today lacks support." The viewpoints in this chapter spotlight some of the debates concerning both the *effectiveness* and *justice* of capital punishment in the United States.

| "Capital punishment for proven premeditated murders . . . is a moral necessity, demanded by justice."

THE DEATH PENALTY IS MORAL

Robert James Bidinotto

In the following viewpoint, Robert James Bidinotto describes the actions, trial, and execution of Pedro Medina, a person who was convicted of a brutal killing. He argues that the principle of proportionality—the idea that criminals should be punished to the extent of the harm they have caused—justifies capital punishment on moral grounds in this and similar cases of premeditated murder. People should support the death penalty not because of utilitarian reasons (such as crime deterrence), but because justice demands it. Bidinotto is a journalist and author of *Freed to Kill*. He edited *Criminal Justice? The Legal System vs. Individual Responsibility*, a critical examination of America's criminal justice system.

As you read, consider the following questions:

1. What unstated moral premises form the basis for arguments against the death penalty, according to Bidinotto?
2. What, in the author's opinion, do the American people believe should govern how much punishment criminals receive?
3. Does Bidinotto believe that executions should be open to public viewing or made deliberately painful?

Reprinted from Robert James Bidinotto, "The Moral Case for Capital Punishment," *LEAA Advocate*, Summer/Fall 1997, by permission of the author.

On March 25, 1997, officials of the Florida Department of Corrections strapped condemned killer Pedro Medina into the electric chair at Florida State Prison. Like 38 other infamous murderers since 1976, including serial killer Ted Bundy, Medina would meet his end in the embrace of "Old Sparky."

This time, however, the 74-year-old oak electric chair more than lived up to its grisly name—and in the process, re-opened the age-old debate over the morality of the death penalty.

THE EXECUTION

After the black leather mask was lowered over Medina's face, the first of three surges of 2,000 volts of electricity jolted his body. He lurched back in the chair. Suddenly flames shot up from the mask, and burned for perhaps ten seconds. The death chamber filled with smoke.

Death penalty opponents immediately cited the gruesome nature of the execution to call once again for an end to capital punishment.

"It was brutal, terrible," declared witness Michael Minerva. "It was a burning alive, literally." Minerva—a defense lawyer for a taxpayer-supported state agency that defends death row inmates—demanded that the governor halt all pending executions.

"When you torture someone to death," added Robyn Blumner, executive director of the Florida chapter of the American Civil Liberties Union, "the Eighth Amendment [barring "cruel and unusual" punishment] clearly has been violated."

Of course, Medina hadn't been "burned alive" or "tortured to death." The medical examiner later said that he'd found no signs that Medina had suffered or felt any prolonged pain; most likely, he had died almost instantly. But the truth hardly mattered; the charges of suffering and torture were only the latest of many spurious arguments employed by death penalty opponents during Medina's long appeal process.

Medina himself had been the most cynical of the claimants. Not only did he maintain his innocence of the murder for which he was convicted; he also argued, on appeal, that he should not have been given the death penalty even if guilty. His reason: the trial court had erred in finding in his crime aggravating factors of "heinous, atrocious, or cruel and for pecuniary gain"—factors necessary for imposing a death-penalty sentence.

A review of the facts, however, suggests otherwise, and provides some telling insights concerning the morality of capital punishment.

You may recall that in 1980, Fidel Castro cleansed his nation of some 125,000 criminals, mentally ill, and other "undesirables" during the notorious "Mariel boatlift." Pedro Medina was among Castro's castoffs.

Once in America, Medina nurtured dreams of upward mobility, symbolized by having a car of his own. Appeals court records describe it as a "tremendous desire," even "an obsession." By 1982, Medina also had a jailed girlfriend, another source of frustration.

He gained the friendship and sympathy of Dorothy James, a 52-year-old mother and schoolteacher. And it turns out that Mrs. James had a car—just the kind of car Medina yearned for.

A simple, direct sort of man, Medina did the only practical thing: in order to obtain the car, he stabbed his "friend," Mrs. James, to death. He wasn't very skilled at it, but he was persistent. In fact, he inflicted a total of ten wounds—six to her chest, one in her neck, another in her abdomen, and two more to her left wrist. Even so, Dorothy James wouldn't die.

Irritated, Medina jammed a gag in her mouth. The medical examiner later determined that Mrs. James, in physical agony, took up to a half hour to die.

Pedro Medina finally had the car of his dreams. Unfortunately, in his excitement, he left his hat behind at the murder scene. Eventually, he decided that it actually might be better to sell the hot car, in order to raise bail for his girlfriend. But negotiations didn't go well with a prospective buyer. So, Medina stabbed and robbed that guy, too.

ARREST AND CONVICTION

Police caught up with Pedro Medina in Lake City, Florida. They found him asleep at the side of the road in Mrs. James' stolen car. At his trial, Medina was asked to try on the hat which had been recovered from the murder scene. It fit perfectly. Being a simple, direct sort of man, Medina then asked the judge if he could keep the hat. "You've got to be kidding!" the judge exclaimed.

He was convicted of murder and given the death penalty.

Years of appeals and endless protestations of innocence failed to sway a small army of appellate judges, who affirmed that his murder of Dorothy James had been "heinous, atrocious, or cruel and for pecuniary gain"—thus meriting the death penalty.

Of course, that didn't persuade death penalty opponents that putting him to death was right and just. They argued, in effect, that however heinous and cruel, Medina's murder of Dorothy James should be irrelevant to the degree of punishment he might receive. He should not be punished in proportion to the harm he had caused an innocent woman; he should not get "revenge," or "just desserts," or "an eye for an eye"; he should not receive justice, but rather, mercy.

UNSTATED PREMISES

This argument, typical of death penalty opponents, is based on several unstated, and usually unchallenged, moral premises:

- that mercy is ethically superior to justice (which they call "revenge");
- that all human life—even that of a killer—has "intrinsic value," so that it's immoral to take another's life under any circumstances; and
- that society's response to a crime shouldn't be proportionate to the harm caused by the criminal, but governed by other considerations.

How do supporters of the death penalty answer such claims? Too often, they ignore or evade these moral questions at the core of the debate, and instead try to advance "practical" (or utilitarian) arguments for capital punishment.

For example, they typically base their case on the notion that capital punishment is a necessary measure for "crime control." From this, they go on to argue (a) that capital punishment incapacitates (or prevents) the killer from ever repeating his crime, and (b) that the existence of a death penalty deters future murders by frightening other would-be killers.

Now it's certainly true that executing a convicted killer will prevent him from ever committing another murder. It's also probably true that some unknown number of potential killers might hesitate, out of fear of being put to death themselves.

But there are two major problems with this line of argument. First, it begs the moral question: it doesn't address the moral claims of death penalty opponents.

Second, as primary objectives of the law, deterrence and incapacitation don't aim primarily to punish a past offense, but rather to prevent future ones. And that can lead to gross injustices.

To elaborate on this second point: as a response to crime, punishment "looks backwards," into the past—to the criminal's specific past crimes and victims.

You punish someone for bad things he already did. By contrast, so-called crime-control measures "look forward," into the future, trying to reduce the rates of future crime. They don't directly address what someone already did; rather, they try indirectly to alter what he might do. They largely forget the criminal's past crimes—and his past victims.

But aren't the past victims of central importance to our system of justice? If preventing future crime is the main goal of the criminal law, then we could easily reduce the number of future murders by blindly imposing brutal penalties on all potential killers—penalties that most people would find to be grossly unfair and disproportionate.

For example, since most killers have escalated from less serious crimes, we might execute all those convicted of any violent crime. That way, we'd be sure to eliminate a significant number of budding killers, and reduce future murder rates. Or, since killers share many psychological characteristics, we might execute any criminal who fit a psychological profile that places them at high risk for future violence. In fact, if reducing the future crime rate were the only consideration in how we punish people, we could simply execute all criminals, from petty to serious. Surely that would be an effective crime control measure. But would anyone think it was fair or just? Should a pickpocket and a serial killer merit exactly the same punishment?

A "crime control" agenda based strictly on deterrence and incapacitation can also lead to unexpected leniency. That's because if reducing future murders is all that matters, then it's not logical or cost-effective to execute those murderers who are unlikely either to repeat their crimes, or to inspire "copycats."

For example, most people would probably agree that Susan Smith, the woman who drowned her own children in October 1994, would be unlikely ever to repeat such an atrocity.

Nor would her unspeakable act be likely to encourage other mothers to drown their own babies, even if she went unpunished. Well, then why bother punishing her at all, let alone with a death penalty?

Solely on the "practical" grounds of deterrence or incapacitation, it doesn't make sense.

Yet most of us would think it obscene to let Susan Smith go totally unpunished for her murders. Sure, we might free Susan Smith tomorrow, on the grounds that she poses "no further threat to society." But is that the issue? Is the point of the criminal justice system simply to render Susan Smith safer to those she may encounter in the future? Or isn't the law also supposed to represent her past victims, her two dead babies? Who speaks for them? Don't they count in any system of justice worthy of the name?

THE PRINCIPLE OF PROPORTIONALITY

Americans are a fair-minded people. They think that a criminal should be punished roughly to the extent of the harm he has caused to people—not more, and not less. This is the principle of proportionality—and most of them intuitively understand that proportionality lies at the heart of justice. That, more than anything else, is what they want, expect, and demand from the criminal justice system. But a utilitarian system, based solely on controlling future crime, invariably sacrifices justice to expediency.

Ironically, many criminal justice "hardliners," who believe in tough deterrence and incapacitation, actually share a common premise with many "bleeding hearts," who believe in rehabilitation and mercy. Hardliners typically want to impose penalties that are much more severe than the damage criminals have actually done to victims. Bleeding hearts want penalties far less severe than the damage done to victims. Both groups believe that the severity of punishments should have no necessary relationship to the seriousness of a crime. Both groups thus reject the principle of proportionality—of justice.

Justice is a punitive response to a criminal that penalizes him in direct proportion to the harm he has done to actual individuals; to reflect back onto him the negative consequences of his criminal actions.

And this brings us back to capital punishment. The moral defense of the death penalty is the principle of justice. In the case of premeditated murder, capital punishment is the only just punishment: it is the only punishment roughly proportionate to the harm that has been done to the murder victim.

Now, anyone who respects life is understandably uneasy about taking even the lives of killers. But the principle of justice demands it, because proportionate punishment for crimes is the moral keystone of any system of justice.

If we undermine or abandon proportionality, how do we then gauge whether to punish someone for a crime, and how much? Why not a hundred lashes of the whip for stealing a loaf of bread—but a mere $5 fine for rape? We are stuck in a trap of arbitrary punishments, of different punishments for the same crime, of punishing someone either too much or too little—and of having our entire legal system lose public credibility and respect, on the grounds that it is inherently unfair and unjust. (That, in fact, is the situation our utilitarian-based legal system finds itself in today.)

To abandon proportionality in sentencing, we abandon the quest for justice itself. And to deny the death penalty for premeditated murder, is to deny the very principle of fitting punishments to offenses. If we abandon the principle of proportionality in the case of murder, the most serious of crimes, then on what grounds do we argue for proportionate punishments for any lesser crimes?

Capital punishment for proven premeditated murders is therefore not immoral; it is not even a "necessary evil"; it is *a moral necessity*, demanded by justice.

Critics of the death penalty—and of punishment in general—often denounce punitivity as arising from "vengeance," or some crude, vindictive notion of "an eye for an eye." But in fact, justice isn't based on revenge; it is based on retribution. The two concepts aren't the same.

The criminal (such as Pedro Medina) wants to gain something unearned and undeserved by force, at the expense of someone else (such as Dorothy James).

Retribution is the moral principle that the harm and injury imposed on the victim should be reflected proportionately back onto the criminal who caused them.

This policy is both moral and practical. Moral—because it upholds the value of innocent human life. Practical—because a policy of reflecting full harm back on the criminal frustrates his goal, which is to profit at someone else's expense. Retribution means that the criminal "won't get away with it."

The principle of proportionality also answers those critics of capital punishment who say they prefer "mercy" to "revenge." First of all, "mercy"—as these people use the term—means a negation of simple justice, by allowing the criminal to bear lower costs for his crimes than the harm he imposes on his victims. This sort of "mercy" actually encourages criminals, because they know that they can gain more from crime than any costs they will have to bear. In this respect, "mercy" (embodied in most "rehabilitation" programs) is utterly immoral.

THE RELATIVE WORTH OF HUMAN LIVES

However, one charge by death penalty opponents is true: the moral case for capital punishment does indeed rest upon making a strong distinction about the relative "worth" of human lives. The concept of justice is incompatible with the view that all human lives are "intrinsically and equally valuable," regardless of the individuals' chosen moral behavior. If that were true, then it would be wrong for an innocent victim to kill an aggressor, even in self-defense or in wartime—because the aggressor's life would be "of equal intrinsic value."

Only human predators could gain from such a policy, and only the innocent could lose. A system that would leave the morally innocent at the mercy of evil predators can be called many things, but "moral" isn't one of them.

On the principle of justice, only the lives of the morally innocent are truly and fully "human." The lives of predators are—by their own choice—subhuman.

A system of justice must make a clear distinction between the two—between the Pedro Medina's and the Dorothy James's of the world—and it must respond accordingly.

America was founded on the principle that each individual is an end in himself. In such a society, premeditated murder is a crime in a class by itself. Murder negates the highest moral end of civil society: the irreplaceable human life.

What possible penalty could be proportionate to such a crime, except the forfeiture of the murderer's own life?

So, in the case of premeditated murder, where there is no question of guilt and no extenuating circumstances, capital punishment should be the standard penalty—on moral grounds.

A Profound Tragedy

We should take no joy in the execution of predators such as Pedro Medina. The taking of a life is a symbol of the ultimate possible waste. It is a profound tragedy, which should be conducted with solemnity, dignity, and privacy. It should not become cause for public participation, celebration, or spectacle.

And it should not involve the deliberate imposition of cruelty or torture: we need not sink to the moral depths of the predators themselves. Executions should be as painless and quick as possible.

But there should be no moral apologies when capital punishment must be employed. Those occasions should be a moral affirmation to the innocent of our common commitment to justice—just as there should be a moral statement to the guilty that there are some crimes no civilized and decent society will ever stoop to tolerate.

> "If we are to have a firm moral
> bedrock for our society, we must
> establish that no one may be
> permitted to kill . . . and that
> includes government."

THE DEATH PENALTY IS IMMORAL

Helen Prejean

Helen Prejean is a Catholic nun and anti-death penalty activist.
Her work as a spiritual advisor to death row inmates formed the
basis for her 1993 book, *Dead Man Walking*. In the following viewpoint, she combines descriptions of her experiences with
Patrick Sonnier, a convicted murderer who was executed in
1982, with general arguments on the morality of the death
penalty. Prejean argues that the death penalty is a fundamentally
unjust taking of a person's life. It is also ethically objectionable
because it falls disproportionately on poor and minority defendants, who are ill served by America's legal system. She concludes that the death penalty can and should be abolished in the
United States.

As you read, consider the following questions:

1. What experiences led the author to become involved with
   death row prisoners?
2. What three central societal issues are connected to the death
   penalty, according to Prejean?
3. What does Prejean assert to be the "essential torture" of the
   death penalty?

Excerpted from Helen Prejean, "Would Jesus Pull the Switch?" *Salt of the Earth*, March
1997. Reprinted with permission from *Salt*, Claretian Publications, 205 W. Monroe St.,
Chicago, IL 60606.

I was scared out of my mind. I went into the women's room because it was the only private place in the death house, and I put my head against the tile wall and grabbed the crucifix around my neck. I said, "Oh, Jesus God, help me. Don't let him fall apart. If he falls apart, I fall apart."

I had never watched anybody be killed in front of my eyes. I was supposed to be Patrick Sonnier's spiritual advisor.

I was in over my head.

All I had agreed to in the beginning was to be a pen pal to this man on Louisiana's death row. Sure, I said, I could write letters. But the man was all alone, he had no one to visit him.

It was like a current in a river, and I got sucked in. The next thing I knew I was saying, "OK, sure, I'll come visit you."

He had suggested that on the prison application form for visitors I fill in "spiritual advisor," and I said, "Sure." He was Catholic, and I'm a Catholic nun, so I didn't think much about it; it seemed right.

But I had no idea that at the end, on the evening of the execution, everybody has to leave the death house at 5:45 p.m., everybody but the spiritual advisor. The spiritual advisor stays to the end and witnesses the execution.

CAPITAL PUNISHMENT AND THE BIBLE

People ask me all the time, "What are you, a nun, doing getting involved with these murderers?" You know how people have these stereotypical ideas about nuns: nuns teach; nuns nurse the sick.

I tell people to go back to the gospel. Look at who Jesus hung out with: lepers, prostitutes, thieves—the throwaways of his day. If we call ourselves Jesus' disciples, we too have to keep ministering to the marginated, the throwaways, the lepers of today. And there are no more marginated, thrown-away, and leprous people in our society than death-row inmates.

There's a lot of what I call "biblical quarterbacking" going on in death-penalty debates: people toss in quotes from the Bible to back up what they've already decided anyway. People want to not only practice vengeance but also have God agree with them. The same thing happened in this country in the slavery debates and in the debates over women's suffrage.

Religion is tricky business. Quote that Bible. God said torture. God said kill. God said get even.

Even the Pauline injunction "Vengeance is mine, says the Lord, I will repay" (Rom. 12:19) can be interpreted as a command and a promise—the command to restrain individual impulses toward revenge in exchange for the assurance that God

176

will be only too pleased to handle the grievance in spades.

That God wants to "get even" like the rest of us does not seem to be in question.

One intractable problem, however, is that divine vengeance (barring natural disasters, so-called acts of God) can only be interpreted and exacted by human beings, *very* human beings.

I can't accept that.

Jesus Christ, whose way of life I try to follow, refused to meet hate with hate and violence with violence. I pray for the strength to be like him.

I cannot believe in a God who metes out hurt for hurt, pain for pain, torture for torture. Nor do I believe that God invests human representatives with such power to torture and kill.

The paths of history are stained with the blood of those who have fallen victim to "God's Avengers." Kings, popes, military generals, and heads of state have killed, claiming God's authority and God's blessing. I do not believe in such a God.

THE SIDE OF THE POOR

But here's the real reason why I got involved with death-row inmates: I got involved with poor people. It took me a while to wake up to the call of the social gospel of Jesus. For years and years when I came to the passages where Jesus identified with poor and marginated people I did some fast-footed mental editing of the scriptures: *poor* meant "spiritually poor."

When I read in Matthew 25, "I was hungry and you gave me to eat," I would say, "Oh, there's a lot of ways of being hungry." "I was in prison, and you came to visit me,"—"Oh, there's a lot of ways we live in prison, you know."

Other members of my religious community woke up before I did, and we had fierce debates on what our mission should be. In 1980, when my religious community, the Sisters of St. Joseph of Medaille, made a commitment to "stand on the side of the poor," I assented, but only reluctantly. I resisted this recasting of the faith of my childhood, where what had counted was a personal relationship with God, inner peace, kindness to others, and heaven when this life was done. I didn't want to struggle with politics and economics. We were nuns, after all, not social workers.

But later that year I finally got it. I began to realize that my spiritual life had been too ethereal, too disconnected. To follow Jesus and to be close to Jesus meant that I needed to seek out the company of poor and struggling people.

So in June 1981 I drove a little brown truck into St. Thomas, a black, inner-city housing project in New Orleans, and began to live there with four other sisters.

Growing up a Southern white girl right on the cusp of the upper class, I had only known black people as my servants. Now it was my turn to serve them.

It didn't take long to see that for poor people, especially poor black people, there was a greased track to prison and death row. As one Mama in St. Thomas put it: "Our boys leave here in a police car or a hearse."

It didn't take long to see how racism worked. When people were killed in St. Thomas and you looked for an account of their deaths in the newspaper, you'd find it buried on some back page as a three-line item. When other people were killed, it was front-page news.

Drug activity took place in the open, but when the sisters went to the mayor's office to complain, the officials would just shrug their shoulders and say, "Well, you know, Sister, every city has a problem with drugs. At least we know where they are."

I began to understand that some life is valued and some life is not.

MEETING PATRICK SONNIER

One day a friend of mine from the Prison Coalition Office casually asked me if I'd be a pen pal to someone on death row in Louisiana.

I said, "Sure." But I had no idea that this answer would be my passport to a strange and bizarre country. God is a mystery, but one of the definite characteristics of God is that God is sneaky.

When I began visiting Patrick Sonnier in 1982, I couldn't have been more naive about prisons. . . .

I wrote Patrick about life at Hope House in St. Thomas, and he told me about life in a 6-by-8½-foot cell, where he and 44 other men were confined 23 hours a day. He said how glad he was when summer was over because there was no air in the cells. He'd sometimes wet the sheet from his bunk and put it on the cement floor to try to cool off; or he'd clean out his toilet bowl and stand in it and use a small plastic container to get water from his lavatory and pour it over his body.

Patrick was on death row four years before they killed him.

I made a bad mistake. When I found out about Patrick Sonnier's crime—that he had killed two teenage kids—I didn't go to see the victims' families. I stayed away because I wasn't sure how to deal with such raw, unadulterated pain. I was a coward. I only met them at Patrick's pardon-board hearing. They were there to demand Patrick's execution. I was there to ask the board to show him mercy. It was not a good time to meet.

Here were two sets of parents whose children had been ripped from them. I felt terrible. I was powerless to assuage their grief. It would take me a long time to learn how to help victims' families, a long time before I would sit at their support-group meetings and hear their unspeakable stories of loss and grief and rage and guilt.

I would learn that the divorce rate for couples who lose a child is over 70 percent—a sad new twist to "until death do us part." I would learn that often after a murder friends stay away because they don't know how to respond to the pain.

THREE WOUNDS

I don't see capital punishment as a peripheral issue about some criminals at the edge of society that people want to execute. I see the death penalty connected to the three deepest wounds of our society: racism, poverty, and violence.

In this country, first the hangman's noose, then the electric chair, and now the lethal-injection gurney have been almost exclusively reserved for those who kill white people.

The rhetoric says that the death penalty will be reserved only for the most heinous crimes, but when you look at how it is applied, you see that in fact there is a great selectivity in the process. When the victim of a violent crime has some kind of status, there is a public outrage, and especially when the victim has been murdered, death—the ultimate punishment—is sought.

But when people of color are killed in the inner city, when homeless people are killed, when the "nobodies" are killed, district attorneys do not seek to avenge their deaths. Black, Hispanic, or poor families who have a loved one murdered not only don't expect the district attorney's office to pursue the death penalty—which, of course, is both costly and time-consuming—but are surprised when the case is prosecuted at all.

In Louisiana, murder victims' families are allowed to sit in the front row in the execution chamber to watch the murderer die. Some families. Not all. Almost never African American families.

Ask Virginia Smith's African American family. She was 14 when three white youths took her into the woods, raped her, and stabbed her to death. None of them got the death penalty. Their fathers knew the district attorney, and they had all-white juries.

In regard to this first and deepest of America's wounds, racism, we'd have to change the whole soil of this country for the criminal-justice system not to be administered in a racially biased manner.

The second wound is poverty. Who pays the ultimate penalty for crimes? The poor. Who gets the death penalty? The poor. After all the rhetoric that goes on in legislative assemblies, in the end, when the net is cast out, it is the poor who are selected to die in this country.

And why do poor people get the death penalty? It has everything to do with the kind of defense they get.

When I agreed to write to Patrick Sonnier, I didn't know much about him except that if he was on death row in Louisiana he had to be poor. And that holds true for virtually all of the more than 3,000 people who now inhabit death-row cells in our country.

Money gets you good defense. That's why you'll never see an O.J. Simpson on death row. As the saying goes: "Capital punishment means them without the capital get the punishment."

I had to learn all this myself. My father was a lawyer. I used to think, "Well, they may not get perfect defense, but at least they get adequate defense."

I tell you it is so shocking to find out what kind of defense people on death row actually have had.

The man I have been going to see on death row now for over six years is a young black man who was convicted for the killing of a white woman in a small community in Many, Louisiana. He had an all-white jury, and he was tried, convicted, and sentenced to death in just one week. Dobie Williams has now been on death row for 10 years, and I believe he's innocent. But it is almost impossible for us to get a new trial for him. Why? Because if his attorney did not raise any objections at his trial, we cannot bring them up in appeals.

Finally, the third wound is our penchant for trying to solve our problems with violence. When you witness an execution and watch the toll this process also takes on some of those who are charged with the actual execution—the 12 guards on the strap-down team and the warden—you recognize that part of the moral dilemma of the death penalty is also: who deserves to kill this man?

On my journey with murder victims' families, I have seen some of them go for vengeance. I have seen families watch executions in the electric chair and still be for vengeance. I have also witnessed the disintegration of families because some parents got so fixated on vengeance that they couldn't love their other children any more or move on with life.

But I have also watched people like Marietta Jaeger of the group Murder Victims for Reconciliation or Lloyd LeBlanc, the father of one of Patrick Sonnier's victims. Although they have been through a white-hot fire of loss and violence, they have been healed by God's grace and been able to overcome their desire for revenge. They are incredible human beings with great courage, and to me they are living witnesses of the gospel and the incredible healing power of Jesus in the midst of violence.

DEATH PENALTY TORTURE

Patrick had tried to protect me from watching him die. He told me he'd be OK. I didn't have to come with him into the execution chamber. "The electric chair is not a pretty sight, it could scar you," he told me, trying to be brave.

But I said, "No, no, Pat, if they kill you, I'll be there.". . .

Being in that death house was one of the most bizarre, confusing experiences I have ever had. It wasn't like visiting somebody dying in a hospital, where you can see the person getting weaker and fading. Patrick was so fully alive, talking and responding to me and writing letters to people and eating.

I'd look around at the polished tile floors—everything so neat—all the officials following a protocol, the secretary typing up forms for the witnesses to sign afterwards, the coffee pot percolating, and I kept feeling that I was in a hospital and the final act would be to save this man's life.

It felt strange and confusing because everyone was so polite. They kept asking Patrick if he needed anything. The chef came by to ask him if he liked his last meal—the steak (medium rare), the potato salad, the apple pie for dessert.

When the warden with the strap-down team came for him, I walked with him. God heard his prayer, "Please, God, hold up my legs." It was the last piece of dignity he could muster. He wanted to walk.

I saw this dignity in him, and I have seen it in the three men I have accompanied to their deaths. I wonder how I would hold up if I were walking across a floor to a room where people were waiting to kill me.

The essential torture of the death penalty is not finally the physical method of death: bullet or rope or gas or electrical current or injected drugs. The torture happens when conscious human beings are condemned to death and begin to anticipate that death and die a thousand times before they die. They are brought close to death, maybe four hours away, and the phone rings in the death house, and they hear they have received a stay of execution. Then they return to their cells and begin the waiting all over again.

The U.N. Universal Declaration on Human Rights states that there are two essential human rights that every human being has: the right not to be tortured and the right not to be killed.

I wish Pope John Paul II in his encyclical "The Gospel of Life" had been as firm and unconditional as the U.N.

The pope still upholds the right of governments to kill criminals, even though he restricts it to cases of "absolute necessity" and says that because of improvements in modern penal systems such cases are "very rare, if not practically nonexistent."

Likewise, the U.S. Catholic bishops in their 1980 "Statement on Capital Punishment," while strongly condemning the death penalty for the unfair and discriminatory manner in which it is imposed, its continuance of the "cycle of violence," and its fundamental disregard for human dignity, also affirm in principle the right of the state to kill.

But I believe that if we are to have a firm moral bedrock for our society, we must establish that no one may be permitted to kill—no one—and that includes government. . . .

The death penalty is still foremost a poor person's issue, and of course it's very controversial. But I've learned that if you try to live the gospel of Jesus, controversy will follow you like a hungry dog.

In this last decade of the 20th century, U.S. government officials kill citizens with dispatch with scarcely a murmur of resistance from the Christian citizenry. In fact, surveys of public opinion show that those who profess Christianity tend to favor capital punishment slightly more than the overall population—Catholics more than Protestants.

True, in recent years leadership bodies of most Christian denominations have issued formal statements denouncing the death penalty, but generally that opposition has yet to be translated into aggressive pastoral initiatives to educate clergy and membership on capital punishment. I do not want to pass judgment on church leaders, but I invite them to work harder to do the right thing.

I also believe that we cannot wait for the church leadership to act. We have to put our trust in the church as the people of God; things have to come up from the grassroots.

The religious community has a crucial role in educating the public about the fact that government killings are too costly for us, not only financially, but—more important—morally. Allowing our government to kill citizens compromises the deepest

moral values upon which this country was conceived: the invio-
lable dignity of human persons.

BOTTOMED OUT?

I have no doubt that we will one day abolish the death penalty in
America. One day all the death instruments in this country—electric chairs, gas chambers, and lethal-injection needles—will be
housed behind velvet ropes in museums.

Today, however, executions are still the order of the day, and
people are being executed at an ever-increasing rate in this
country.

People are scared of crime, and they've been manipulated by
politicians who push this button for all it's worth. For politicians, the death penalty is a convenient symbol and an easy way
to prove how tough they are on criminals and crime. It allows
them to avoid tackling the complex issue of how to get to the
roots of crime in our communities.

But we may be close to bottoming out, which has to happen
before momentum can build in the other direction. Right now we
may be at just the beginning of the dawning of consciousness.

The death penalty is firmly in place, but people are beginning
to ask, "If this is supposed to be the solution, how come we're
not feeling any better? How come none of us feels safer?"
People are beginning to realize that they have been duped and
that the death penalty has not so much to do with crime as it
has to do with politics.

The bottoming out that has to happen is kind of like in the
12-step program: the first step is to admit that as a society we
have a problem and need help.

People are capable of change, and the beauty and the power
of the gospel is that when people hear it, they will respond to it.

When people support executions, it is not out of malice or ill
will or hardness of heart or meanness of spirit. It is, quite simply, that they don't know the truth of what is going on.

And that is not by accident. The secrecy surrounding executions makes it possible for executions to continue. I am convinced
that if executions were made public, the torture and violence
would be unmasked and we would be shamed into abolishing
executions.

LAST RITES

When you accompany someone to the execution, as I have done
three times as a spiritual advisor, everything becomes very crys-
tallized, distilled, and stripped to the essentials. You are in this

building in the middle of the night, and all these people are organized to kill this man. And the gospel comes to you as it never has before: Are you for compassion, or are you for violence? Are you for mercy, or are you for vengeance? Are you for love, or are you for hate? Are you for life, or are you for death?

And the words of Jesus from the gospel kept coming to me that night: "And the last will be first" and "This too is my beloved son, hear him." On death row I grasped with such solidity and fire the grace of God in all human beings, the dignity in all human beings.

I am not saying that Patrick Sonnier was a hero. I do not want to glorify him. He did the most terrible crime of all. He killed. But he was a human being, and he had a transcendence, a dignity. He—like each of us—was more than the worst thing he had done in his life. And I have one consolation: he died well. I hope I die half as well. . . .

In his last words he expressed his sorrow to the victims' family. But then he said to the warden and to the unseen executioner behind the plywood panel, "but killing me is wrong, too."

> "To fight and deter crime effectively, individuals must have every tool government can afford them, including the death penalty."

THE DEATH PENALTY DETERS CAPITAL CRIMES

George Pataki

George Pataki, an avowed supporter of capital punishment, was elected governor of New York in 1994. The following year he signed legislation reinstituting the death penalty in the state (New York's previous governors, Hugh Carey and Mario Cuomo, had consistently vetoed such legislation). In the following viewpoint, he credits the death penalty for helping to reduce crime rates in New York. The death penalty deters crime by sending the message to potential murderers that their own lives may be taken, he asserts. It also prevents situations in which convicted killers serving life sentences are free to kill again upon their escape or parole from prison.

As you read, consider the following questions:

1. What, in Pataki's view, happened in New York during the two decades in which the death penalty could not be used?
2. What does the case of Arthur Shawcross illustrate, according to the author?
3. What factors must juries consider in determining whether to impose the death penalty, according to Pataki?

Excerpted from George Pataki, "Death Penalty Is a Deterrent," USA Today magazine, March 1997. Reprinted by permission of the Society for the Advancement of Education, ©1997.

Sept. 1, 1995 [when the state of New York became authorized to carry out executions], marked the end of a long fight for justice in New York and the beginning of a new era in our state that promises safer communities, fewer victims of crime, and renewed personal freedom. For 22 consecutive years, my predecessors had ignored the urgent calls for justice from our citizens—their repeated and pressing demands for the death penalty in New York State. Even after the legislature passed a reinstatement of the capital punishment law, it was vetoed for 18 years in a row. (Twelve of those vetoes came from the pen of former Gov. Mario Cuomo.)

That was wrong. To fight and deter crime effectively, individuals must have every tool government can afford them, including the death penalty. Upon taking office in January 1995, I immediately began the process of reinstating the death penalty. Two months later, I signed the death penalty into law for the most heinous and ruthless killers in our society.

THE DUTY OF GOVERNMENT

Protecting the residents of New York against crime and violence is my first priority. Indeed, it is the most fundamental duty of government. For too long, coddling of criminals allowed unacceptable levels of violence to permeate the streets. They were not subject to swift and certain punishment and, as a result, violent criminal acts were not deterred.

For more than two decades, New York was without the death penalty. During this time, fear of crime was compounded by the fact that, too often, it largely went unpunished.

No more. In New York, the death penalty has turned the tables on fear and put it back where it belongs—in the hearts of criminals. Within just one year, the death penalty helped produce a dramatic drop in violent crime. Just as important, it has restored New Yorkers' confidence in the justice system because they know their government genuinely is committed to their safety.

Honest, hard-working people share my vision for a safer New York, a place where children can play outside without worry; parents can send their kids to school with peace of mind; people can turn to each other on any street corner, in any subway, at any hour, without casting a suspicious eye; and New York citizens—of all races, religions, and ages—pull together and stand firm against crime.

In short, we are creating a state where law-abiding citizens have unlimited freedom from crime—a state where all can raise a family and follow their dreams in neighborhoods, streets, and schools that are free from the scourge of crime and violence. We've made tremendous progress. Although the death penalty has contributed to that progress, it's just one facet of New York's broad anti-crime strategy.

Other major reforms include substantially increasing the sentences for all violent criminals; eliminating parole eligibility for virtually all repeat violent offenders; barring murderers and sex offenders from participating in work release programs; toughening penalties for perpetrators of domestic violence; notifying communities as to the whereabouts of convicted sex offenders; overturning court-created criminal-friendly loopholes to make it easier to prosecute violent criminals; and allowing juries to impose a sentence of life without parole for killers.

These new laws are working. Since I took office in 1995, violent crime has dropped 23%, assaults are down 22%, and murders have dropped by nearly one-third. New Yorkers now live in safer communities because we finally have begun to create a climate that protects and empowers our citizens, while giving criminals good cause to fear arrest and conviction. I believe this has occurred in part because of the strong signal that the death penalty and our other tough new laws sent to violent criminals and murderers: You will be punished with the full force of the law.

Shortly before the death penalty went into effect, I listened to the families of 20 murder victims as they told of their pain. No loved ones should have to go through such a wrenching experience. I never will forget the words of Janice Hunter, whose 27-year-old daughter, Adrien, was stabbed 47 times by serial killer Nathaniel White in 1992. Mrs. Hunter spoke for every family member when she said, "It' s a heartache that all parents suffer. I have to go to the cemetery to see my daughter. Nathaniel White's mother goes to jail to see him and I don't think it's fair."

Although no law can bring back Mrs. Hunter's daughter, our laws can and must take every responsible step to prevent others from enduring the heartache suffered by her and her family. Before becoming Governor, I supported the death penalty because of my firm conviction that it would act as a significant deterrent and provide a true measure of justice to murder victims and their loved ones.

SAVING LIVES

I know, as do most New Yorkers, that by restoring the death penalty, we have saved lives. Somebody's mother, somebody's brother, somebody's child is alive today because we were strong enough to be tough enough to care enough to do what was necessary to protect the innocent. Preventing a crime from being committed ultimately is more important than punishing criminals after they have shattered innocent lives.

No case illustrates this point more clearly than that of Arthur Shawcross. In 1973, Shawcross, one of New York's most ruthless serial killers, was convicted of the brutal rape and murder of two children in upstate New York. Since the death penalty had been declared unconstitutional, Shawcross was sentenced to prison. After serving just 15 years—an absurd prison term given the crime—he was paroled in 1988. In a horrific 21-month killing spree, Shawcross took 11 more lives. That is 11 innocent people who would be alive today had justice been served 24 years ago; 11 families that would have been spared the pain and agony of losing a loved one.

By reinstating the death penalty, New York has sent a clear message to criminals that the lives of our children are worth more than just a 15-year prison term. Moreover, it has given prosecutors the legal wherewithal to ensure New York State never has another Arthur Shawcross.

APPLYING THE ULTIMATE PUNISHMENT

Too often, we are confronted with wanton acts of violence that cry out for justice. The World Trade Center bombing and the murderous rampage on the Long Island Rail Road by Colin Ferguson are but two examples. The slaying of a police officer in the line of duty is another. To kill a police officer is to commit an act of war against civilized society.

A person who knowingly commits such a heinous act poses a serious threat to us all, for government can not protect citizens without doing everything it can to protect those charged with our safety. Police officers put their lives on the line, not knowing whether their next traffic stop or call to duty will be their last.

Under New York's death penalty law, those who murder a police officer; a probation, parole, court, or corrections officer; a judge; or a witness or member of a witness' family can face the death penalty. Someone who murders while already serving life in prison, escaping from prison, or committing other serious felonies can face the death penalty.

Contract killers, serial murderers, those who torture their victims, or those who have murdered before also can be sentenced to death. In determining whether the death penalty should be imposed on anyone convicted of first-degree murder, the bill expressly authorizes juries to hear and consider additional evidence whenever the murder was committed as part of an act of terrorism or by someone with two or more prior serious felony convictions.

New York's death penalty is crafted carefully so that only the most inhuman murderers are eligible for it. Upon the conviction of the defendant, a separate sentencing phase is conducted during which the original jury, or a new jury under special circumstances, weights the facts of the case.

The jury must consider the defendant's prior criminal history, mental capacity, character, background, state of mind, and the extent of his or her participation in the crime. It then compares this evidence with the facts. For the death penalty to be imposed, the jury must reach a verdict unanimously and beyond a reasonable doubt.

Our state lived without adequate protection for 22 years. That is 22 years too long. Now, finally, we have begun to empower New Yorkers with the legal tools they need to make their communities safe.

At the same time, we have put lawless sociopaths like Arthur Shawcross on notice. The time that Shawcross spent in prison was not punishment; it was a mere inconvenience that offered New Yorkers nothing more than a 15-year moratorium from his murderous acts.

Our resolve to end crime is only as strong as the laws we pass to punish criminals. By making the death penalty the law of the land in New York, we have demonstrated that resolve, thus strengthening the promise that our children and future generations will grow up in a state that is free of violence.

"*Actual experience . . . establishes beyond a reasonable doubt that the death penalty does not deter murder.*"

THE DEATH PENALTY DOES NOT DETER CAPITAL CRIMES

Hugo Adam Bedau

The following viewpoint is excerpted from a 1997 pamphlet authored by Hugo Adam Bedau for the American Civil Liberties Union (ACLU), a private civil liberties organization that opposes the death penalty as an unconstitutional practice of "cruel and unusual punishment." Bedau rebuts the claim that the death penalty prevents crime, arguing that to be an effective deterrent to criminals, the death penalty must be used in much greater frequency and with less delay between crime and execution than is currently the case. Such a state of affairs can only be attained by jettisoning procedural safeguards and constitutional rights of defendants, Bedau contends, risking the execution of innocent people. He concludes that long-term imprisonment without parole is a sufficiently punitive and less inhumane alternative to the death penalty. Bedau, a professor of philosophy at Tufts University in Massachusetts, has written extensively on capital punishment.

As you read, consider the following questions:

1. How must capital punishment be administered and employed to be an effective deterrent, according to Bedau?
2. What have studies comparing Wisconsin and Iowa (non-death penalty states) and Illinois revealed about the relationship between the death penalty and homicide rates, according to the author?
3. How frequent, according to Bedau, are cases in which convicted murderers kill a second time?

Excerpted from Hugo Adam Bedau, *The Case Against the Death Penalty*, a pamphlet published by the American Civil Liberties Union, revised edition, 1997. Reprinted by permission of the American Civil Liberties Union. (Endnotes in the original have been omitted in this reprint.)

C apital punishment is not a deterrent to capital crimes. Deterrence is a function not only of a punishment's severity, but also of its certainty and frequency. The argument most often cited in support of capital punishment is that the threat of execution influences criminal behavior more effectively than imprisonment does. As plausible as this claim may sound, in actuality the death penalty fails as a deterrent for several reasons.

APPLYING THE DEATH PENALTY

1) A punishment can be an effective deterrent only if it is consistently and promptly employed. Capital punishment cannot be administered to meet these conditions.

- *The proportion of first-degree murderers who are sentenced to death is small, and of this group, an even smaller proportion of people are executed.* Although death sentences in the mid-1990s have increased to about 300 per year, this is still only about one percent of all homicides known to the police. Of all those convicted on a charge of criminal homicide, only 3 percent—about 1 in 33—are eventually sentenced to death.
- *Mandatory death row sentencing is unconstitutional.* The possibility of increasing the number of convicted murderers sentenced to death and executed by enacting mandatory death penalty laws was ruled unconstitutional in 1976 (*Woodson v. North Carolina*, 428 U.S. 280).
- *A considerable time between the imposition of the death sentence and the actual execution is unavoidable, given the procedural safeguards required by the courts in capital cases.* Starting with selecting the trial jury, murder trials take far longer when the ultimate penalty is involved. Furthermore, post-conviction appeals in death-penalty cases are far more frequent than in other cases. These factors increase the time and cost of administering criminal justice.

We can reduce delay and costs only by abandoning the procedural safeguards and constitutional rights of suspects, defendants, and convicts—with the attendant high risk of convicting the wrong person and executing the innocent.

2) Persons who commit murder and other crimes of personal violence either may or may not premeditate their crimes.

- *When crime is planned, the criminal ordinarily concentrates on escaping detection, arrest, and conviction.* The threat of even the severest punishment will not discourage those who expect to escape detection and arrest. It is impossible to imagine how the threat of any punishment could prevent a crime that is not premeditated. Gangland killings, air piracy, drive-by shootings, and kidnapping for ransom are among the graver felonies that continue to be committed because some individuals think they are too clever to get caught.

- *Most capital crimes are committed in the heat of the moment.* Most capital crimes are committed during moments of great emotional stress or under the influence of drugs or alcohol, when logical thinking has been suspended. In such cases, violence is inflicted by persons heedless of the consequences to themselves as well as to others. Furthermore, the death penalty is a futile threat for political terrorists because they usually act in the name of an ideology that honors its martyrs.

- *Capital punishment doesn't solve our society's crime problem.* Threatening capital punishment leaves the underlying causes of crime unaddressed, and ignores the many political and diplomatic sanctions (such as treaties against asylum for international terrorists) that could appreciably lower the incidence of terrorism.

- *Capital punishment is a useless weapon in the so-called "war on drugs."* The attempt to reduce murders in the drug trade by threat of severe punishment ignores the fact that anyone trafficking in illegal drugs is already risking his life in violent competition with other dealers. It is irrational to think that the death penalty—a remote threat at best—will avert murders committed in drug turf wars or by street-level dealers.

LONG-TERM IMPRISONMENT

3) If, however, severe punishment can deter crime, then long-term imprisonment is severe enough to deter any rational person from committing a violent crime.

- *The vast preponderance of the evidence shows that the death penalty is no more effective than imprisonment in deterring murder and that it may even be an incitement to criminal violence.* Death-penalty states as a group do not have lower rates of criminal homicide than non-death-penalty states. During the early 1970's death-penalty states averaged an annual rate of 7.9 criminal homicides per 100,000 population; abolitionist states averaged a rate of 5.1.

- *Use of the death penalty in a given state may actually increase the subsequent rate of criminal homicide.* In Oklahoma, for example, reintroduction of executions in 1990 may have produced "an abrupt and lasting increase in the level of stranger homicides" in the form of "one additional stranger-homicide incident per month," writes John K. Cochran, Mitchell B.

Chamlin, and Mark Seth in *Criminology* (1994). Why? Perhaps because "a return to the exercise of the death penalty weakens socially based inhibitions against the use of lethal force to settle disputes. . . ."

- *In adjacent states—one with the death penalty and the other without it—the state that practices the death penalty does not always show a consistently lower rate of criminal homicide.* For example, between 1990 and 1994, the homicide rates in Wisconsin and Iowa (non-death-penalty states) were half the rates of their neighbor, Illinois—which restored the death penalty in 1973, and by 1994 had sentenced 223 persons to death and carried out two executions.

- *On-duty police officers do not suffer a higher rate of criminal assault and homicide in abolitionist states than they do in death-penalty states.* Between 1973 and 1984, for example, lethal assaults against police were not significantly more, or less, frequent in abolitionist states than in death-penalty states. There is, according to William C. Bailey and Ruth D. Peterson, "no support for the view that the death penalty provides a more effective deterrent to police homicides than alternative sanctions. Not for a single year was evidence found that police are safer in jurisdictions that provide for capital punishment."

- *Prisoners and prison personnel do not suffer a higher rate of criminal assault and homicide from life-term prisoners in abolition states than they do in death-penalty states.* Between 1992 and 1995, 176 inmates were murdered by other prisoners; the vast majority (84%) were killed in death penalty jurisdictions. During the same period about 2% of all assaults on prison staff were committed by inmates in abolition jurisdictions. Evidently, the threat of the death penalty "does not even exert an incremental deterrent effect over the threat of a lesser punishment in the abolitionist states," writes Wendy P. Wilson.

Actual experience thus establishes beyond a reasonable doubt that the death penalty does not deter murder. No comparable body of evidence contradicts that conclusion.

DEATH PENALTY STUDIES

Using methods pioneered by economists, three investigators [Isaac Ehrlich, David P. Phillips and Stephen K. Layson] concluded that capital punishment does deter murderers. Subsequently, however, several qualified investigators [Ruth D. Peterson and William C. Bailey, William J. Bowers, James Alan Fox and Michael L. Radelet] independently examined these claims—and all rejected them. In its thorough report on the effects of criminal sanctions on crime rates, the National Academy of Sciences concluded: "It seems unthinkable to us to base decisions on the use of the death penalty" on such "fragile" and "uncertain" results. "We see too many plausible explanations for [these] findings . . . other than the theory that capital punishment deters murder."

Furthermore, there are clinically documented cases in which the death penalty actually incited the capital crimes it was supposed to deter. These include instances of the so-called suicide-by-execution syndrome—persons who wanted to die but feared taking their own lives, and committed murder so that the state would kill them.

Although inflicting the death penalty guarantees that the condemned person will commit no further crimes, it does not have a demonstrable deterrent effect on other individuals. Further, it is a high price to pay when studies show that few convicted murderers commit further crimes of violence. Researchers examined the prison and post-release records of 533 prisoners on death row in 1972 whose sentences were reduced to incarceration for life by the Supreme Court's ruling in Furman (Furman v. Georgia, 408 U.S. 238). This research showed that seven had committed another murder. But the same study showed that in four other cases, an innocent man had been sentenced to death.

Recidivism among murderers does occasionally happen, but it occurs less frequently than most people believe; the media rarely distinguish between a convicted offender who murders while on parole, and a paroled murderer who murders again. Government data show that about one in twelve death row prisoners had a prior homicide conviction. But as there is no way to predict reliably which convicted murderers will try to kill again, the only way to prevent all such recidivism is to execute every convicted murderer—a policy no one seriously advocates. Equally effective but far less inhumane is a policy of life imprisonment without the possibility of parole.

"Bias and discrimination warp our nation's criminal justice system at the very time it matters most—in matters of life and death."

THE DEATH PENALTY DISCRIMINATES AGAINST AFRICAN AMERICANS

Jesse Jackson

Jesse Jackson is a minister and civil rights activist who ran for the Democratic presidential nomination in both 1984 and 1988. The following viewpoint is excerpted from his 1996 book *Legal Lynching: Racism, Injustice and the Death Penalty*. Jackson argues that because there are no firm objective rules to govern prosecutors, jurors, and judges in seeking and implementing the death penalty, it will inevitably be administered in ways that discriminate against members of America's minority groups, especially African Americans. He cites statistical studies that indicate that black defendants are more likely than white defendants convicted of the same crime to receive the death penalty. Other studies, he argues, demonstrate how the race of murder victims affects death penalty sentencing, with murderers of whites being more likely to be executed than murderers of blacks. People's lives should not be at risk because of a racially biased criminal justice system, Jackson concludes.

As you read, consider the following questions:

1. What misconceptions do Americans who support the death penalty have on how it is administered, according to Jackson?
2. What statistics does the author cite in arguing that the death penalty is utilized unfairly in the states of Alabama and Georgia?
3. What message is America's judicial system communicating about African Americans, according to Jackson?

The death penalty is essentially an arbitrary punishment. There are no objective rules or guidelines for when a prosecutor should seek the death penalty, when a jury should recommend it, and when a judge should give it. This lack of objective, measurable standards ensures that the application of the death penalty will be discriminatory against racial, gender, and ethnic groups.

The majority of Americans who support the death penalty believe, or wish to believe, that legitimate factors such as the violence and cruelty with which the crime was committed, a defendant's culpability or history of violence, and the number of victims involved determine who is sentenced to life in prison and who receives the ultimate punishment. The numbers, however, tell a different story. They confirm the terrible truth that bias and discrimination warp our nation's judicial system at the very time it matters most—in matters of life and death. The factors that determine who will live and who will die—race, sex, and geography—are the very same ones that blind justice was meant to ignore. This prejudicial distribution should be a moral outrage to every American. . . .

RACE AND THE DEATH PENALTY

The relationship between race and capital punishment is much more complex than most people suppose. One surprise for many people is that more white defendants than black defendants have been executed. Since 1976, according to the Death Penalty Information Center, 56 percent of the condemned prisoners executed have been white, 38 percent have been black, and 6 percent have been Hispanic, Native American, or Asian. And death row population statistics reflect similar percentages. As of January 1996, 48 percent of the inmates on death row were white, 41 percent were black, 7.5 percent were Hispanic, and 3.5 percent were listed as "other.". . .

These statistics are simply the beginning of a chain that is not generally reported by the media, and so is not known by the public. Numerous researchers have shown conclusively that African American defendants are far more likely to receive the death penalty than are white defendants charged with the same crime. For instance, African Americans make up 25 percent of Alabama's population, yet of Alabama's 117 death row inmates, 43 percent are black. Indeed, 71 percent of the people executed there since the resumption of capital punishment have been black.

The population of Georgia's Middle Judicial Circuit is 40 percent black, but 77 percent of the circuit's capital decisions have been found against black defendants. The Ocmulgee Judicial Circuit posts remarkably similar numbers. In 79 percent of the cases in which the district attorney sought the death penalty, the defendant was black, despite the fact that only 44 percent of the circuit's population is black. More ominously, in the cases where black defendants faced capital prosecution, 90 percent of the district attorney's peremptory strikes were used to keep African Americans off the juries.

And this disproportion in capital sentencing is not just a Southern problem, for the results of the 1988 federal law providing for a death penalty for drug kingpins are telling. In 1993, all nine defendants approved for capital prosecution were African Americans. Of the first 36 cases in which prosecutors sought the death penalty under this new legislation, four of the defendants were white, four were Hispanic, and 28 were black. . . .

RACE OF THE VICTIMS

It is not just the race of the defendant that affects the state's decision of whether to seek the death penalty and whether it is meted out. The race of the victim—more specifically, whether or not the victim was white—can have an even stronger influence.

Dr. David Baldus of the University of Iowa has studied over 2,500 Georgia murder cases. Controlling for 230 nonracial factors in the cases, he found that defendants accused of murdering a white victim are 4.3 times more likely to receive the death penalty than defendants accused of killing blacks. Baldus determined that the race of the murderer was less important than the race of the victim. Fewer than 40 percent of the homicide victims in Georgia are white, yet fully 87 percent of the cases resulting in the death penalty involved white victims.

Baldus cited one judicial circuit in Georgia where, despite the fact that 65 percent of the homicide cases involved African American victims, 85 percent of the cases in which the district attorney sought the death penalty were against murderers of whites. Overall, this particular district attorney sought the death penalty in 34 percent of the cases involving white victims but a mere 5.8 percent of the cases in which the victim was black.

Georgia is not the only state where the color of the victim's skin can mean the difference between life and death. Nationwide, even though 50 percent of murder victims are African American, says the Death Penalty Information Center, almost 85 percent of the victims in death penalty cases are white. And in their 1989 book *Death and Discrimination: Racial Disparities in Capital Sentencing*, Samuel Gross and Robert Mauro analyzed sentencing in capital cases in Arkansas, Florida, Georgia, Illinois, Mississippi, North Carolina, Oklahoma, and Virginia during a period when these states accounted for 379 of the 1,011 death penalties nationwide. They found widespread discrepancies in sentencing based on the victim's race in all eight states.

Defendants in Florida, for example, who killed whites received the death penalty eight times more often than those defendants convicted of killing African Americans. In Bay County, blacks are the victims of 40 percent of the murders, yet in all 17 cases between 1975 and 1987 in which a death sentence was handed down, the victims were white.

As one study after another confirmed the correlation between the race of the homicide victim and whether the defendant would receive a capital sentence, the evidence became so overwhelming that Congress's General Accounting Office decided to take up the question itself. In its February 1990 report *Death Penalty Sentencing*, the GAO reviewed 28 studies based on 23 sets of data and concluded, "In eighty-two percent of the studies, race of the victim was found to influence the likelihood of being charged with capital murder or receiving the death penalty, i.e., those who murdered whites were found more likely to be sentenced to death than those who murdered blacks."

And when a case involves interracial murder, the bias against black homicide defendants multiplies the effects of the bias against the murderers of white victims. Since 1976, only four white defendants have been executed for killing a black person, yet 75 black defendants have been executed for murdering a white person. Astoundingly, African Americans who murder whites are 19 *times as likely to be executed* as whites who kill blacks.

THE CASE OF WARREN MCCLESKY

In 1987, Warren McClesky, a black man armed with formidable evidence linking the victim's race with the distribution of the death penalty, appealed to the Supreme Court to overturn his death sentence. He argued that the fact his victim was white played an important role in his sentencing. Although the Court acknowledged that the correlation of the victim's race and the imposition of the death penalty was "statistically significant in the system as a whole" (*McClesky v. Kemp*, 481 U.S. 279), it denied McClesky's petition saying that the burden is on the defendant to prove his individual sentence was based on his victim's race. . . . McClesky was executed on September 25, 1991.

In response to the *McClesky* decision, the Racial Justice Act was introduced in Congress in 1994. The purpose of the act was to allow condemned prisoners to appeal their death sentences using evidence of past discriminatory sentencing—the kind of evidence that failed to save McClesky. After passing in the House 217–212, the bill failed in the Senate. To date, there has been no precedent set for citing biased sentencing patterns to successfully appeal a death sentence. [Editor's note: In 1998 Kentucky became the first state to pass legislation allowing for death penalty appeals on the basis of racial disparity in sentencing.]

With black men nearly eight times more likely to be victims of homicide than white men, could there be a more blatant message from the criminal justice system that it values some lives more highly than others? Not in a loud voice that would attract undue attention, but quietly and methodically, one prosecution at a time, our judicial system is telling us that African American life is less important than white life, and its annihilation less tragic. Our judicial system is demonstrably, institutionally racist in the end result, and the end result—killing a disproportionate number of black males—matters. . . .

We are confronted with the undeniable evidence that the death penalty is handed down unjustly. The reaction of most state governments to this evidence has been to assert that the death penalty is still necessary, and that what is needed is a way of ensuring that it is distributed fairly and handed down for the right reasons. At this time, the Supreme Court agrees with the majority of the states. The goal of implementing a fair system for imposing the death penalty, however, has proved very elusive. . . .

Thirty-five years in the civil rights struggle has taught me that you can't legislate acceptance, objectivity, or morality. How then, at the moment between life and death, is society to erase a lifetime of social conditioning, assumptions, and attitudes the judges and jurors may not even realize they hold? There is no way the states, the federal government, or the judicial system can ensure that every prosecuting attorney, every jury member, and every judge involved in every homicide case is impartial and unbiased. And in the case of the death penalty, the stakes are just too high for even one life to be lost to prejudice and hatred.

"Contrary to popular belief, the evidence indicates that African-American murder defendants are no more likely to get death sentences than are whites."

THE DEATH PENALTY DOES NOT DISCRIMINATE AGAINST AFRICAN AMERICANS

David Andrew Price

Many death penalty opponents have argued that capital punishment is administered in the United States in a manner that discriminates against African Americans. In the following viewpoint, attorney and legal affairs journalist David Andrew Price rebuts this claim. He contends that little evidence exists indicating that blacks are more likely to receive death sentences than whites or that racism plays any role in the implementation of the death penalty. African Americans constitute a larger share of the death-row inmate population because blacks commit a disproportionate share of violent crimes. Price also responds to the argument that convicted killers of poor blacks are less likely to receive the death penalty than murderers of whites; he asserts that such disparities, if they exist, are a reason for pursuing more death penalty sentences rather than abolishing capital punishment.

As you read, consider the following questions:
1. What percentage of Americans supports the death penalty, according to Price?
2. What did the General Accounting Office conclude about race and the death penalty in a 1990 study review, according to the author?

Reprinted from David Andrew Price, "Death Penalty Is a Black and White Issue," *USA Today*, November 19, 1998, by permission of the author.

True or false: The death penalty in America discriminates against African-American defendants?

The answer is important. The number of prisoners on death row is at its highest since 1965. Four defendants are scheduled for execution this week in November 1998—in Maryland, Texas, Virginia and North Carolina.

Today, one opinion poll after another shows that upward of 70% of Americans support the death penalty for the most heinous offenses. Against that consensus, the charge of racism is the most cutting and effective argument used by the penalty's opponents—from the Rev. Jesse Jackson to Sister Helen Prejean in her book *Dead Man Walking*. But if you answered "true," don't be too sure. There's precious little support for the mythology that prosecutors are more zealous about seeking the death penalty against African-Americans, or that biased juries are sending African-Americans to death row more often.

LITTLE EVIDENCE OF RACIAL BIAS

Contrary to popular belief, the evidence indicates African-American murder defendants are no more likely to get death sentences than are whites.

According to a 1985 analysis by the Justice Department's Bureau of Justice Statistics, whites who are arrested for murder or manslaughter (other than negligent manslaughter) are more prone to be sentenced to death than blacks arrested for those offenses—1.6% of whites vs. 1.2% of African-Americans.

When Congress' General Accounting Office reviewed 53 studies on the subject in 1990, it could only conclude that the evidence was "equivocal": Some researchers found white defendants more likely to go to death row, some found African-Americans more likely.

Another inconvenient fact for those playing the race card: White death-row prisoners are more likely than African-Americans to have their death sentences carried out. From 1977-1996, 7.2% of white prisoners were executed, compared to 5.9% of African-Americans.

Claims of wrongful convictions—of whites or minorities—in death-penalty cases typically involve decades-old cases, dating back to the era before the legal safeguards mandated by the Supreme Court.

And in the modern-day cases cited by opponents, like those of Leonel Herrera and Jesse Jacobs, the supposed "innocence" of the defendants often dissipates under scrutiny.

If, in fact, the justice system were systematically biased in giving the death penalty to African-American defendants who don't deserve it, you would expect to find that African-American prisoners on death row have cleaner criminal records, on average, than their white counterparts.

But the opposite is true, Justice Department data show. African-American prisoners are 10% more likely than whites to have had felony convictions prior to the crimes that put them on death row. The disparity is even higher for prior homicides: African-American prisoners on death row are 20% more likely to have prior homicide convictions.

It's clear the criminal justice system has come a long way since grand juries and trial juries were selected on the basis of race, and when African-American police officers and prosecutors were unheard of.

THE RIGHT POINT OF COMPARISON

Yes, African-Americans do make up a larger share of death row than their share of the general population: at the end of 1996, 42% of death-row inmates were African-American. But that isn't the relevant point of comparison. Otherwise, the fact that men make up 98.5% of death-row inmates, but only half of the population, would "prove" that the death penalty discriminates against men.

The right point of comparison is the share of crimes committed by the group you're talking about. Although men make up around half the population, they commit most of the country's heinous, violent offenses. Hence, they're more heavily represented on death row. It's the same story, unfortunately, when you look at race.

According to federal statistics, the defendants in 43.2% of violent crime cases in 1996—and 54.9% of all murder cases—were African-American. In that light, the fact that 42% of death-row inmates are African-American does not seem like evidence of racism at work.

For reasons not fully understood, but which are undoubtedly tied to social problems facing the urban poor, the sad truth is that a disproportionate share of violent crimes are committed by African-Americans—mostly against other African-Americans. That, and not racist application of the death penalty, seems to account for the share of African-Americans on death row.

THE VICTIMS ISSUE

Hence, more sophisticated opponents of the death penalty have taken a different tack. While tacitly conceding that the death penalty doesn't tend to discriminate against African-American defendants, they argue that it discriminates against African-American victims. These opponents point to evidence that killers of whites are more likely to get a death sentence than killers of African-Americans. That, they argue, shows the system values African-American lives less than white lives.

But not all studies of the issue have had similar results. For instance, a statistical study by Stephen Klein of the think-tank RAND in California found that neither the race of the victim nor the race of the defendant appeared to affect death-penalty sentencing in that state.

But assuming it's true that killers of African-Americans are less likely to get the death penalty, what do you make of that? As Justice Sandra Day O'Connor has noted, such a pattern hardly argues for abolishing the death penalty; it argues for pursuing it in more cases involving African-American victims.

That solution, of course, isn't exactly what death-penalty opponents have in mind. For them, the alleged disparities are just a useful argumentative device—not a shortcoming that they would actually want society to fix by applying the death penalty more generally.

But that course is the right one. If prosecutors are failing to pursue the death penalty in some murder cases just because the victim was a poor inner-city resident—one whose death rated only a brief article on an inside page of the next day's newspaper—that needs to change. Our society has reached a consensus on the death penalty it has reached on few other issues, and that consensus holds death to be the just punishment for the worst crimes.

SHOULD ASSISTED SUICIDE BE LEGAL?

Chapter Preface

On September 17, 1998, Jack Kevorkian killed Thomas Youk by injecting him with a lethal combination of drugs. Houk was suffering from amyotrophic lateral sclerosis (Lou Gehrig's disease), a terminal illness that causes gradual paralysis. According to his family, Houk was suffering from pain and fear of choking on his own saliva, and he wanted to end his suffering by ending his life. "I don't want to die," his brother later quoted him as saying, "but I don't want to live like this." Kevorkian's act of euthanasia or "mercy killing" on Houk was videotaped and later broadcast to millions of Americans in a November 1998 episode of the venerable television newsmagazine "60 Minutes."

The videotaped killing was the latest of many controversial writings and actions by Kevorkian, a retired pathologist who by his own admission had helped 130 people to die. In previous cases Kevorkian provided drugs and devices which patients could use to kill themselves. Such "physician-assisted suicide," as it has come to be called, is legal as of 1999 in only one state, Oregon, which legalized the practice in 1997. Kevorkian had been tried four times in Michigan for helping people to die, but those trials ended in acquittals or mistrials.

Houk's case (which also occurred in Michigan) differed from Kevorkian's previous activities not only because of its television exposure, but also because Kevorkian himself injected the fatal drug combination. Such an act of euthanasia (as opposed to assisted suicide) is illegal in all states, including Oregon. Kevorkian was charged with murder, and was found guilty of second-degree murder by a Michigan jury in March 1999.

The actions and trials of Kevorkian have stimulated much public debate over whether Kevorkian should be imprisoned for his actions, or whether physician-assisted suicide and/or euthanasia should be made legal. Many people believe that Houk and people in similar situations should have the option of ending their own lives, and that Kevorkian's actions, both in assisting in the suicide of others and the direct killing of Houk, were justified. "I believe it is wrong to prevent a person from having a choice at the end of life, when they cannot get relief from their suffering," argues Sallie Troy, president of the San Diego chapter of the Hemlock Society, an organization that advocates the personal right to die. Others note that the withdrawal or withholding of life-sustaining treatment (such as a respirator) is legal and ethically acceptable by most people, and contend that such "passive euthanasia" differs little from the "active euthanasia" that was performed by Kevorkian on Houk.

Kevorkian's critics declare that resorting to euthanasia or suicide cheapens the value attached to human life. "The legal acceptance of the voluntary killing of one member of society by another member," concludes a March 1999 report by the Roman Catholic Church, "overturns at its roots one of the fundamental principles of co-existence in society." Others warn that permitting assisted suicide or euthanasia increases the chances of terminally ill or disabled patients' being killed without their consent. In addition, opponents of assisted suicide and euthanasia argue that such actions are unnecessary because people's concerns over the circumstances of their own dying can be met through better palliative and psychiatric care.

Some critics of assisted suicide note that people who request it often do so for reasons other than pain and terminal illness. According to religious writer and activist Beverly LaHaye, one person who committed suicide with Kevorkian's help, for instance, did not turn out to suffer from any terminal illness or pain, but instead was a victim of an abusive husband and depression about her weight. "There was nothing dignified or humane about that woman's death," LaHaye concluded, arguing that legalizing suicide or euthanasia could lead to similar cases.

As America's elderly population grows and medical technology advances, the question of whether to legalize assisted suicide and euthanasia promises to endure. The viewpoints in this chapter examine some of the major debates surrounding these contentious end-of-life issues.

"No matter how good the care gets,
there still will be a need to have an
assisted death as one choice."

PHYSICIAN-ASSISTED SUICIDE SHOULD BE LEGALIZED

Faye Girsh

In 1997 Oregon became the first state in the United States to legalize physician-assisted suicide. In the following viewpoint, Faye Girsh argues that other states should follow Oregon's example and permit terminally ill patients to receive the assistance of a doctor in hastening their death. Fears that such legislation would create a "culture of death" are belied by Oregon's experience and the safeguards contained in Oregon's assisted suicide law, she contends. Legalizing assisted suicide would enable patients to take greater control over their own lives and to manage the circumstances of their dying. Girsh is executive director of the Hemlock Society, an organization that supports the legalization of physician-assisted suicide for the terminally ill.

As you read, consider the following questions:

1. What levels of public support exist for assisted suicide, according to Girsh?
2. How has the right-to-die movement affected the quality of health care for the terminally ill, according to the author?
3. According to Girsh, what policy objectives would be accomplished by legalizing physician aid in dying?

Many people agree that there are horrifying situations at the end of life which cry out for the help of a doctor to end the suffering by providing a peaceful, wished-for death. But, opponents argue, that does not mean that the practice should be legalized. They contend that these are the exceptional cases from which bad law would result.

PAIN AND SUFFERING

I disagree. It is precisely these kinds of hard deaths that people fear and that happen to 7 to 10 percent of those who are dying that convince them to support the right to choose a hastened death with medical assistance. The reason that polls in this country—and in Canada, Australia, Great Britain and other parts of Europe—show 60 to 80 percent support for legalization of assisted suicide is that people want to know they will have a way out if their suffering becomes too great. They dread losing control not only of their bodies but of what will happen to them in the medical system. As a multiple-sclerosis patient wrote to the Hemlock Society: "I feel like I am just rotting away. . . . If there is something that gives life meaning and purpose it is this: a peaceful end to a good life before the last part of it becomes even more hellish."

Even with the best of hospice care people want to know that there can be some way to shorten a tortured dying process. A man whose wife was dying from cancer wrote, "For us, hospice care was our choice. We, however, still had 'our way,' also our choice, as 'our alternative.' We were prepared. And the 'choice' should be that of the patient and family."

It is not pain that causes people to ask for a hastened death but the indignities and suffering accompanying some terminal disorders such as cancer, stroke and AIDS. A survey in the Netherlands found that the primary reason to choose help in dying was to avoid "senseless suffering."

Hospice can make people more comfortable, can bring spiritual solace and can work with the family, but—as long as hospice is sworn neither to prolong nor hasten death—it will not be the whole answer for everyone. People should not have to make a choice between seeking hospice care and choosing to hasten the dying process. The best hospice care should be available to everyone, as should the option of a quick, gentle, certain death with loved ones around when the suffering has become unbearable. Both should be part of the continuum of care at the end of life.

We have the right to commit suicide and the right to refuse

unwanted medical treatment, including food and water. But what we don't have—unless we live in Oregon—is the right to get help from a doctor to achieve a peaceful death. As the trial judge in the Florida case of *Kirscher vs McIver*, an AIDS patient who wanted his doctor's help in dying, said in his decision: "Physicians are permitted to assist their terminal patients by disconnecting life support or by prescribing medication to ease their starvation. Yet medications to produce a quick death, free of pain and protracted agony, are prohibited. This is a difference without distinction."

The Oregon example has shown us that, although a large number of people want to know the choice is there, only a small number will take advantage of it. During the first eight months of the Oregon "Death With Dignity" law, only 10 people took the opportunity to obtain the medications and eight used them to end their lives. In the Netherlands it consistently has been less than 5 percent of the total number of people who die every year who choose to get help in doing so from their doctor.

In Switzerland, where physician-assisted death also is legal, about 120 people die annually with the help of medical assistance. There is no deluge of people wanting to put themselves out of their misery nor of greedy doctors and hospitals encouraging that alternative. People want to live as long as possible. There are repeated testimonials to the fact that people can live longer and with less anguish once they know that help will be available if they want to end it. Even [controversial euthanasia activist] Jack Kevorkian, who says he helped 130 people die since 1990, has averaged only 14 deaths a year.

To the credit of the right-to-die movement, end-of-life care has improved because of the push for assisted dying. In Oregon, end-of-life care is the best in the country: Oregon is No. 1 in morphine use, twice as many people there use hospice as the national average and more people die at home than in the hospital. In Maine there will be an initiative on the ballot in 2000 to legalize physician aid in dying, and in Arizona a physician-assisted-dying bill has been introduced. In both states the Robert Woods Johnson Foundation has awarded sizable grants to expand hospice care and to improve end-of-life care.

It is gratifying that the specter of assisted dying has spurred such concern for care at the end of life. Clearly, if we take the pressure off, the issue will disappear back into the closet. No matter how good the care gets, there still will be a need to have an assisted death as one choice. The better the care gets, the less that need will exist.

A CULTURE OF DEATH?

The pope and his minions in the Catholic Church, as well as the religious right, announce that assisted dying is part of the "culture of death." Murder, lawlessness, suicide, the cheapening of life with killing in the media, the accessibility of guns, war—those create a culture of death, not providing help to a dying person who repeatedly requests an end to his or her suffering by a day or a week. Not all religious people believe that. The Rev. Bishop John Shelby Spong of the Episcopal Diocese of Newark, N.J., said: "My personal creed asserts that every person is sacred. I see the holiness of life enhanced, not diminished, by letting people have a say in how they choose to die. Many of us want the moral and legal right to choose to die with our faculties intact, surrounded by those we love before we are reduced to breathing cadavers with no human dignity attached to our final days. Life must not be identified with the extension of biological existence. [Assisted suicide] is a life-affirming moral choice."

The Catholic belief that suicide is a sin which will cause a person to burn in hell is at the root of the well-financed, virulent opposition to physician aid in dying. This has resulted in expenditures of more than $10 million in losing efforts to defeat the two Oregon initiatives and a successful campaign to defeat the 1998 Michigan measure [to legalize assisted suicide]. And $6 million was spent in Michigan, most of which came from Catholic donors, to show four TV ads six weeks before voters saw the issue on the 1998 ballot. . . . Surely that money could have been spent to protect life in better ways than to frustrate people who have come to terms with their deaths and want to move on. The arguments that life is sacred and that it is a gift from God rarely are heard now from the opposition. Most Americans do not want to be governed by religious beliefs they don't share, so the argument has shifted to "protection of the vulnerable and the slippery slope." Note, however, that the proposed death-with-dignity laws carefully are written to protect the vulnerable. The request for physician-assisted death must be voluntary, must be from a competent adult and must be documented and repeated during a waiting period. Two doctors must examine the patient and, if there is any question of depression or incompetence or coercion, a mental-health professional can be consulted. After that it must be up to the requester to mix and swallow the lethal medication. No one forces anyone to do anything!

The same arguments were raised in 1976 when the first "living-will" law was passed in California. It again was raised in

1990 when the Supreme Court ruled that every American has the right to refuse medical treatment, including food and hydration, and to designate a proxy to make those decisions if they cannot. This has not been a downhill slope in the last 22 years but an expansion of rights and choices. It has not led to abuse but rather to more freedom. Those who raise the specter of the Nazis must remember that we are in greater danger of having our freedoms limited by religious dogma than of having them expanded so that more choices are available. When the state dictates how the most intimate and personal choices will be made, based on how some religious groups think it should be, then we as individuals and as a country are in serious trouble.

One observer said about the Oregon Death With Dignity law: "This is a permissive law. It allows something. It requires nothing. It forbids nothing and taxes no one. It enhances freedom. It lets people do a little more of what they want without hurting anyone else. It removes a slight bit of the weight of government regulation and threat of punishment that hangs over all of us all the time if we step out of line."

REGULATING ASSISTED DYING

Making physician aid in dying legal as a matter of public policy will accomplish several objectives. Right now we have a model of prohibition. There is an underground cadre of doctors—of whom Kevorkian is the tip of the iceberg—who are helping people die. The number varies, according to survey, from 6 to 16 percent to 20 to 53 percent. The 53 percent is for doctors in San Francisco who work with people with AIDS where networks for assisted dying have existed for many years. This practice is not regulated or reported; the criteria and methods used are unknown. There is some information that the majority of these deaths are done by lethal injection. Millions of viewers witnessed on 60 Minutes the videotape of Kevorkian using this method to assist in the death of Thomas Youk. If the practice is regulated, there will be more uniformity, doctors will be able to and will have to obtain a second opinion and will have the option of having a mental-health professional consult on the case. Most importantly for patients, they will be able to talk about all their options openly with their health-care providers and their loved ones.

Another consequence is that desperately ill people will not have to resort to dying in a Michigan motel with Kevorkian's assistance, with a plastic bag on their heads, with a gun in their mouth or, worse, botching the job and winding up in worse shape and traumatizing their families. They won't have to die the way someone else wants them to die, rather than the way they choose. As [law and philosophy professor] Ronald Dworkin said in *Life's Dominion*: "Making someone die in a way others approve, but he believes a horrifying contradiction of his life, is a devastating, odious form of tyranny."

"Broad legalization of physician-assisted suicide and euthanasia would have the paradoxical effect of making patients seem to be responsible for their own suffering."

PHYSICIAN-ASSISTED SUICIDE SHOULD NOT BE LEGALIZED

Ezekiel Emanuel

Ezekiel Emanuel is an associate professor at Harvard Medical School. He is also the author of *The Ends of Human Life: Medical Ethics in a Liberal Polity*. In the following viewpoint, he asserts that arguments in favor of physician-assisted suicide are based on misunderstandings and misinformation about the practice. Contrary to widespread belief, most people request assisted suicide because of depression and psychological distress, not pain as is commonly believed. Such patients should not be killed but rather be given psychiatric intervention and better health care, he contends. Furthermore, he asserts that in the Netherlands, permitting doctor-assisted suicide has led to the involuntary euthanasia of children and others who did not request it. Emanuel recommends that physician-assisted suicide and euthanasia should be kept illegal.

As you read, consider the following questions:

1. What distinctions does the author draw between physician-assisted suicide, euthanasia, and withholding life-support technology to patients that have requested it?
2. What are the four major myths surrounding the case for legalizing assisted suicide and euthanasia, according to Emanuel?
3. What are some of the social risks inherent in legalizing assisted suicide and euthanasia, according to the author?

Reprinted from Ezekiel Emanuel, "Whose Right to Die?" *The Atlantic Monthly*, March 1997, by permission of the author.

In physician-assisted suicide a doctor supplies a death-causing means, such as barbiturates, but the patient performs the act that brings about death. In voluntary euthanasia the physician performs the death-causing act after determining that the patient indeed wishes to end his or her life. Neither term applies to a patient's refusal of life-support technology, such as a respirator or artificial nutrition, or a patient's request that it be withdrawn; these have had ethical and constitutional sanction nationwide for years. And neither term applies to what is sometimes called indirect euthanasia, when the administration of drugs primarily for pain relief may have the secondary effect of causing death, as the physician is well aware. This practice, too, is ethically and legally sanctioned. . . .

MISTAKEN ASSUMPTIONS

[Arguments for assisted suicide and voluntary euthanasia] are based on misreadings of history, misinterpretations of survey data, mistaken reasoning, and simple misinformation.

Myth No. 1: It is primarily advances in biomedical technology—especially life-sustaining technology—that have created unprecedented public interest in physician-assisted suicide and voluntary euthanasia. . . .

Physician-assisted suicide and euthanasia have been profound ethical issues confronting doctors since the birth of Western medicine, more than 2,000 years ago. All the arguments made today to justify—or condemn—the two practices were articulated before any modern biomedical technology existed. . . .

Even in America legalized euthanasia, rather than being a new issue, has been publicly debated and rejected. . . . Modern interest in euthanasia in the United States began in 1870, when a commentator, Samuel Williams, proposed to the Birmingham Speculative Club that euthanasia be permitted "in all cases of hopeless and painful illness" to bring about "a quick and painless death." The word "painless" is important: the idea of euthanasia began gaining ground in modern times not because of new technologies for agonizingly prolonging life but because of the discovery of new drugs, such as morphine and various anesthetics for the relief of pain, that could also painlessly induce death. Over the next three decades Williams's proposal was reprinted in popular magazines and books, discussed in the pages of prominent literary and political journals, and debated at the meetings of American medical societies and nonmedical professional associations. . . .

Thus, decades before the discovery of penicillin (1928) and

the development of mechanical respirators (1929), dialysis (1945), and other life-sustaining technologies, serious public discussions of physician-assisted suicide and euthanasia took place in the United States (and also in European countries). These discussions were couched in the same language we use today—"patients' rights," "the relief of pain and suffering," "the loss of dignity."

Indeed, rather than creating a perceived need for physician-assisted suicide and euthanasia, advances in life-sustaining technology should help to obviate them. Patients who are being kept alive by technology and want to end their lives already have a recognized constitutional right to stop any and all medical interventions, from respirators to antibiotics. They do not need physician-assisted suicide or euthanasia.

POPULAR SUPPORT FOR EUTHANASIA

Myth No. 2: Legalizing physician-assisted suicide and euthanasia is widely endorsed. . . .

Yes, polls show that a majority of Americans support physician-assisted suicide and euthanasia—indeed, have supported legalizing them for almost twenty-five years. But the support is neither strong nor deep. Careful analysis of the polling data suggests that there is a "rule of thirds": a third of Americans support legalization under a wide variety of circumstances; a third oppose it under any circumstances; and a third support it in a few cases but oppose it in most circumstances.

Americans tend to endorse the use of physician-assisted suicide and euthanasia when the question is abstract and hypothetical. . . .

Other, more carefully designed questions can elicit majority support for physician-assisted suicide and euthanasia, but only when patients are described as terminally ill *and* experiencing unremitting physical pain. Support dwindles when the public is asked about physician-assisted suicide and euthanasia in virtually any other situation. Two thirds of Americans oppose physician-assisted suicide or euthanasia when a terminally ill patient has no pain but wants to die because of concern about being a burden to his or her family, or because he or she finds a drawn-out dying process meaningless. . . .

WHY IS ASSISTED SUICIDE REQUESTED?

Myth No. 3: It is terminally ill patients with uncontrollable pain who are most likely to be interested in physician-assisted suicide or euthanasia. . . .

The empirical studies of physician-assisted suicide and euthanasia in the Netherlands (where the practices have long been accepted), the United States, and elsewhere indicate that pain plays a minor role in motivating requests for the procedures. A 1996 update of the comprehensive and rigorous 1991 Remmelink Report on euthanasia practices in the Netherlands revealed that in only 32 percent of all cases did pain play any role in requests for euthanasia; indeed, pain was the sole reason for requesting euthanasia in no cases. A study of patients in nursing homes in the Netherlands revealed that pain was among the reasons for requesting physician-assisted suicide or euthanasia in only 29 percent of cases and was the main reason in only 11 percent. A study of physicians in Washington State who admitted to having received requests for physician-assisted suicide or euthanasia revealed that severe pain played a role in only about a third of the requests. A study of HIV-infected patients in New York found that interest in physician-assisted suicide was not associated with patients' experiencing pain or with pain-related limitations on function. My own study of cancer patients, conducted in Boston, reveals that those with pain are more likely than others to oppose physician-assisted suicide and euthanasia. These patients are also more likely to say that they would ask to change doctors if their attending physician indicated that he or she had performed physician-assisted suicide or euthanasia. No study has ever shown that pain plays a major role in motivating patient requests for physician-assisted suicide or euthanasia.

What does motivate requests? According to studies, depression and general psychological distress. . . .

These studies highlight an important conflict between people's actual attitudes and likely medical practice. Many Americans say they would support physician-assisted suicide or euthanasia for patients in pain; they oppose the practices for patients who worry about being a burden, about life's being meaningless, about hopelessness. But patients with depression and psychological distress are most likely to request death; patients in pain are less likely to request it.

The Netherlands Experience

Myth No. 4: The experience with euthanasia in the Netherlands shows that permitting physician-assisted suicide and euthanasia will not eventually get out of hand. . . .

The slippery slope feared by opponents and supporters alike is the route from physician-assisted suicide or euthanasia for terminally ill but competent adults to euthanasia for patients who cannot give consent: the unconscious, the demented, the mentally ill, and children. Because the Netherlands is the one developed democracy that has experience with sanctioned euthanasia, advocates and adversaries alike invoke it to defend their points of view. What does the Dutch experience actually show?

Contemporary Dutch policy regarding voluntary euthanasia had its origins in 1973, with the case of a physician, Geertruida Postma, who injected a deaf, partially paralyzed seventy-eight-year-old woman with morphine, ending her life. The patient happened to be Postma's mother. Postma was convicted of murder but given a suspended sentence of one week in jail and one year on probation, a sentence that effectively exonerated her. A subsequent case in 1981 resulted in an agreement between Dutch prosecutors and the Royal Dutch Medical Society, under the terms of which physicians who participated in physician-assisted suicide or euthanasia would not be prosecuted for murder if they adhered to certain guidelines. The main guidelines, parts of which have been incorporated into proposals for outright legalization in other countries, are that 1) the patient must make an informed, free, and explicit request for physician-assisted suicide or euthanasia, and the request must be repeated over time; 2) the patient must be experiencing unbearable suffering—physical or psychological—that cannot be relieved by any intervention except physician-assisted suicide or euthanasia; 3) the attending physician must have a consultation with a second, independent physician to confirm that the case is appropriate for physician-assisted suicide or euthanasia; and 4) the physician must report the facts of the case to the coroner, as part of a notification procedure developed to permit investigation and to ensure that the guidelines have been followed.

It is important to recognize that despite a widespread perception to the contrary, euthanasia has not been legalized under the Dutch penal code—it remains a crime, albeit one that will not be prosecuted if performed in accordance with the guidelines. . . .

Not until 1990, a decade after the Dutch rules were promulgated, was the comprehensive and reliable empirical study done of physician-assisted suicide and euthanasia in the Netherlands which resulted in the Remmelink Report. The 1996 update of this report reveals that of about 9,700 requests for physician-assisted suicide or euthanasia made each year in the Netherlands, about 3,600 are acceded to, accounting for 2.7 percent of all deaths in the Netherlands (2.3 percent from euthanasia, 0.4 percent from physician-assisted suicide). . . .

The 1996 data show small increases in the numbers of requests for physician-assisted suicide and euthanasia since 1990, but the overall changes are undramatic. The new research does indicate, however, that problems identified by the Remmelink Report have by no means been eliminated.

First, the update found that beyond the roughly 3,600 cases of physician-assisted suicide and euthanasia reported in a given year, there are about 1,000 instances of nonvoluntary euthanasia. Most frequently, patients who were no longer competent were given euthanasia even though they could not have freely, explicitly, and repeatedly requested it. Before becoming unconscious or mentally incompetent about half these patients did discuss or express a wish for euthanasia; nevertheless, they were unable to reaffirm their wishes when the euthanasia was performed. Similarly, a study of nursing-home patients found that in only 41 percent of physician-assisted suicide and euthanasia cases did doctors adhere to all the guidelines. Although most of the violations were minor (usually deviations in the notification procedure), in 15 percent of cases the patient did not initiate the request for physician-assisted suicide or euthanasia; in 15 percent there was no consultation with a second physician; in seven percent no more than one day elapsed between the first request and the actual physician-assisted suicide or euthanasia, violating the guideline calling for repeated requests; and in nine percent interventions other than physician-assisted suicide or euthanasia could have been tried to relieve the patient's suffering.

Second, euthanasia of newborns has been acknowledged. The reported cases have involved babies suffering from well-recognized fatal or severely disabling defects, though the babies were not in fact dying. Precisely how many cases have occurred is not known. One estimate is that ten to fifteen such cases occur each year. Whether ethically justified or not, providing euthanasia to newborns (upon parental request) is not voluntary euthanasia and does constitute a kind of "mercy killing."

The Netherlands studies fail to demonstrate that permitting physician-assisted suicide and euthanasia will not lead to the nonvoluntary euthanasia of children, the demented, the mentally ill, the old, and others. Indeed, the persistence of abuse and the violation of safeguards, despite publicity and condemnation, suggest that the feared consequences of legalization are exactly its inherent consequences. . . .

U.S. POLICY

What, then, should be U.S. policy regarding physician-assisted suicide and euthanasia? Magazine and television stories about patients who want to end their suffering by means of physician-assisted suicide or euthanasia help to reinforce the seemingly inherent link between pain and such interventions. As an oncologist I have often personally cared for patients who suffer despite all available treatment. Only the callous and insensitive would deny that in such cases physician-assisted suicide or euthanasia can offer obvious benefits—can end a life that is worse than death.

But these cases distort the picture. The question is not about whether intervention is right for this or that particular patient. In any given case it may be the ethical thing to do, whatever the law says—and should be done. The question confronting the United States is one of policy: Should we broadly legalize physician-assisted suicide and euthanasia? We must not be swayed by a few—or even a few thousand—wrenching cases in which such intervention seems unequivocally right.

Most of the patients interested in physician-assisted suicide or euthanasia will not be suffering horrific pain. As noted, depression, hopelessness, and psychological distress are the primary factors motivating the great majority. Should their wishes be granted? Our usual approach to people who try to end their lives for reasons of depression and psychological distress is psychiatric intervention—not giving them a syringe and life-ending drugs.

Legalizing physician-assisted suicide and euthanasia, some argue, would not benefit only those who eventually made use of these procedures; it would also provide "psychological comfort" or "reassurance" to millions of other Americans, who would know that if they were dying and things got really bad, they could end their lives. However, the one study we have—the Boston study mentioned previously—shows that for every cancer patient who is likely to be reassured by a discussion of physician-assisted suicide or euthanasia, another patient finds that such a discussion would decrease his or her trust in the care being provided.

DANGERS OF LEGALIZATION

Whatever the benefits of legalized physician-assisted suicide and euthanasia, they must be measured against the dangers of legalization. In considering dangers we must consider more than potential violations of safeguards. . . . (It is hardly surprising that, according to surveys, those who are most opposed to physician-assisted suicide and euthanasia include those most likely to experience abuse and coercion: the old, the less well off, and minorities.) For instance, how would legalization affect our society's already tenuous commitment to providing quality health care for the millions of people who die every year?

Providing the terminally ill with compassionate care and dignity is very hard work. It frequently requires monitoring and adjusting pain medications, the onerous and thankless task of cleaning people who cannot control their bladders and bowels, and feeding and dressing people when their every movement is painful or difficult. It may require agonizing talks with dying family members about their fears, their reflections on life and what comes after, their family loves and family antagonisms. Ending a patient's life by injection, with the added solace that it will be quick and painless, is much easier than this constant physical and emotional care. If there is a way to avoid all this hard work, it becomes difficult not to use it.

Broad legalization of physician-assisted suicide and euthanasia would have the paradoxical effect of making patients seem to be responsible for their own suffering. Rather than being seen primarily as the victims of pain and suffering caused by disease, patients would be seen as having the power to end their suffering by agreeing to an injection or taking some pills; refusing would mean that living through the pain was the patient's decision, the patient's responsibility. Placing the blame on the patient would reduce the motivation of caregivers to provide the extra care that might be required, and would ease guilt if the care fell short. Such an easy, thoughtless shift of responsibility is probably what makes most hospice workers so deeply opposed to physician-assisted suicide and euthanasia.

BUDGETARY PRESSURES

There is one final matter to consider: the possibility that euthanasia not only would be performed on incompetent patients in violation of the rules—as an abuse of the safeguards—but would become the rule in the context of demographic and budgetary pressures on Social Security and Medicare as the Baby Boom generation begins to retire, around 2010.

Once legalized, physician-assisted suicide and euthanasia would become routine. Over time doctors would become comfortable giving injections to end life and Americans would become comfortable having euthanasia as an option. Comfort would make us want to extend the option to others who, in society's view, are suffering and leading purposeless lives. The ethical arguments for physician-assisted suicide and euthanasia, advocates of euthanasia have maintained, do not apply to euthanasia only when it is voluntary; they can also be used to justify some kinds of nonvoluntary euthanasia of the incompetent.

Euthanasia would come to be seen as "one end of a spectrum of caring for dying patients," as the philosopher and euthanasia defender Dan Brock writes. "When viewed in this way," he goes on, "it will be difficult to deny euthanasia to a patient for whom it is seen as the best or most appropriate form of care simply because that patient is now incompetent and cannot request it."

Advocates of physician-assisted suicide and euthanasia urge legalization for reasons of compassion, but there is no guarantee that the reasons offered in 1997 would remain the justification even a few years ahead, under different social and economic circumstances. The confluence of ethical arguments, medical practice, demographic and budgetary pressures, and a social ethos that views the old and sick as burdens would seem capable of overwhelming any barriers against euthanasia for incompetent patients.

THE CORRECT POLICY

The proper policy, in my view, should be to affirm the status of physician-assisted suicide and euthanasia as illegal. In so doing we would affirm that as a society we condemn ending a patient's life and do not consider that to have one's life ended by a doctor is a right. This does not mean we deny that in exceptional cases interventions are appropriate, as acts of desperation when all other elements of treatment—all medications, surgical procedures, psychotherapy, spiritual care, and so on—have been tried. Physician-assisted suicide and euthanasia should not be performed simply because a patient is depressed, tired of life, worried about being a burden, or worried about being dependent. All these may be signs that not every effort has yet been made.

By establishing a social policy that keeps physician-assisted suicide and euthanasia illegal but recognizes exceptions, we would adopt the correct moral view: the onus of proving that everything had been tried and that the motivation and rationale were convincing would rest on those who wanted to end a life. Such a policy would recognize that ending a life by physician-assisted suicide or euthanasia is an extraordinary and grave event. To recognize a legal right to physician-assisted suicide or euthanasia transforms the practices into routine interventions that can be administered without the need for a publicly acceptable justification. Doctors who end patients' lives would no longer bear the burden of having to prove the appropriateness of their action, if called upon to do so, but could simply justify their action as a legally sanctioned procedure.

Advocates for legalization might find a policy that permits exceptions to embody a double standard. But crafting a social policy in this way would also embody what we know: not all cases are the same, and among the millions of Americans who die each year there are morally relevant differences that cannot be captured in an inflexible rule. We must ensure that moral judgments are made in individual cases, and that those who make them will be accountable before the law.

| "We should not permit our hubris of thinking we can overcome the suffering of dying to keep the physician from acceding to the patient's request for a lethal dose."

ASSISTED SUICIDE CAN BE A COMPASSIONATE RESPONSE TO THE DYING

Arthur Rifkin

Arthur Rifkin is a professor of psychiatry at the Albert Einstein College of Medicine in the Bronx, New York. In the following viewpoint, he argues that while quality medical care can relieve much of the suffering of the terminally ill, it is impossible to eliminate all suffering. Permitting physician aid in suicide for dying patients who desire a hastened death—subject to safeguards to prevent the unethical killing of people without their consent or good reason—may be the only compassionate response in some cases, he concludes.

As you read, consider the following questions:

1. What advantages and disadvantages has technology created for patients, according to Rifkin?
2. In what respects do humans already refuse to "let nature take its course," according to the author?
3. How does Rifkin respond to concerns that permitting physician-assisted suicide creates a "slippery slope" leading to unethical killing?

Reprinted from Arthur Rifkin, "Spiritual Aspects of Physician-Assisted Suicide," *Friends Journal*, October 1997, by permission of *Friends Journal*.

Physician-assisted suicide in a concrete fashion forces us to consider and act on what we consider ultimate. It not only makes us question whether someone should commit suicide, but whether another person should help.

Do we "play God" when we seek to end life? The typical instance concerns someone terminally ill who considers life meaningless because of pain and mental and physical impediments. Technology, as in many areas, creates advantages and disadvantages. We live longer and more comfortably because of medical advances, such as renal dialysis, organ transplantations, joint replacement, and antidepressants. But technology, as well, can simply prolong dying. Where pneumonia, "the old man's friend," would kill a debilitated person relatively quickly, we, often, can prevent this. Mechanical ventilation and parenteral nutrition extend life, even for long periods of unconsciousness or stupor.

CAN RELIEVE SOME SUFFERING

We can reduce suffering. Optimal treatment of pain can remove much discomfort, although many patients don't receive optimal pain management because of the mistaken concern that tolerance will develop to the analgesic effect or worry about addiction. Much suffering comes from unkind treatment, from insensitive caregivers, neglect from family and friends, and unpleasant surroundings. Much suffering comes from the narrowing of areas that sustain interest and pleasure, by sensory loss, invalidism, and lack of intellectual and social opportunities. Compassionate, intelligent care in pleasant surroundings would alleviate much suffering.

However, for many people we cannot mitigate the suffering. We think unrealistically if we expect to make all dying free of severe suffering.

The situation is not hopeless: some very painful conditions remit, even if the patient does not recognize that this can occur. This raises the very difficult question of determining if the dying person has the mental capacity to make the decision to end his or her life. We would not honor the decision to commit suicide by minors or people with mental disorders, which includes everything from alcohol intoxication to Alzheimer's Disease. The difficult issue is assessing depression. We rightly protect a depressed person from committing suicide because his or her judgement is impaired, and most depressions eventually lift.

How do we distinguish depression from existential despair in the dying?

If the dying person no longer enjoys usual activities, has a poor appetite, sleeps poorly, cannot concentrate well, feels hopeless, and wants to die, are these symptoms of a mental disorder (depression) or understandable and reasonable responses to the illness and its treatment, and/or the result of the illness or treatment? Can we make the case for a mental disorder? Do the symptoms hang together, are the course, family history, and response to treatment predictable? Several studies have shown that depression associated with physical illness does respond to antidepressant drugs, but no studies have included terminally ill patients.

Some psychiatrists aver that the wish to die in a terminally ill patient always represents a treatable mental disorder: if not depression then demoralization—a sense of unrealistic pessimism. This assumes that the realistic suffering of dying can be ameliorated, a questionable assumption.

As I assess the situation, there are inadequate psychiatric reasons for considering all instances of suicidal desires instances of psychopathology, and we cannot ameliorate all terrible suffering and lack of dignity in dying persons, although we can do a lot more than we have. The hospice movement shows that much can be done.

ALTERING NATURE'S COURSE

Do we play God by terminating a natural process? I think not. We hardly live in some pure state of nature. In small and large ways we don't "let nature take its course." We foster death by many unhealthful practices. We forestall death by healthful living, environment changes, and medical treatment.

Most people, and all courts, recognize that patients can request discontinuation of life support measures. Do we cross some qualitative bridge between ending life support measures and assisting in suicide, or is this more a quantitative difference, or is it no difference? It seems very late in the day to concern ourselves with altering nature. For better or worse, we have grasped the helm of much that determines our lives. It seems like cowardice and hypocrisy to lift our hands away from the rudder and say, "Now God, you take over."

GOD'S PURPOSE

Is opposition to physician-assisted suicide the last gasp of the "God of the gaps," pinning on God what we remain ignorant of, namely how to make our deaths a deeply spiritually meaningful event and not horrendous torture we would never think of inflicting on anyone? Does it serve God's purpose for us to lose, at the ends of our lives, that which characterizes us at our spiritual best: intentionality, seeking the Light Within to lead us to our culmination? This should be our time of letting go and deepest insight, not a time of agony, stupor, undignified dependence, a prisoner of tighter restrictions than inmates of a maximum security prison endure. Must we become slaves to our failing bodies?

The 22nd Psalm aptly describes a horrible death:

I am poured out like water,
and all my bones are out of joint;
my heart is like wax;
     it is melted within my breast;
my mouth is dried up like a potsherd,
     and my tongue sticks to my jaws;
     you lay me in the dust of death.

This psalm then leads to the magnificent, stately 23rd, filled with peaceful gratitude:

Even though I walk through the darkest
     valley,
     I fear no evil;
for you are with me;
     your rod and your staff,
     they comfort me.

Is it stretching too far to say that the shepherd's rod at the time of death could be the physician's lethal dose of medication?

MUST GUARD AGAINST ABUSE

A treatment of ultimate finality—physician-assisted suicide—must have the most stringent safeguards against misuse. Although distinguishing reversible depression from nonreversible existential anguish is difficult, psychiatrists should use care to recognize and treat reversible depression. We should try to create an ambience most conducive to a meaningful death. We should have a method of paying for healthcare that does not drain away remaining resources. We should provide caretakers who view it as a privilege to competently and compassionately use technical skills and understanding to assist the dying patient.

We should not permit our hubris of thinking we can overcome the suffering of dying to keep the physician from acceding to the patient's request for a lethal dose. We hear misguided claims that following the Hippocratic Oath would keep physicians from assisting in suicide. The spirit of the Hippocratic Oath says the physician should be devoted to the patient's interests. How we define those interests today should not be limited by our understanding of medicine over two millennia ago.

What of the slippery slope? Does physician-assisted suicide open the door to unethical practices of killing people without consent and without good cause? The answer to unintelligent, unscrupulous behavior is intelligence and scrupulous concern for the patient's interest and not manacles to prevent ethical, useful acts. The history of humankind is a widening circle of compassionate and just concerns. We have recognized the need to free ourselves from the injustice of slavery, mistreatment of children, unequal treatment of women, and ethnic and religious bigotry. Now the horizon of concern has reached a group often treated as unfairly and sadistically as any of the foregoing groups: the dying. Let us grasp the chance boldly.

| "In helping the terminally ill to kill
themselves, we're colluding not only
in their dehumanization, but our
own."

ASSISTED SUICIDE IS AN IMMORAL RESPONSE TO THE DYING

Charles J. Chaput

The euthanasia campaigns of Nazi Germany demonstrate how compassion for the dying can be manipulated to justify mass killing, argues Charles J. Chaput in the following viewpoint. A truly merciful and compassionate response to the dying, he asserts, would be to relieve their pain and restore meaning to their lives—not assist in killing them. Permitting physician-assisted suicide would give doctors too much power and destroy trust between patients and their physicians. Chaput is the Roman Catholic archbishop of Denver, Colorado.

As you read, consider the following questions:

1. What example of euthanasia propaganda does Chaput describe?
2. What statement does the author make about the evils of suffering?
3. What is missing from the debate over doctor-assisted suicide, according to Chaput?

Reprinted from Charles J. Chaput, " Eugenics to Euthanasia," Crisis, October 1997, by permission of Crisis magazine. To order, call 800-852-9962.

See if this story sounds familiar: A happily married couple—she is a pianist; he a rising scientist—have their love suddenly tested by a decline in the wife's health. Diagnosed with multiple sclerosis, she falls victim to a steady loss of muscle control and paralysis. The desperate husband uses all his professional skills to save her. But ultimately he must watch her deteriorate in hideous pain. The wife worries that she will soon no longer be "a person anymore—just a lump of flesh—and a torture" for her husband. She begs her husband to kill her before that happens. And eventually, worn down, the reluctant husband releases his wife from her misery with poison.

The husband is indicted for murder. But the understanding judge and jury soon agree that, given the circumstances, the husband is not a killer, and the law needs to be reformed. Meanwhile, in impassioned public comments, the husband attacks "the proponents of outmoded beliefs and antiquated laws" who inflict unnecessary anguish on the terminally ill, "who suffer without hope and whose death would be deliverance for them."

LEARNING FROM HISTORY

The story fits comfortably with today's medical headlines. It could easily be a 20/20 segment or a page from Jack Kevorkian's latest trial. But it comes from another era. Produced in 1941, it's the plot line of *I Accuse*, one of the Third Reich's most effective propaganda films. *I Accuse* was created for one reason only: to advance the Nazi campaign of euthanasia for the mentally and physically handicapped, "antisocial elements," and the terminally ill. And it worked. It was a big box-office success. It's also the classic example of how compassion can be manipulated to justify mass killing—first in the name of mercy, then in the name of cost and utility.

Obviously, America in 1997 is not Germany in 1941. Americans have a practical sense of justice that favors the weak and the little guy. But if we want to keep it that way, we shouldn't assume that merely knowing about a past tragedy prevents us from repeating it. We need to learn from history. And in reflecting on physician-assisted suicide, the first lesson for our lawmakers is that any killing motivated by a distorted sense of mercy—no matter how many reasonable and honeyed words endorse it—leads to killing that has nothing at all to do with the best interests of those killed.

Let's examine a few simple facts.

First, every one of us fears the image of a dying patient stripped of dignity and trapped in a suffering body. But today, no one needs to suffer excruciating pain in a terminal illness. Modern pain-suppression drugs can ensure the comfort of persons even in the final stages of dying. Hospice care, focused on ensuring a natural death with comfort and dignity, is increasingly available. It's true that some doctors underprescribe pain medication or seek to artificially prolong life beyond reasonable hope of recovery. But that is an issue of training. Patients have the right to decline extraordinary means of treatment. They also have a right to be free of mind-numbing pain. Both these goals can be accomplished without killing them.

Second, terminally ill persons seeking doctor-assisted suicide usually struggle with depression, guilt, anger, and a loss of meaning. They need to be reassured that their lives and their suffering have purpose. They don't need to be helped toward the exit. We should also remember that in helping the terminally ill to kill themselves, we're colluding not only in their dehumanization, but our own. Moreover, the notion that suffering is always evil and should be avoided at all costs is a very peculiar idea. Six thousand years of Judeo-Christian wisdom show that suffering can be—and often is—redemptive, both for the person who suffers and for the family and friends of the one in need. In any case, it is very odd to try to eliminate suffering by killing those who suffer.

Third, the Hippocratic Oath has very good reasons for binding physicians to "do no harm." Doctors wield enormous power over their patients. And that power quickly corrupts the profession unless it is rigorously held in check. That is one of the reasons the American Medical Association has rightly, and so strongly, opposed physician-assisted suicide.

A DANGEROUS ALTERNATIVE

The alternative is immensely dangerous. The doctors who killed their patients in Nazi Germany may be written off as the product of a special and terrible time. But what about the doctors in the Netherlands—right now, today—who admit to killing patients without their approval?

Physician-assisted suicide among the Dutch has been quietly tolerated for some time. But no one was prepared for the number of Dutch doctors who have taken it beyond that, proactively dispatching the terminally ill without their knowledge. The point is: The logic behind doctor-assisted suicide naturally expands. Can anyone honestly argue that physician-assisted suicide will limit itself to voluntary candidates in an era of ruthless medical cost-efficiency? And do we really want a society where patients aren't sure they can trust their physicians?

One final point: While the Supreme Court upheld state bans against physician-assisted suicide in Washington and New York in June 1997, the debate is far from over. Missing from too much of today's discussion of doctor-assisted suicide is the presence of God. Yet God, in the view of the great majority of Americans, is the author of life and its only true "owner." Life is God's gift, and he alone is its Lord. However wounded or attenuated it may seem, life is precious. Every life is sacred, from conception to natural death. We rarely understand life. We certainly don't own it. But if this sad century has taught us anything, it's that we have no right to dispose of it—however good the alibi.

> "The rising cost of health care is a societal reality that has promoted . . . interest in constructing a new culture of dying . . . focusing on shortening the dying process for those who want it."

LEGALIZING ASSISTED SUICIDE MAY BECOME NECESSARY TO CUT HEALTH CARE COSTS

Derek Humphry and Mary Clement

Derek Humphry is the founder of the Hemlock Society and a well-known advocate of euthanasia. He and Mary Clement, an attorney, are co-authors of *Freedom to Die: People, Politics, and the Right-to-Die Movement*, from which the following viewpoint is excerpted. Humphry and Clement argue that the issue of physician-assisted suicide has become prominent in part because of the rising costs of health care for elderly people in the last days of life. The financial and emotional tolls of caring for the dying are straining the resources of individual families and of society, leading many people to consider physician-assisted suicide and voluntary euthanasia to be acceptable options. A social taboo exists against openly expressing economic arguments for euthanasia, the authors contend, but such issues cannot ultimately be ignored. For more information, visit www.finalexit.org.

As you read, consider the following questions:

1. What are some of the factors that Humphry and Clement say are contributing to rising health care costs?
2. How do people in other cultures deal with the elderly, according to Humphry and Clement?

It is politically incorrect to use economics as an argument in favor of the right to choose the time and manner of one's death—for the moment, at least. Even now, however, people are beginning to question the common sense of keeping someone alive, at great societal and personal expense, who prefers to forgo the final hours or weeks of an intolerable existence. To what purpose? Might not money be better spent on preventive treatment, medicine for the young, educating the youth of the nation, or for that matter, the children in the patient's own family. Is there, in fact, a duty to die—a responsibility within the family unit—that should remain voluntary but expected nevertheless? Rationing of health care already exists, but how much limitation on services will the nation tolerate?

UNSPOKEN ARGUMENTS

Like it or not, the connections between the right-to-die and the cost, value, and allocation of health care resources are part of the political debate, albeit frequently unspoken. Policies are emerging more or less simultaneously; and policies in one arena implicate those in another. Physician-assisted suicide is an idea whose time has come, even if legalization occurs gradually. While government is contemplating these policy issues, the right-to-die movement is gaining momentum in response to a legitimate societal problem—the emotional, physical, and economic toll of the dying experience on not only government, employers, hospitals, and insurance companies, but on families as well.

RISING COSTS OF HEALTH CARE

Medical expenditures used to be small, not because doctors were stingy or inefficient, but because there was very little that medicine could offer—no matter how much the public was willing or able to spend. Since the 1940s, every year has brought new medical advances: new diagnostic techniques to identify problems; new surgical procedures to correct problems that could previously only be allowed to run their course; and new therapies that cure or at the very least alleviate conditions. With the assistance of medical technology, Americans seem able to cheat death in the short term, but the resulting quality of life is often seriously degraded and prohibitively expensive.

In 1970 the U.S. spent 7 percent of its gross domestic product (GDP) on medical care. National health care spending totaled $949.4 billion or almost 14 percent of the gross domestic product in 1994. Health care spending has increased well over

30 percent since 1990, rising much faster than the economy as a whole. By the year 2000 the amount spent on health care is estimated to be $1.5 trillion. Health care is expected to consume 18 percent of the GDP by 2005. . . .

Consider the rising cost of health care, skewed in the direction of the seriously ill elderly patient who will die within a short time regardless of the medical intervention implemented. Medical expenditures at the end of life are disproportionately high, while the elderly consume a disproportionate amount of health care resources. These two facts combine to raise serious concerns about our economic future. Health care dollars spent on futile care during the last days and weeks of life are largely responsible for the increasing interest in right-to-die issues. Many are questioning the vast amounts of money spent on temporary rescue services for the dying and the elderly, while health care costs are spiraling out of control and other medical needs like prenatal care and preventive medicine, are going unaddressed. . . .

COST CONTAINMENT

The United States is being forced to consider methods of cost containment. The potential savings to society if advance directives were universally used are enormous. One method of cost containment, and one that will eventually become mandatory, will be for insurance companies and Medicare to require that patients execute a Living Will, clearly articulating what kind of life-sustaining treatment they want and do not want if they become incompetent and unable to make their own medical decisions.

Information shows that getting people to plan ahead for the medical care they want as they approach death, can save an average of more than $60,000 per patient. . . .

A second method of cost containment is doctor-assisted suicide. While no one is suggesting assisted suicide against the patient's wishes, both advance directives and physician-assisted suicide (PAS) propose a voluntary shortening of the dying experience and therefore come under the umbrella of the right-to-die. The proposal has been floated that if a mentally competent terminally ill adult wishes to hasten his or her inevitable death with the aid of a physician, then why not allow it? The patient gets what he or she wants, and society saves money that would otherwise be spent on expensive and, most important, *unwanted* end-of-life care. Compassion and dignity are sufficient justifications for its legalization. . . .

As the cost of health care soars and the population ages, there are equally unsustainable hardships on the family as on the nation's economy and business community. Many dying people report that their one remaining goal in life is to not be a burden on loved ones, yet 7 million Americans, largely women, take care of an ailing or chronically ill parent or spouse.

Dr. Kenneth E. Covinsky, assistant professor of medicine at Case Western Reserve University Medical Center in Cleveland, worries about the family. "We talk a good deal about the financial costs of dying for hospitals, for government, and for insurance companies. But what about the cost of the families? The cost of serious illness we are not measuring is the cost and the burden of suffering to the patient's family," he cautions.

The lives of loved ones are usually seriously compromised by having to care for the ill. The ramifications are physical, emotional, and financial. The burdens of providing constant care, twenty-four hours a day, seven days a week, are overwhelming. When this kind of caregiving goes on for years, with no life or time for herself, the caregiver becomes exhausted and her health is often destroyed. It can also be emotionally devastating to live with a spouse who is increasingly unresponsive and unreachable. The needs of the caregiver suffer. The needs of other family members go unmet. Social life evaporates. Support systems vanish. It becomes impossible to leave home and see friends, while the caregiver's home ceases to be a welcome place to visit.

The financial burdens can be devastating. While most discussions focus solely on the needs of the patient, to the exclusion of the caregiver's concerns and difficulties, John Hardwig, professor of ethical and social/political philosophy, and medical ethics at East Tennessee State University, points to the caregiver's situation:

> We must also acknowledge that the lives of our loved ones can be devastated just by having to pay for health care for us. One part of the SUPPORT [Study to Understand Prognosis and Preferences for Outcomes and Risks in Treatment] study documented the financial aspects of caring for a dying member of a family. Only those who had illnesses severe enough to give them less than a 50% chance to live six more months were included in this study. When these patients survived their initial hospitalization and were discharged, about one-third required considerable caregiving from their families; in 20% of cases a family member had to quit work or make some other major lifestyle change, *almost one-third of these families lost all of their savings; and just under 30% lost a major source of income.* If talking about money sounds venal or trivial, remember that much more than money is normally at stake here. When someone has to quit work, she may well lose her career. Savings decimated late in life cannot be recouped in the few remaining years of employability, so the loss compromises the

quality of the rest of the caregiver's life. For a young person, the chance to go to college may be lost to the attempt to pay debts due to an illness in the family, and this decisively shapes an entire life.

Long-term medical care can wipe out the savings of the elderly and the children of the elderly in no time at all, causing severe economic hardship to the entire family. The cost of long-term care insurance is prohibitive for most people. The average nursing-home bill nationwide is more than $100 a day, with New York State averaging $130 to $230 a day and a nursing home in Manhattan or on Long Island exceeding $100,000 per year.

Not everyone is willing to burden his or her family with futile treatment. Many patients show enormous compassion for their survivors. When faced with economic hardship, patients and family members often opt against certain kinds of care—the kind of care that costs more money. . . .

A Duty to Die?

Until recently, the notion of forgoing treatment or actively seeking a physician's help in dying, motivated by a duty to die, was rarely considered, and certainly not voiced aloud. The unmentionable is unmistakably on the table for discussion as we approach the end of the twentieth century. The normally conservative *Hastings Center Report* asked, in its cover story in the spring of 1997, "Is There A Duty To Die?" Hardwig, the author, answered in the affirmative:

> Many people were outraged when Richard Lamm (the former Governor of Colorado) claimed that old people had a duty to die. As modern medicine continues to save more of us from acute illness, it also delivers more of us over to chronic illnesses, allowing us to survive far longer than we can take care of ourselves. It may be that our technological sophistication coupled with a commitment to our loved ones generates a fairly widespread duty to die.

Hardwig, like a growing number of other people, believes there is a duty to refuse life-sustaining treatment if there is no hope of recovery, and also a duty to complete advance directives requesting others to refuse it for you. However, it is not to this group that the author is writing. He is addressing the person who may want to live, even though debilitated, facing dementia, or undergoing treatment that is futile. It is directed to the patient who has bought "the individual fantasy"; that fantasy that leads one to imagine that lives are separate and unconnected, the fantasy that assumes the ailing patient is the only one affected by his or her health care decision. Most discussions of an illness in the family sound as though responsibility is a one-way street. Not so, writes Hardwig. Illness is a two-way street with obligations and responsibilities going both ways. . . .

A rational argument can be made for allowing PAS in order to offset the amount society and family spend on the ill, *as long as it is the voluntary wish* of the mentally competent terminally and incurable ill adult. There will likely come a time when PAS becomes a commonplace occurrence for individuals who *want* to die and feel is it the right thing to do by their loved ones. There is no contradicting the fact that since the largest medical expenses are incurred in the final days and weeks of life, the hastened demise of people with only a short time left would free resources for others. Hundreds of billions of dollars could benefit those patients who not only *can* be cured but who also *want* to live. What possible sense does it make to use limited resources on people who *cannot* be helped and who *do not want* to be helped, either because they themselves have had "enough" or because they believe it is the morally correct thing to do for their family?

It is this kind of thinking that concerns critics of an assisted death. Opponents of the practice are repelled by the thought of assisted suicide as an answer to shrinking health care resources. Supporters of the practice respond that no one is forcing, coercing, or encouraging anyone to do anything. Assisted death is totally *voluntary*—a matter to be decided with the family and with the patient's conscience. The debate goes round and round, and few, if any, change their minds.

DEATH IN OTHER CULTURES

Whether one approves or not, however, American society is inching toward allowing the elderly and infirmed to make choices about curtailing life. Economic necessity is forcing us to evaluate medical services in a cost effective manner. This is not a unique concept. Cross-cultural studies reveal patterns of full support and respect for elders until such time as they become dependent on others for survival and perceived as a burden by society. In the past, Japanese elders, ordinarily highly respected by the community, had an obligation to commit suicide when they became a burden, frequently with the assistance of a relative. It is virtually only in those cultures where the Judeo-Christian sanctity-of-life and redemption-in-suffering arguments predominate that behavior like this is prohibited.

Research shows that in many "primitive" societies, once an elder's life has no further economic value to the community and may indeed be an economic liability, the community hastens death by refusing financial and other support to the dependent elder. Eskimo elders are highly revered and nurtured by the community as long as they can contribute to the general good of the group and add to its resources. Once they are no longer productive, however, they are abandoned by the community or assisted in their death. Necessity, rather than indifference or animosity, motivates this behavior. . . .

The American public is uncomfortable talking about the money connection, focusing instead on the right of the patient to a dignified death. Herein lies the unspoken argument for physician aid in dying. The rising cost of health care is a societal reality that has promoted a rush of populist interest in constructing a new culture of dying in the United States, focusing on shortening the dying process for those who want it. It is the unspoken connection of value to cost—for the nation, business, and the family unit. In advocating for an assisted death, one is beginning to hear the argument that says: "Look, let's face facts. The nation's economy is about to break under the growing cost of health care and the situation will get markedly worse as baby boomers become elderly and infirmed patients eating at the subsidized table. Families are suffering. Even if reform takes place, how comprehensive will it be? Politicians know it's a losing issue at the ballot box. If someone wants to bail out a little early, why should we stop them? Let's put our energies toward guidelines that will enable the practice to go as smoothly as possible. We certainly won't encourage people to hasten their death, but why should we stop them? Physician-assisted suicide is a win-win situation." Spend some time on the subject, and this unspoken argument will surface—on an ever more frequent basis. It is a pragmatic argument and one that deserves an answer.

> "In evaluating the right-to-die movement, one should not overlook the fundamental importance of money."

CUTTING HEALTH CARE COSTS CANNOT JUSTIFY LEGALIZING ASSISTED SUICIDE

Evan J. Kemp Jr.

In the following viewpoint, Evan J. Kemp Jr. argues that because of the economic pressures that drive America's health care institutions, permitting assisted suicide will result in the rationing of health care. People without health insurance or those who have disabilities may be coerced into "choosing" suicide to save society the costs of caring for them. The risks of allowing doctors to assist in suicide therefore outweigh any potential benefits, he concludes. Kemp, who suffers from a progressive neuromuscular disease, served as chairman of the Equal Employment Opportunity Commission under President George Bush.

As you read, consider the following questions:

1. What experiences have disabled patients had with hospitals concerning "do-not-resuscitate" (DNR) orders, according to Kemp?
2. Who does Kemp believe controls decisions on health care spending in America?
3. Why has the American Medical Association opposed physician-assisted suicide, according to Kemp?

Reprinted from Evan J. Kemp Jr., "Could You Please Die Now?" *The Washington Post National Weekly Edition*, January 13, 1997, by permission of the author.

On Jan. 8, 1997, the Supreme Court heard oral arguments in *Washington v. Glucksberg* and *Vacco v. Quill*. At issue is the question of whether or not "terminally ill" individuals have an inherent "right to die." And, if so, should a licensed physician be granted the legal right to assist in the "suicide" of a patient? [Editor's note: The U.S. Supreme Court ruled in June 1997 that the Constitution does not guarantee a "right to die."]

As the case was argued inside the court, thousands will be keeping vigil outside the court. I will be among them.

You might ask, "Why would a conservative Republican who served as the chair of the U.S. Equal Employment Opportunity Commission in the Bush administration join Clinton Democrats, representatives of the Catholic Church, Orthodox Jews, civil rights advocates, and a large congregation of disabled and elderly people in a noisy street demonstration?"

The answer is simple: I do not believe that doctors should kill their patients.

At the outset, I must acknowledge that the right-to-die proponents have a certain undeniable logic to their argument. I agree with the proposition that every individual has a right to control his or her life. Unfortunately, this logic does not take into account the institutional ramifications of physician-assisted suicide and thus misses a much more basic point. In this age of soaring health care costs, I believe the right-to-die option inevitably will be transformed into a means of rationing health care.

A SLIPPERY SLOPE

As a matter of fact, we've already taken our first few steps down this exceedingly steep and slippery slope. At present, a patient checking into a hospital is routinely given the option of signing a "do not resuscitate" order (DNR), requesting that "heroic measures," such as cardiopulmonary resuscitation, not be taken should such measures be required to keep the person alive.

DNR consent is supposed to be voluntary. In practice, however, that has not always been the case. Some disabled people report instances in which hospitals have pressured patients—most notably, people with disabilities, the uninsured, and the severely ill—to sign DNR orders.

In some cases, the DNR is not explained clearly. The patient, or the patient's family or other representative, is not adequately informed of the nature of the order—especially the fact that it is supposed to be voluntary. The DNR is often included with other routine administrative papers to be signed. This cannot be construed as "informed consent."

Joe Ehman, a news reporter in Rochester, New York, who uses a wheelchair, told me he was "literally hounded by social workers" to sign a DNR when he was hospitalized in 1995 for back surgery. "A few hours after surgery, still delirious from the anesthesia and from postsurgical morphine and demerol, I had to hear from yet another social worker who wanted to force-feed me a DNR. I mustered my strength and screamed, 'I'm 30 years old. I don't want to die!'"

Maria Matzik, a woman in her thirties who lives and works in Dayton, Ohio, says she had a frightening battle with nurses during a 1993 hospital stay. "They kept asking me to sign a DNR order," she told me. "When I wouldn't sign it, they said it didn't matter anyway. Because I use a ventilator, they told me nothing would be done if I had a cardiac arrest." Matzik escaped that fate, but others have not.

Marjorie Nighbert, a 76-year-old Florida woman, was hospitalized in 1996 after a stroke. Before her hospital admission, she signed an advance directive that no "heroic measures" should be employed to save her life. On the basis of that directive and at the request of her family, the hospital denied Nighbert's requests for food and water, according to reports in the *Northwest Florida Daily News*. A hurriedly convened hospital ethics committee ruled that she was "not medically competent to ask for such a treatment." Until her death more than 10 days later, Nighbert was restrained in her bed to prevent her from raiding other patients' food trays.

The larger point is that, in evaluating the right-to-die movement, one should not overlook the fundamental importance of money. In the *Washington v. Glucksberg* decision, federal judge Stephen Reinhardt tried to put the best possible face on the economic pressures involved in life and death decisions: ". . . in a society in which the costs of protracted health care can be so exorbitant, we are reluctant to say that it is improper for competent, terminally ill adults to take the economic welfare of their families and loved ones into consideration."

THE ECONOMICS OF DYING

When it comes to spending money on health care, however, "families and loved ones" often are not in a position to call the shots. Insurance companies, hospitals, nursing homes and HMOs are—and they would prefer that the dirty little secret of money be kept out of the public debate about assisted suicide. After all, it's much easier for them to justify their actions on the basis of humanitarian principle than financial self-interest. Once physician-assisted suicide is given the sanction of law, our health care institutions are likely to devise contractual mechanisms that make sure members of targeted groups die as efficiently as possible.

All of this will be justified by the holy grail of the right-to-die movement: "choice." But the laws of economics virtually guarantee that, in practice, those who "choose" assisted suicide will disproportionately come from the lower end of the socio-economic ladder: people without health insurance, as well as from people who are said to possess a low "quality of life"—i.e., people with disabilities.

As former Surgeon General C. Everett Koop declared at a Washington, D.C., press conference in November 1996, "Toleration of doctor-assisted suicide can lead to acceptance of involuntary euthanasia."

As a disabled person, I am especially sensitive to the "quality of life" rationale that is frequently introduced in the debate. For the past 47 years, I have lived with a progressive neuromuscular disease that first began to manifest itself when I was 12. My disease, Kugelburg Weylander Syndrome, has no known cure, and I have no hope for "recovery."

Upon diagnosis, my parents were informed by the physicians treating me that I would die within two years. Later, another group of physicians was certain that I would live only to the age of 18. Yet here I am at age 59, continuing to have an extraordinarily high quality of life.

And my case is by no means unique. The majority of families I have encountered in my lifetime, and who have been close enough to share details of their extended family life, have had at least one member who defied the medical establishment by living a far longer and more productive life than expected. Should we permit the medical establishment to assist these individuals with disabilities to die before their time at the hands of their physicians? I don't think so.

PAYING FOR SUICIDE

If physician-assisted suicide is decriminalized, the next question to arise will be how to pay for the service. If the suicide services, dubbed "obitiatry" by Dr. Jack Kevorkian, become billable, those services could dovetail all too well with our nation's current drive to cut health care costs. Health maintenance organizations may view the cost of obitiatry as especially cost-effective in that the practice will require neither referrals to specialists nor repeat visits to physicians' offices.

In managed-care parlance, the portion of the premium dollar spent on medical care is called the "medical-loss ratio." Insurance companies and health maintenance organizations could cut that ratio by providing assisted suicide rather than bypass surgeries and the like. After all, many people are cheaper dead than alive.

The American Medical Association has twice affirmed its opposition to physician-assisted suicide and recently filed an amicus brief with the Supreme Court. The AMA wishes for physicians to maintain their role as healers, and not to become potential killers, even for reasons of mercy.

The experience of Nazi Germany is relevant here, not because the advocates of assisted suicide are incipient fascists (they're not) but because of the historical fact that the Holocaust had its beginnings in the systematic elimination of Germans with disabilities. As Hugh Gregory Gallagher noted in his 1990 book, *By Trust Betrayed: Physicians, Patients and the License to Kill in the Third Reich*, Adolf Hitler's order of September 1939 called for physicians to assist in the killings of citizens with illnesses and disabilities. Nazi propagandists, led by a small number of physicians, said that such citizens were "useless eaters" and "life unworthy of life." Today American health planners, while driven by a very different ideology, also speak a dehumanizing language about "health care consumers" and the dubious "quality of life" of our citizens with illnesses and disabilities.

From where I sit, it is undeniably clear that giving physician-assisted suicide the sanction of law will have unintended consequences which vastly outweigh any benefits that might accrue. As Koop puts it, "Society must not allow doctors to be killers as well as healers."

CHAPTER 7

SHOULD LIMITS BE PLACED ON GENETIC ENGINEERING?

CHAPTER PREFACE

"Most people, I suspect, regard genetic engineering as something that will happen tomorrow," writes science journalist Charles C. Mann in a 1998 article. "They are wrong. Biotechnology is here today." In 1973, geneticists announced that they had spliced a gene from a toad into a bacterium, creating the first "transgenic" organism. Since then scientists and researchers have made remarkable and rapid progress in manipulating genes—the basic biochemical building blocks that govern all life forms. By the end of the twentieth century more than 4,600 genetically modified organisms—most developed for agricultural purposes—had been field-tested; and genetically engineered tomatoes, potatoes, and other foods had found their way to American supermarkets. The amount of U.S. farmland planted with genetically modified seeds grew from 6 million acres in 1996 to 58 million in 1998. Bacteria have been genetically modified to produce vaccines, drugs, insulin, and other medical substances.

In addition to changing how foods and drugs are produced, genetic engineering research is rapidly approaching the point of directly affecting human reproduction and evolution. Cloning—the making of exact genetic copies of organisms—occurs naturally in plants and simple animals such as bacteria. A 1997 announcement that a sheep had been cloned from an adult sheep cell, however, prompted much speculation and debate over the prospect of human cloning (previous animal cloning research had used cells of embryos). The government-sponsored Human Genome Project and private corporations are racing to decipher the hundred thousand genes that constitute the genetic makeup of humans, gathering information that could soon make it possible for scientists to genetically alter people as they have already engineered other species. Some day, many predict, parents could conceivably control the genetic makeup of their children, making them free of genetic disorders—or simply taller and smarter.

The potential powers of genetic engineering raise ethical questions that have led many people to question whether genetic engineering research—especially experiments that are performed on humans—should be allowed to go forward without restriction. Some oppose genetic engineering on religious grounds. Prince Charles of Great Britain, for instance, has stated that tampering with genes "takes mankind into realms that belong to God and God alone." Others have argued that the rights of children should be paramount, and that it is not in their best interest to be the subjects of genetic experiments—or to be a cloned copy of a parent, famous athlete, or anybody else. A 1997 *Time*/CNN poll found 93 percent of Americans expressing disapproval of human cloning. Defenders of genetic engineering research argue that banning or restricting this line of scientific inquiry would deprive humanity of many potential benefits, ranging from new sources of food to the elimination of genetic diseases. Others argue that restrictions on cloning and genetic engineering unfairly limit reproductive freedom. "There may be problems," argues James Watson, co-discoverer of the structure of genes, "but I don't believe we can let the government start dictating the decisions people make about what sorts of families they'll have." The viewpoints in this chapter debate whether the risks of genetic engineering outweigh its benefits and whether it should be subject to regulation or restriction.

"If appropriate go-ahead signals
come, the first resulting gene-
bettered children will in no sense
threaten human civilization."

GENETIC ENGINEERING OF HUMANS SHOULD BE PERMITTED

James D. Watson

James D. Watson, a biochemist, shared the Nobel Prize for
medicine in 1962 for his work in discovering the molecular
structure of deoxyribonucleic acid (DNA), the substance that
makes up genetic material in humans and all other organisms.
From 1989 to 1992, he directed the National Center for Human
Genome Research, an agency of the National Institutes of
Health. In the following viewpoint, Watson argues that baseless
fears about genetic engineering in the 1970s unnecessarily delayed important scientific research. He goes on to state that
while genetic engineering is now generally recognized as safe,
research into inserting genetic material into human sperm and
egg cells is still not being conducted because of apprehension
about possible harmful consequences of tampering with humanity's genetic makeup. Watson asserts that forgoing such research because of ill-defined fears of what might happen will
deprive society of important medical advances.

As you read, consider the following questions:
1. What comparison does Watson make between the discovery
   of DNA and the discovery of atomic energy?
2. What moral does the author draw from the experiences of
   genetic engineering researchers and critics during the 1970s?
3. For what uses will genetic engineering of humans most likely
   be applied, according to Watson?

There is lots of zip in DNA-based biology today. With each passing year it incorporates an ever increasing fraction of the life sciences, ranging from single-cell organisms, like bacteria and yeast, to the complexities of the human brain. All this wonderful biological frenzy was unimaginable when I first entered the world of genetics. In 1948, biology was an all too descriptive discipline near the bottom of science's totem pole, with physics at its top. By then [Albert] Einstein's turn-of-the-century ideas about the interconversion of matter and energy had been transformed into the powers of the atom. If not held in check, the weapons they made possible might well destroy the very fabric of civilized human life. So physicists of the late 1940s were simultaneously revered for making atoms relevant to society and feared for what their toys could do if they were to fall into the hands of evil.

Such ambivalent feelings are now widely held toward biology. The double-helical structure of DNA, initially admired for its intellectual simplicity, today represents to many a double-edged sword that can be used for evil as well as good. No sooner had scientists at Stanford University in 1973 begun rearranging DNA molecules in test tubes (and, equally important, reinserting the novel DNA segments back into living cells) than critics began likening these "recombinant" DNA procedures to the physicist's power to break apart atoms. Might not some of the test-tube-rearranged DNA molecules impart to their host cells disease-causing capacities that, like nuclear weapons, are capable of seriously disrupting human civilization? Soon there were cries from both scientists and nonscientists that such research might best be ruled by stringent regulations—if not laws.

As a result, several years were to pass before the full power of recombinant-DNA technology got into the hands of working scientists, who by then were itching to explore previously unattainable secrets of life. Happily, the proposals to control recombinant-DNA research through legislation never got close to enactment. And when anti-DNA doomsday scenarios failed to materialize, even the modestly restrictive governmental regulations began to wither away. In retrospect, recombinant-DNA may rank as the safest revolutionary technology ever developed. To my knowledge, not one fatality, much less illness, has been caused by a genetically manipulated organism.

The moral I draw from this painful episode is this: Never postpone experiments that have clearly defined future benefits for fear of dangers that can't be quantified. Though it may sound at first uncaring, we can react rationally only to real (as opposed to hypothetical) risks. Yet for several years we postponed important experiments on the genetic basis of cancer, for example, because we took much too seriously spurious arguments that the genes at the root of human cancer might themselves be dangerous to work with.

Though most forms of DNA manipulation are now effectively unregulated, one important potential goal remains blocked. Experiments aimed at learning how to insert functional genetic material into human germ cells—sperm and eggs—remain off limits to most of the world's scientists. No governmental body wants to take responsibility for initiating steps that might help redirect the course of future human evolution. These decisions reflect widespread concerns that we, as humans, may not have the wisdom to modify the most precious of all human treasures—our chromosomal "instruction books." Dare we be entrusted with improving upon the results of the several million years of Darwinian natural selection? Are human germ cells Rubicons that geneticists may never cross?

Unlike many of my peers, I'm reluctant to accept such reasoning, again using the argument that you should never put off doing something useful for fear of evil that may never arrive. The first germ-line gene manipulations are unlikely to be attempted for frivolous reasons. Nor does the state of today's science provide the knowledge that would be needed to generate "superpersons" whose far-ranging talents would make those who are genetically unmodified feel redundant and unwanted. Such creations will remain denizens of science fiction, not the real world, far into the future. When they are finally attempted, germ-line genetic manipulations will probably be done to change a death sentence into a life verdict—by creating children who are resistant to a deadly virus, for example, much the way we can already protect plants from viruses by inserting antiviral DNA segments into their genomes.

If appropriate go-ahead signals come, the first resulting gene-bettered children will in no sense threaten human civilization. They will be seen as special only by those in their immediate circles, and are likely to pass as unnoticed in later life as the now grownup "test-tube baby" Louise Brown does today. If they grow up healthily gene-bettered, more such children will follow, and they and those whose lives are enriched by their existence will rejoice that science has again improved human life. If, however, the added genetic material fails to work, better procedures must be developed before more couples commit their psyches toward such inherently unsettling pathways to producing healthy children.

Moving forward will not be for the faint of heart. But if the twenty-first century witnesses failure, let it be because our science is not yet up to the job, not because we don't have the courage to make less random the sometimes most unfair courses of human evolution.

| "The world is not a safe enough place to let this particular genie out of the bottle."

GENETIC ENGINEERING OF HUMANS SHOULD NOT BE PERMITTED

David King

David King is a British geneticist who has written and spoken extensively on the ethical issues of genetic engineering. In the following viewpoint, King expresses reservations about experimenting with human "germ line" cells (the cells involved in human reproduction). He argues that such genetic engineering has relatively little utility in eliminating genetic diseases and involves significant health risks. In addition, germ line engineering, if successful, gives humanity the enormous power of consciously designing human beings—a power King believes could be dangerously abused.

As you read, consider the following questions:

1. What safety risks does King state are created by germ line engineering?
2. What alternative methods to genetic engineering exist to prevent genetic diseases, according to King?
3. Why is it impossible to ensure that genetic engineering would be used only for medical, rather than cosmetic, purposes, according to the author?

Reprinted from "No to Genetic Engineering of Humans!" by David King, at www.users.globalnet.co.uk/~cahge/back1.htm (1999), by permission of the author. For further information, contact *GenEthics News* at 101561.3476@compuserve.com, or the Campaign Against Human Genetic Engineering at www.users.globalnet.co.uk/~cahge.

One of the recurrent horror scenarios of genetic engineering is the creation of armies of engineered blond 'super-soldiers'. As geneticists are often at pains to point out, we are very far from realising such a scenario. It does not seem necessary to explain why the attempt to create 'super races' is undesirable, but there are already many people arguing that genetic engineering of humans could be used for medical benefit. At present [1999] the technology does exist to introduce genes into human cells, and a massive industry is being created around the still very experimental technology of gene therapy. So far, only somatic cells (body cells other than the 'germ line'—the cells that give rise to sperm and eggs) have been manipulated in this way in humans. But in animals, engineering of the germ line, to create transgenic animals, particularly mice, is commonplace. In Britain, the Human Fertilisation and Embryology Act prohibits genetic engineering of human embryos, after fertilisation, but is silent on attempts to engineer eggs and sperm.

With some exceptions, the current consensus in the medical and scientific world seems to be that germ line engineering (GLE) should not be permitted at present, for reasons of safety. It is impossible to guarantee that such manipulation would not itself have harmful effects on the child. The primary danger arises from the fact that new DNA integrates randomly into chromosomes: in doing so it may 'land' in the middle of vital genes, causing mutations which may be harmful or lethal. There is a large catalogue of such unexpected and sometimes horrific mutations in transgenic mice. Until some way is found of controlling the integration of DNA into chromosomes, it is unlikely that human germ line engineering will be officially sanctioned. Nonetheless, there seems to be a widespread expectation that it will be technically and ethically possible to create a reliable GLE system. The objection on the grounds of safety is entirely different from a principled objection to GLE as such.

NOT THE ONLY SOLUTION

One of the flaws in the argument of those who support the possibility of GLE for medical purposes is that there seem to be very few good examples where it is the only solution to the medical problem of genetic disease. The main advantage of GLE is said to be the elimination of disease genes from a family. This must surely refer to 'dominant' disease genes where even if only one copy is present disease will occur. There is no medical benefit to a family from eliminating 'recessive' genes like the cystic fibrosis (CF) gene which do not cause disease when only one of the two copies is harmful. In this case, existing technologies of pre-natal and preimplantation testing allow the avoidance of actual disease, so the benefit of eliminating the CF gene would be purely psychological: not having to worry about CF anymore. Such psychological benefits surely do not justify GLE. In fact, even in the case of dominant genes, prenatal screening is only inadequate to guarantee the birth of an unaffected child in the very rare case where one partner has two copies of the domi-nant, disease-causing gene. Other proposed candidates for GLE are likewise extremely rare.

Furthermore, there is always another solution for those cou-ples who are certain to produce a genetically disabled child and cannot, or do not want to deal with this possibility. They can choose not to have children, or to adopt a child. Parenthood is not the only way to create fulfilment through close, intimate and long lasting relationships with children. Although this may be an inferior solution for some, the question we have to ask is whether this rather minor and rare consideration justifies devel-oping the technology for GLE, with all the incalculable conse-quences that may flow from it. We have become too used to the assumption that people's desires for a child come before the needs of society at large.

Given the lack of good candidates for GLE on medical grounds, one is tempted to question the insistence on the part of many doctors and geneticists that GLE should not be banned indefi-nitely. Assuming that such individuals are not using purported medical benefits as a cover for an urge to indulge in cosmetic or 'enhancement' engineering, it seems most likely that the driving force is blind technophilia, or the desire to wield the awesome power that GLE would bring.

Can We Control It?

Germ line manipulation opens up, for the first time in human history, the possibility of consciously designing human beings, in a myriad of different ways. I am not generally happy about using the concept of playing God, but it is difficult to avoid in this case. The advocates of genetic engineering point out that humans constantly 'play God', in a sense, by interfering with na-ture. Yet the environmental crisis has forced us to realise that many of the ways we already do this are not wise, destroy the environment and cannot be sustained.

Once it was available, how would it be possible to ensure that GLE was used for purely medical purposes? The same problem applies to prenatal genetic screening and to somatic gene therapy, and not only are there no accepted criteria for deciding what constitutes a medical condition, but in a free market society there seems to be no convincing mechanism for arriving at such decision. The best answer that conventional medical ethics seems to have is to 'leave it up to the parents'.

As a result of the free market, sophisticated medical technology and medical personnel are employed in increasingly fashionable cosmetic surgery; and at the same time, due to aggressive marketing by its makers, genetically engineered human growth hormone, developed to remedy the medical condition of growth hormone deficiency, is routinely prescribed in the USA to normal short children with no hormone deficiency. If these pressures already exist, how much stronger will they be for a technology with as great a power to manipulate human life as GLE? And of course, once the technology was described in the scientific literature, it would be possible for, for example, dictators to abuse it, with horrific consequences.

In short, the world is not a safe enough place to let this particular genie out of its bottle and it would be irresponsible in the extreme to do so. This does not imply an absolutist opposition to genetic engineering. . . . I am not opposed to genetic engineering per se. However, there are some aspects of genetic engineering, the consequences of which are far too dangerous to contemplate. This is one of them.

3

| "Human cloning is something neither
to fool around with nor to attempt."

HUMAN CLONING SHOULD BE BANNED

John F. Kilner

Scientists have successfully cloned mice, sheep, and monkeys, raising questions as to whether humans could be next. In March 1997 President Bill Clinton banned the use of federal money for cloning humans and urged a moratorium on all human cloning research. In the following viewpoint, John F. Kilner supports Clinton's actions and argues that human cloning should not be allowed. Cloning research, he asserts, would destroy the lives of human embryos and infants. In addition, he contends that making genetic copies of humans for utilitarian purposes is unethical and demeaning. Kilner is director of the Center for Bioethics and Human Dignity in Bannockburn, Illinois.

As you read, consider the following questions:

1. How would cloning research cause the death of human beings, according to Kilner?
2. What questions does Kilner say are raised by the prospect of human cloning?
3. How might children be harmed by being the result of cloning, according to Kilner?

Reprinted from John F. Kilner, "Stop Cloning Around," *Christianity Today*, April 28, 1997, with permission from the author.

Cigar, the champion racehorse, is a dud as a stud. Attempts to impregnate numerous mares have failed. But his handlers are not discouraged. They think they might try to have Cigar cloned.

If a sheep and a monkey can be cloned—and possibly a racehorse—can human clones be far behind? The process is novel, though the concept is not.

We have long known that virtually every cell of the body contains a person's complete genetic code. The exception is sperm or egg cells, each of which contains half the genetic material until the sperm fertilizes the egg and a new human being with a complete genetic code begins growing.

We have now learned that the partial genetic material in an unfertilized egg cell may be replaced by the complete genetic material from a cell taken from an adult. With a full genetic code, the egg cell behaves as if it has been fertilized. At least, that is how Dolly, the sheep cloned in Scotland, came to be [in an experiment publicized in February 1997]. Hence, producing genetic copies of human beings now seems more likely.

We have been anticipating this possibility in humans for decades and have been playing with it in our imaginations. The movie The Boys from Brazil was about an attempt to clone Adolf Hitler. And in Aldous Huxley's novel Brave New World, clones were produced to fulfill undesirable social roles. More recently the movie Multiplicity portrayed a harried man who jumped at the chance to have himself copied—the better to tend to his office work, his home chores, and his family relationships. It all seems so attractive, at first glance, in our hectic, achievement-crazed society.

THE COSTS OF CLONES

But how do we achieve this technologically blissful state? Multiplicity is silent on this matter, implying that technique is best left to scientists, as if the rest of us are interested only in the outcome. But the experiments of Nazi Germany and the resulting Nuremberg Trials and Code taught us long ago that there is some knowledge that we must not pursue if it requires the use of immoral means.

The research necessary to develop human cloning will cause the deaths of human beings. Such deaths make the cost unacceptably high. In the process used to clone sheep, there were 277 failed attempts—including the deaths of several defective clones. In the monkey-cloning process, a living embryo was intentionally destroyed by taking the genetic material from the embryo's eight cells and inserting it into eight egg cells whose partial genetic material had been removed. Human embryos and human infants would likewise be lost as the technique is adapted to our own race.

GOAL RUSH

Yet, as we press toward this new mark, we must ask: Is the production of human clones even a worthwhile goal? As movies and novels suggest, and godly wisdom confirms, human cloning is something neither to fool around with nor to attempt.

Cloning typically involves genetically copying some living thing for a particular purpose—a wheat plant that yields much grain, a cow that provides excellent milk. Such utilitarian approaches may be fine for cows and corn, but human beings, made in the image of God, have a God-given dignity that prevents us from regarding other people merely as means to fulfill our desires. We must not, for instance, produce clones with low intelligence (or low ambition) to provide menial labor, or produce clones to provide transplantable organs (their identical genetic code would minimize organ rejection). We should not even clone a child who dies tragically in order to remove the parents' grief, as if the clone could actually be the child who died.

All people are special creations of God who should be loved and respected as such. We must not demean them by fundamentally subordinating their interests to those of others.

There is a host of problems with human cloning that we have yet to address. Who are the parents of a clone produced in a laboratory? The donor of the genetic material? The donor of the egg into which the material is transferred? The scientist who manipulates cells from anonymous donors? Who will provide the necessary love and care for this embryo, fetus, and then child—especially when mistakes are made and it would be easier simply to discard it?

The problems become legion when having children is removed from the context of marriage and even from responsible parenthood. For instance, Hope College's Allen Verhey asks "whether parenting is properly considered making children to match a specific design, as is clearly the case with cloning, or whether parenting is properly regarded as a disposition to be hospitable to children as given." Clearly, from a biblical perspective, it is the latter.

Further, the Bible portrays children as the fruit of a one-flesh love relationship, and for good reason. It is a context in which children flourish—in which their full humanity, material and nonmaterial, is respected and nourished. Those who provide them with physical (genetic) life also care for their ongoing physical as well as nonphysical needs.

As Valparaiso University's Gilbert Meilaender told *Christianity Today*, this further separation of procreating from marriage is bad for children. "The child inevitably becomes a product," says ethicist Meilaender, someone who is made, not begotten.

"To beget a child is to give birth to one who is like us, equal in dignity, for whom we care, but whose being we do not simply control. To 'make' a child is to create a product whose destiny we may well think we can shape. Hence, the 'begotten, not made' language of the creed is relevant also to our understanding of the child and of the relation between the generations.

"If our purpose is to clone people as possible sources of perfectly matching organs," says Meilaender, "that clearly shows how we could come to regard the clone as a being we control—as simply an 'ensemble of parts or organs.'"

XEROXING MICHAEL

It is all too easy to lose sight of the fact that people are more than just physical beings, Meilaender's ensembles of organs. What most excites many people about cloning is the possibility of duplicate Michael Jordans, Mother Teresas, or Colin Powells. However, were clones of any of these heroes to begin growing today, those clones would not turn out to be our heroes, for our heroes are not who they are simply because of their DNA. They, like us, were shaped by genetics and environment alike, with the spiritual capacity to evaluate, disregard, and at times to overcome either or both. Each clone would be subject to a unique set of environmental influences, and our loving God would surely accord each a unique personal relationship with him.

The problem with cloning is not the mere fact that technology is involved. Technology can help us do better what God has for us to do. The problem arises when we use technology for purposes that conflict with God's. And, as C.S. Lewis argued, technology never merely represents human mastery over nature; it also involves the power of some people over other people. This is as true in the genetic revolution as it was in the Industrial Revolution. When human cloning becomes technically possible, who will control who clones whom and for what ends? Like nuclear weaponry, the power to clone in the "wrong hands" could have devastating consequences.

There is wisdom in President Bill Clinton's immediate move to forestall human cloning research until public debate and expert testimony have been digested and policies formulated. But there is even greater wisdom in never setting foot on the path that leads from brave new sheep to made-to-order organ donors, industrial drones, and vanity children.

| "At this early stage in the development of mammalian cloning, a ban on all human cloning is both imprudent and unjustified."

HUMAN CLONING SHOULD NOT BE BANNED

John A. Robertson

John A. Robertson is a law professor at the University of Texas School of Law at Austin. His writings on legal and bioethical issues include the book *Children of Choice: Freedom and the New Reproductive Technologies*. In the following viewpoint, he argues that cloning research is still at a very early stage and that it is too soon to make broad pronouncements banning or criminalizing human cloning research. The cloning of humans in the future may be of significant help for infertile couples desiring children, he argues. The fact that cloning can be used to influence the child's genetic makeup does not preclude its use, Robertson asserts, because people already influence their child's genes in a variety of ways.

As you read, consider the following questions:

1. What three general areas does Robertson address in his evaluation of human cloning?
2. What are some of the possible beneficial uses of cloning that the author describes?
3. How does the author respond to the argument that cloned children may be treated as means rather than ends?

Reprinted from John A. Robertson, Pro & Con, *Congressional Digest*, February 1998.

The successful cloning of an adult sheep in February 1997 has startled the public in the speed of its arrival, and in the potential it offers to select and control the genome of offspring. The initial reaction has been hostility and repugnance, and a skepticism that anything but abuse and harm could ensue from human cloning. A more considered response would recognize that there are potential benefits to infertile couples and others from human cloning, and that the harms alleged to flow from cloning are too vague and speculative at this point to justify a ban on cloning or on cloning research.

A crucial point is that it is much too early in the development cycle to make global judgments about human cloning, much less to ban all human cloning research or to declare that anyone who clones another is a criminal. It is still unclear whether the initial successes with cloning sheep and primates will be replicated in those or other nonhuman species.

Even if they are, cloning by nuclear transfer may not extend easily to humans, or there may be very little demand for any application, much less the applications that stir the public. Rather than rush to judgment with bans that could deter important research in cloning and related areas, it is important that government officials, advisors, and policymakers proceed carefully and fully assess the issues before determining public policy.

An optimal public policy on human cloning would respect human rights and individual freedom and dignity, including scientific freedom. It would permit cloning to occur where substantial benefit to families or patients would result or important individual freedoms are involved. It would limit or restrict it when tangible harm to others is likely. In assessing harm, deviation from traditional methods of reproduction, including genetic selection of offspring characteristics, is not itself a compelling reason for restriction when tangible harm to others is not present. However, moral or symbolic concerns unrelated to actual harm to persons may appropriately be taken into account when determining the types of research and services to be supported by public funds.

A rational assessment of cloning would address (1) how cloning relates to current reproductive and genetic practices; (2) possible beneficial uses, and their relation to prevailing conceptions of procreative liberty; and (3) the harms that cloning could produce.

RELATION TO EXISTING PRACTICES

In significant ways, cloning is not qualitatively different from prebirth genetic selection techniques that are now in widespread use. Indeed, cloning appears much less intrusive than the ability to alter and manipulate genes that will follow the development of germline gene therapy that is on the near horizon. Because cloning is situated in a web of other genetic selection practices, there is a danger that in legislating or making policy for cloning alone, practices which now are or will become acceptable will also be restricted.

We now engage in a wide variety of practices to control, influence, or select the genes and characteristics of offspring. Most of these techniques involve carrier and prenatal screening and operate in a negative way by avoiding the conception, implantation, or birth of children with particular characteristics. But there is a large amount of active genetic selection, albeit at the gross level, that occurs in choosing mates or gametes for reproduction, or in deciding which embryos or which fetuses will survive and go to term.

Cloning does differ in some ways from existing selection technology. Because it actively seeks to replicate DNA, it involves positive choice rather than negative deselection, as occurs with most other means of genetic selection. In addition, it selects or replicates the entire genome (except for mitochondria), rather than focus on the presence or absence of particular genes. Yet neither of these differences are qualitatively different from the genetic selection that now occurs in reproductive medicine. If cloning does not lead to tangible harm to others, it should be no less legally available than existing practices are.

Furthermore, cloning is much less radical than the gene alteration technologies on the horizon. Cloning enables a child with the genome of another embryo or person to be born. The genome is taken as it is. Genetic alteration, on the other hand, will change the genome of a person who could have been born with their genome intact.

It would be a serious mistake to make policy for cloning without situating it within the range of genetic selection practices that now occur or are likely to occur as gene therapy is perfected. Sorting out the good and the bad uses of genetic selection across the range of situations in which it arises is a complex matter. . . .

POSSIBLE BENEFICIAL USES

Since few scientists and physicians had previously considered the prospect of human cloning, and considerable research remains before human cloning by blastomere separation or nuclear substitution is safe and available, the contributions which cloning might make to treatment of infertility and other diseases are still unclear.

Yet several reasonable grounds for seeking to replicate a human genome are easily imagined. Embryos might be cloned to provide an infertile couple with enough embryos to achieve pregnancy. In that case cloning an embryo could lead to the simultaneous or delayed birth of twins. Temporal separation of the birth of the twins is not necessarily harmful, and may lead to a special form of sibling bonding.

There may be other situations of merit, such as creating embryos from which a child may be able to obtain needed organs or tissue, or creating a twin of a previous child who died. Cloning may also enable a couple seeking an embryo donation to choose more precisely the genome of offspring, thus assuring both that the resulting child has a good genetic start in life and the couple a happy rearing experience. In addition, cloning research is likely to generate insights and knowledge about cellular and genetic development generally, with therapeutic applications beyond treating infertility.

In assessing possible beneficial uses of cloning, a major distinction exists between cloning that occurs in the course of IVF [in vitro fertilization] treatment for infertility and cloning to select the genome of a child for rearing.

CLONING OF EMBRYOS

There are several reasons why a couple going through IVF might choose to clone embryos, by blastomere separation or by nuclear transfer. One would be to obtain enough embryos to achieve pregnancy. Another would be to obtain embryos without going through an additional cycle of hormonal stimulation and egg retrieval. A third would be to have a backup supply of tissue or organs or a replacement child if a tragedy befalls the first.

A cloned embryo may be transferred to the uterus at the same time as its source, thus raising the possibility of intentionally created twins. Or the infertile couple could transfer them at a later time, as might occur if the first cycle failed; if it succeeded and the couple wants a second child; or if it succeeded and the first child died or is in need of tissue or organs. The couple could also donate cloned embryos to other infertile couples who are seeking an embryo donation.

An important point is that requests by couples undergoing IVF to clone by embryo splitting or nuclear transfer may fall within their fundamental freedom to decide whether or not to have offspring. If the ability to clone an embryo and transfer it to a uterus is essential to whether the couple has offspring, then cloning should receive the same protection that other forms of assisted reproduction and genetic selection receive. In that case, dislike or repugnance at how a couple is reproducing will not be a sufficient reason to ban the practice. Unless tangible harm to others is likely to occur, the freedom to use noncoital techniques to reproduce is left to the individuals directly involved. If cloning is essential to a couple's reproduction, it should be similarly treated.

CLONING AS A FORM OF GENETIC SELECTION

In addition to enhancing fertility or obtaining a child for rearing, a reason for cloning would be to produce a child that has a healthy genome. Cloning for this purpose—eugenic cloning—would require that an embryo first be created from existing DNA. In that case an egg would have to be obtained, be denucleated, and the DNA from the source cell removed and placed in it. The resulting cell would then have to be made operable and transferred to a uterus to enable it to come to term. One or more persons would then have to be prepared to rear the resulting child.

Cloning for genetic selection is also closely related to widely accepted practices that now exist. However, eugenic cloning also has the greatest potential for deviation from those practices, and has generated the most bizarre scenarios and fears. Since only a few forms of eugenic cloning closely relate to current practices, there may be little demand for this form of cloning, even if human cloning technology is perfected.

A situation in which cloning for selection or eugenic purposes is closely related to current practices would arise with a couple who need an embryo donation because both lack viable gametes, but the wife has a functioning uterus and wishes to carry a pregnancy. Ordinarily they would be candidates for an embryo donation. Instead of receiving an embryo left over from another infertile couple's attempts at IVF, which may not be healthy or have been adequately screened for infectious disease or genetic factors, they might well prefer that the embryo they gestate and rear be created from the cell of an adult or child with desirable genes. Or they may request a donation of a cloned embryo from another couple. To proceed with cloning in either case, they would need the consent of the clone source or its parents.

The acceptability of this form of cloning depends first on the acceptability of embryo donation itself. Given a general consensus in favor of embryo donation, a second question concerns whether couples should be free to select the embryos that they are willing to gestate and rear. Since we now allow individuals wide choice over the mates they choose and over the gametes used in assisted reproduction, a strong argument can be made for allowing recipients of embryo donation some choice in the embryos they receive.

Accordingly, it is plausible to view cloning existing DNA as a reasonable means of embryo selection to assure that a couple seeking an embryo donation will have a healthy child to rear. Strictly speaking, that couple will not be engaged in genetic reproduction, but they will be involved in having a child whom they will gestate and rear, and thus should be treated equivalently to infertile couples who also provide egg or sperm in forming a family.

The most problematic situation of eugenic cloning would arise if the cloning were not designed to produce a healthy child for rearing by loving parents. Scenarios of abuse and narcissism or excessive power involve such cases. They also illustrate that not all cases of human cloning need be treated similarly, for they are not all equivalent in importance or in their impact on the clone source or on the resulting child. Thus cloning of self as a form of genetic selection might pose different problems and deserve different treatment than cloning embryos in order to treat infertility.

Policymakers should distinguish among the differing uses, and prohibit only those which pose a threat of serious harm, not those which serve legitimate needs of infertile couples seeking a healthy child to rear.

If a loving family will rear the child, it is difficult to see why cloning for genetic selection (eugenic cloning) is per se unacceptable. We engage in many forms of genetic selection already, most of which are designed to make sure that a child will be healthy and have good chances in life. Eugenic cloning is but another form of genetic selection, and should not be banned on that ground alone.

HARM CAUSED BY CLONING

Given that there are potentially beneficial uses of cloning that fall within current practices in assisted reproduction and genetic selection, a ban on all cloning or on all cloning research can be justified only if cloning always or invariably caused great harm to others. Yet opponents of cloning have been very nonspecific and speculative about harms. The most florid critics imagine power-hungry tycoons or dictators narcissistically cloning themselves, or cloning a race of permanent servants or replicants of limited ability, à la Aldous Huxley's *Brave New World* or Ridley Scott's *Bladerunner*.

More moderate opponents talk about the importance of having a unique genome, and how cloning might rob children of a unique identity. At the same time, however, they want to deny the importance of genes alone in creating identity.

A more considered view of the potential harms of human cloning must address three issues. The first issue concerns the rights and status of persons born after cloning by embryo splitting or nuclear transfer. In the most likely cloning scenarios, parents will be seeking a child whom they will love for itself. But even in less benign situations, any resulting child would be a person with all the moral and legal rights of persons and no more would be the property or subject of the person who commissions or carries out the cloning than any other child.

A second issue concerns whether the child will be harmed because it will have the same DNA as another person, either living or dead. Most negative views of cloning assume that the clone will be exactly identical to the clone source, like the multiple copies of a Xeroxed document. But the child who results from cloning will not be the same person as the clone source, even if the two share many physical characteristics, for its rearing environment and experiences will be different. Indeed, religious commentators have noted that such a child will have its own soul. Given the importance of nurture in making us who we are, the danger that the person cloned will be a mere copy or replica is highly fanciful.

A key issue in assessing harm to the child who results from cloning (whether by nuclear transfer or embryo splitting) is that that child would not have existed but for the cloning procedure at issue. Prior to the cloning, it did not exist. It came into being only as a result of cloning. In a crucial sense it has not been harmed because it has no other way to be born but with the DNA chosen for it. Nor can it be said to be harmed because its life itself is so full of suffering or confused identity that any existence as a clone is less preferable than nonexistence.

Of course, it might be preferable if parents had had a child whose DNA has not been copied from another. Yet that option will usually not be present in many of the situations involving cloning which couples face. It will be either the clone or no child at all. A policy requiring no child at all would interfere with their procreative liberty. It could not be justified as protecting the child with the DNA of another, for such a child would exist only if the cloning occurred.

A third issue is the need to recognize that the great discomfort with cloning—and calls for its prohibition—may be rooted in the discomfort felt by the deliberate and intentional choice of another's genome that cloning represents. This discomfort arises regardless of whether harm to offspring or families can be shown. The very idea of selecting a child's DNA appears too instrumental or manipulative, and risks treating children as means rather than ends. To prevent such an attitude toward children, some persons would ban all cloning and all cloning research.

There are two problems with this view of harm. One is that it is subjective and personal, reflecting a view about our relationship to offspring that is not universally or even necessarily widely shared. Depending on the needs and purposes which cloning serves, people will vary in their perceptions of whether it instrumentalizes or commodifies children.

A second problem with this view is that it paints with too broad a brush. If taken seriously, this view would condemn all deliberate decisions to have children, whether by current assisted reproductive and genetic screening practices or by coital conception. For infertile couples and couples at risk of offspring with severe genetic disease, the children they seek are truly children of choice and could be said to serve selfish ends. Indeed, the same can be said of most cases of having children. There is no basis for singling out cloning as the most egregious form of instrumentalization of offspring, if it is one at all.

In sum, it is difficult to show actual harm to offspring, families, or society from the cloning scenarios most likely to occur. There may be harm or offense to particular notions of how conception and children should be chosen and born. But such purely moral or symbolic concerns are not a sufficient basis for overcoming procreative choice or banning beneficial uses, even though they may appropriately enter into Federal research funding policy.

A CLONING BAN IS UNJUSTIFIED

At this early stage in the development of mammalian cloning, a ban on all human cloning is both imprudent and unjustified. Enough good uses can be imagined that it would be unwise to ban all cloning and cloning research because of vague and highly speculative fears. Nor need all cases of cloning be treated the same, for they differ in their intent and effects on the clone source and resulting individual. As with other technological innovations, science fiction should not drive science policy.

"We should postpone large-scale commercialization of genetic engineering in agriculture until we know that the benefits will outweigh the hazards."

RESTRICTIONS SHOULD BE PLACED ON THE GENETIC ENGINEERING OF FOOD

John B. Fagan

John B. Fagan is a professor of molecular biology at the Maharishi University of Management in Fairfield, Iowa. In the following viewpoint, he argues that genetically engineered foods are starting to be marketed in the United States without adequate assessment of their health and environmental risks. Placing new genes into foods has unpredictable effects on their nutritional value, he asserts, which can include creating toxins and allergens. In addition, releasing genetically modified organisms into the environment may have disastrous ecological consequences. Fagan concludes that genetically modified food products should not be sold until they are shown to be safe, and that consumers should be informed on whether food products have been produced using genetic engineering technology.

As you read, consider the following questions:

1. What are some of the dangers of the genetic engineering of food, according to Fagan?
2. What opinions does Fagan say American consumers have about genetically engineered foods.
3. What makes the effects of genetic engineering different from chemical or nuclear pollution, according to the author?

From John B. Fagan, "Genetically Engineered Food: Hazardous to Health and the Environment," paper at http://online.sfsu.edu/~rone/GE Essays/GEF Health Risk Fagan.htm. Revised by the author July 1999. Reprinted with permission.

What is genetic engineering? Genes are the blueprints for every part of an organism. Genetic engineering is the process of artificially modifying these blueprints. By cutting and splicing DNA—genetic surgery—genetic engineers can isolate genes from virtually any organism on the planet and transfer those genes into any other organism. The characteristics encoded by those genes are thereby transferred to the recipient organism.

Why do it? Biotechnologists use genetic engineering to confer upon an organism new characteristics that they consider desirable. For example, they might transfer a gene that will make a crop resistant to an herbicide or resistant to an insect pest.

Does cost/benefit analysis give the green light? Close examination reveals that the use of genetic engineering carries with it tremendous potential for unanticipated and uncontrollable adverse side effects. At present, insufficient research has been carried out to adequately assess these potential negative impacts. The precautionary principle dictates that we should postpone large-scale commercialization of genetic engineering in agriculture until we know that the benefits will outweigh the hazards.

Why does genetic engineering generate adverse side effects? Because living organisms are highly complex, genetic engineers cannot reliably predict all of the effects of introducing new genes into them. This is so for even simple bacteria, not to mention more complex plants and animals.

We cannot reliably predict the results of genetic engineering because:

- the introduced gene may act differently when working within its new host
- the original genetic blueprints of the host will be disrupted by the insertion of the new gene
- the new combination of the host genes and the introduced gene may have unpredictable effects

Therefore, it is impossible to predict either the short-term or the long-term effects of genetically engineered foods on the health of those who eat them or on the environment.

What are the potential dangers?

- New toxins in genetically engineered foods
- New allergens in genetically engineered foods
- Reduced nutritional value of genetically engineered foods
- Increased use of agro-chemicals, resulting in increased contamination of soil, food and water
- Creation of herbicide-resistant weeds
- Creation of new diseases and agricultural pests
- Loss of biodiversity—both agricultural biodiversity and biodiversity in the wider ecosystem

- Disruptions of the ecosystem
- Irreversible transmission and perpetuation of genetic engineering-related problems. Once released, genetically engineered organisms will be self-perpetuating, and cannot be recalled.

NEW FOOD BEING INTRODUCED

Engineered foods are on the grocers' shelves now. Genetically engineered foods have already penetrated deep into the U.S. food market. These include tomatoes, squash, canola oil, yeast, corn, potatoes, and soybeans. These are ingredients in at least 70% of all processed foods, including bread, pasta, candies, ice cream, pies, biscuits, margarine, meats and meat substitutes. Genetically engineered organisms are also used to produce cheeses, artificial sweeteners, and other products.

Proponents of genetic engineering have convinced the food industry and government that they can assume that these new foods are not substantially different from existing foods and pose no special health or environmental risks. As a consequence, current federal regulations call for only minimal safety evaluation (voluntary consultations) for some foods, and none at all for others. In no case do regulations require direct assessment of human health impacts or evaluation of long-term effects.

Surveys consistently find that 85-90% of consumers want clear labeling of all genetically engineered foods. Yet, current regulations in the U.S. do not require genetically engineered foods to be labeled. Thus, food producers and manufacturers have already introduced genetically engineered ingredients into many foods without informing consumers.

HARMFUL SIDE EFFECTS

Genetic engineering is no different than any other technology. The current rapid introduction of engineered foods into the U.S. food supply—without adequate safety or environmental testing and without labeling—is predicated on the assumption that this technology is going to behave differently than any other technology in the history of human life. It is predicated on the assumption that genetic engineering will have no significant harmful side effects.

However, unexpected harmful side effects are inevitable with any technology. If we do not take this into account when we commercialize genetic engineering, we are courting disaster. Why would we expect genetic engineering to be different from the chemical, nuclear, electronic, and pharmaceutical technologies that have given rise to adverse unanticipated effects such as nuclear pollution, global warming, the toxic effects of pesticides and herbicides, and the health-damaging side effects of many medicines? In every case, hazardous side effects emerge and must be reckoned with.

Already problems are arising as a result of genetic engineering, including the following:

- Pollen from genetically engineered corn, deposited on milkweed the natural forage of monarch butterfly larvae, has been shown to reduce survival and slow the growth of these larvae.
- Unexpected problems with genetically engineered cotton have resulted in millions of dollars of lost crop revenues to American farmers in Texas, Alabama, and Mississippi in 1997 and 1998.
- Genetic pollution has been detected in Canada, Denmark, and Scotland, and research has shown that the problems are potentially very large. This pollution is due to cross-pollination between genetically engineered and conventional canola and between genetically engineered canola and wild related plant species.
- Genetically engineered bovine growth hormone has been shown to have highly adverse effects on health, reproductive potential, and longevity of dairy cattle, and evidence suggests that consumption of milk from cows treated with this hormone may increase cancer risk for humans.
- Genetically engineered potatoes fed to rats were found to stunt their growth and suppress their immune systems.
- Genetically engineered soybeans have been shown to be highly allergenic to a significant subsection of the population.
- A dietary supplement produced by genetically engineered bacteria was found to contain a toxin that killed 37 Americans and permanently disabled 1500 more.

A precautionary approach is needed. Genetic engineering poses the greatest danger of any technology yet introduced, because many of the damaging effects of genetic engineering are irreversible. This irreversibility dictates that we must adopt a more forward-thinking stance: We must adopt a precautionary approach designed to prevent problems before they arise.

What is needed to protect our health:

- Safety testing of genetically engineered foods must be made much more rigorous; commercialization should be contingent on passing stringent safety tests.

271

- Genetically engineered foods should be labeled as such. No testing program can give a 100% guarantee of safety. Labeling provides consumers with the information that they need to choose to accept or avoid the risks associated with genetically engineered foods.

What is needed to protect the environment:

- All genetically engineered organisms should be subjected to thorough environmental assessment before they are commercialized.
- Consent to commercialize applications of genetic engineering that involve intentional release of genetically engineered organisms into the environment should be based on open and transparent discussions that actively involve all segments of society, and should be given only after extensive, long-term evaluation.

THE FACTS ON AGRICULTURAL GENETIC ENGINEERING

- *Genetic engineering is not natural*—Gene-technology proponents claim that their manipulations are a natural extension of traditional breeding techniques. However, genetic engineering is not a natural process, but a laboratory procedure that enables the engineer to bring about genetic alterations that would never happen via natural means. The cross-species gene transfers that genetic engineering allows, such as between fish and tomatoes, or between potatoes and insects, illustrate this. Bringing genes together from such divergent species greatly increases the likelihood that unanticipated side effects may occur, including the creation of new toxins or allergens in foods, and new viruses and agricultural pests.
- *Genetic engineering is not precise and controlled, but random and uncontrolled*—Proponents of genetic engineering claim their methods are precise and highly controlled. Although it is possible to cut and splice genes with precision in the test tube, the process of inserting those engineered genes into the cells of a living organism is quite random and uncontrolled, and can cause mutations to the normal genes of the organism. Genetic research shows that disease and pest susceptibilities in crops and livestock have their origin in defects (mutations) in their genetic blueprints. Therefore, the random damage resulting from genetic engineering is likely to result in harmful side effects to the crop, the livestock, to the consumer, and to the environment. Scientists have assessed these risks to be substantial. . . .

- *Genetic engineering gives rise to unpredictable adverse effects*—When genetic engineers insert a new gene into any organism there are "position effects" which can lead to unpredictable changes in the pattern of gene expression and genetic function. The protein product of the inserted gene may interact in unexpected ways with other cellular components, thereby producing harmful effects, such as allergens, toxins, and reduced nutritional value. There is also serious concern about the dangers of using genetically engineered viruses as delivery vehicles (vectors) in the generation of transgenic plants and animals. This could destabilize the genome of the plant/animal, leading to a host of unanticipated side effects. Damaging effects on food safety and the environment are summarized in the following two points. . . .
- *Genetically engineered foods are more risky than conventional foods*—The process of genetic engineering can introduce dangerous new allergens and toxins into foods, and can reduce nutritional value. Already, one genetically engineered soybean variety has been found to cause serious allergic reactions. A bacterium genetically engineered to produce large amounts of the food supplement tryptophan has produced toxic contaminants that killed 37 people and permanently disabled 1,500 more. . . .
- *Genetic engineering can create new pests and weeds, and can accelerate pollution of food, soil, and the water supply*—More than 50% of the crops developed by biotechnology companies have been engineered to be resistant to herbicides. Use of herbicide-resistant crops will lead to a threefold increase in the use of herbicides, resulting in even greater pollution of our food and water with toxic agrochemicals. These engineered crops also perpetuate the farmer's dependence on the chemical approach to agriculture, which is widely recognized as environmentally and economically unsustainable. In addition, genetically engineered crops can exacerbate weed and other pest problems. For instance, canola that is genetically engineered to be herbicide resistant has already begun to behave as a weed in Canada. This phenomenon, along with cross-pollination and the increased use of herbicides, will result in the development of additional herbicide-resistant weeds, which will be a nuisance to farmers. . . .
- *Genetic pollution may damage the environment*—When new genetic information is introduced into plants, bacteria, insects or other animals, it can easily be passed into related organisms through processes such as cross pollination. This process

may create a wide range of adverse effects on the ecosystem, including "super weeds" and the displacement of existing species from the ecosystem, as happened with genetically engineered Klebsiella soil bacteria. . . .

- *Crops are being engineered to produce their own pesticides*—This will promote the more rapid appearance of resistant insects and lead to excessive destruction of useful insects and soil organisms, thus disrupting the ecosystem. For instance, recent research shows that pollen from these toxic plants kill monarch butterfly larvae when deposited on milkweed leaves. In addition, the pesticides produced by plants may be harmful to the health of consumers. . . .

- *Genetically engineered crops are a threat to global and national food security*—Genetic manipulations can generate unanticipated harmful side effects. Yet, genetically engineered foods are not tested sufficiently to eliminate those that are dangerous to health and the environment or that may be unreliable agronomically. As a consequence, the current rapid commercialization of genetically engineered foods not only jeopardizes the health of individuals, but could also lead to national or even global food shortages and large-scale health threats. Already, unanticipated defects in genetically engineered cotton varieties have resulted in crop failures in both 1997 and 1998, which resulted in millions of dollars of lost revenues to farmers. There is no logical scientific justification for exposing society to the risk currently associated with agricultural genetic engineering. There are better, more effective approaches to feeding humanity. The primary benefit of this technology is economic gain for the biotech industry. They are currently harvesting short-term economic gain at the expense of the health of the population, the safety of the ecosystem, and the security of the world's food supply.

- *Government regulation is inadequate*—Biotech proponents claim that genetically engineered foods must be safe, since they have been scrutinized by government regulatory bodies. However, the facts show that regulators are not protecting the public adequately. In the U.S., safety assessment is left to the discretion of industry; the U.S. Food and Drug Administration (FDA) merely "encourages" genetic engineers to participate in voluntary safety consultations with FDA staff. These deficiencies are becoming obvious to regulators in other nations. For instance, the Canadian ministry of health recently reviewed the FDA's safety assessment of the genetically engineered hormone, rBGH (recombinant bovine growth hormone). They found significant deficiencies in the FDA's safety assessment, and, on that basis, rejected an industry application to allow the use of this hormone in Canada. Regulators do not have strong records with respect to other technologies either. For instance, DDT, Thalidomide, and genetically engineered L-tryptophan all complied with U.S. safety regulations but were all damaging to consumers. Recently it was found that 80% of supermarket milk contained traces of illegal medicines, antibiotics, or hormones, including genetically engineered bovine growth hormone (rBGH). . . .

- *Damaging effects of genetic engineering will continue forever*—Unlike chemical or nuclear contamination, genetic pollution is self-perpetuating. Once a living genetically engineered organism is introduced into the ecosystem, it cannot be recalled but will perpetuate itself and may transfer its genes to other members of the ecosystem. Thus harmful effects cannot be reversed or cleaned up, but will be passed on to all future generations.

- *Ethical concerns*—The broader social/cultural/economic impacts of the genetic engineering raise a wide range of ethical problems. One example is the transfer of animal genes into plants, which raises important ethical issues for vegetarians and some religions. Another is the probability that genetically engineered crops will disrupt third-world economies by displacing key agricultural products. For instance genetically engineered, high-laurate canola oil produced in North America is likely to displace palm and coconut oil, which are central to the agricultural economy of Indonesia, Malaysia, and the Philippines.

"Biotechnology in agriculture will help to eliminate most of the remaining hunger in the world."

RESTRICTIONS SHOULD NOT BE PLACED ON THE GENETIC ENGINEERING OF FOOD

Dennis Avery

The world faces the challenge of providing enough food, including meat, for a growing population, argues Dennis Avery in the following viewpoint. He contends that genetic engineering can help farmers improve their productivity in raising crops and livestock and thus help both to end world hunger and preserve wild habitat. Genetic engineering can be used to increase the meat production of hogs and other animals and to boost yields of rice, tomatoes, and other crops. Such progress in biotechnology, he asserts, should not be blocked by onerous regulations. Avery directs the Center for Global Food Issues, an organization created by the Hudson Institute, a public policy research organization.

As you read, consider the following questions:

1. What factors does Avery list that make genetic engineering difficult and complex?
2. What is the biggest farming challenge facing the world, according to the author?
3. What do American consumers believe about genetic engineering, according to Avery?

Excerpted from Dennis Avery, "Feeding the World with Biotech Crops." This article appeared in the May 1998 issue of, and is reprinted with permission from, *The World & I*, a publication of The Washington Times Corporation, copyright ©1998.

Genetic engineering is likely to be a major factor in raising the per-acre yields of crops and livestock during the twenty-first century—perhaps the major factor.

World rice yields have been stagnant for 15 years but, thanks to biotechnology, may now soar dramatically. Researchers from Cornell have managed to insert two genes from wild relatives of the rice plant into the top-yielding Chinese hybrid rice varieties. Each of the two wild genes increased the yields of its test variety by 17 percent. Used together, the wild genes are expected to boost the world's potential rice yields by 20–40 percent. That may save more than 123 million acres of the world's wild-lands—or four times the land area of Pennsylvania—from being plowed for rice production.

How did the researchers raise the yields? They already had the seeds of the rice plant's wild relatives in gene banks, but the wild relatives wouldn't interbreed with the domestic rice varieties. (Over time, they had become too different.) So the researchers used genetic engineering to create a "wide cross"—an arranged marriage between different species.

The higher crop yields do require more plant nutrients, which simply means that farmers need to apply higher levels of fertilizers containing the nitrogen, phosphate, potash, and 26 trace minerals important to plant growth.

FARMING IN THE TROPICS

The tropics are urgently short of good cropland. This is the main reason poor farmers take their families into the tropical rain forests in a desperate effort to grub out a subsistence amid heat, humidity, snakes, and disease.

Now genetic researchers in Mexico have found a way to overcome the aluminum toxicity that debilitates crop plants in much of the best potential cropland throughout the tropics. Raising yields on the land already being farmed will take much of the food production pressure off the tropical rain forests.

Plant breeders had long known that some plants succeed on the big acid-soil savannas in the tropics because they secrete citric acid from their roots. (The acid ties up the aluminum ions.) Plant breeders had been searching for existing plants they could crossbreed for the citric acid feature but hadn't found any.

Instead, the Mexican researchers took the direct route, through genetic engineering. They took a gene from a bacterium that codes for citric acid and inserted it directly into tobacco and papaya plants (along with the genetic programming that causes a gene to be expressed in the roots). Presto, they came up with crops for the tropics that fend off aluminum with their own citric acid secretions. The researchers are now working to add the acid secretion to corn, wheat, and other key crops.

This represents a huge advance, because aluminum toxicity cuts crop yields by up to 80 percent on 30–40 percent of the world's cropland!

HOW GENETIC ENGINEERING WORKS

Nothing demonstrates the speed of modern science better than our sudden breakthrough in biotechnology.

Until 1947, we had no clear idea how nature transmitted its incredibly complicated instructions telling new organisms how to grow. Then researchers discovered that we each inherit a double coil of DNA—deoxyribonucleic acid. DNA, and the sequence of genes within it, determine our biological heritage.

Today, we can insert DNA into organisms with short electric pulses or with DNA–coated gold beads shot from "gene guns." Even high school students routinely separate the bits of DNA that carry genetic instructions.

That doesn't mean genetic engineering is simple or easy:

• Most of the world's biodiversity is in tropical forests, mountain microclimates, and remote, fetid swamps, so gathering the DNA can be slow, and dangerous, work.

• Preserving the world's DNA resources in gene banks where researchers can get at them is itself a costly and demanding endeavor.

• The greatest challenge is figuring out what pieces of DNA to put where to achieve a beneficial result. (No one is suggesting crossing an elephant with a saber-tooth tiger to produce a big, vicious predator. Nor crossing crabgrass with poison ivy to create an itching, pervasive nuisance. That's why genetic engineering experiments are carefully regulated.)

Still, the technology is becoming more and more practicable.

THE PROTEIN CHALLENGE

Some critics say we shouldn't take the risks of "playing God" with biotechnology. But the agricultural world is now facing another huge hurdle: how to produce enough high-quality protein.

The biggest farming challenge was in 1960, when we feared much of the world would starve before 1980. Plant breeders, using standard crossbreeding techniques, produced the green revolution and made it possible to triple the yields on the world's best cropland. As a result of that valiant effort, per capita calories in the Third World have increased by 35 percent—during the greatest surge of population growth the world will ever see.

Today the world's population growth is tapering off rapidly. The trends say we'll peak at about 8.5 billion people by 2035 or before. The average births per woman in the developing countries have already dropped from 6.5 in 1960 to about 3.1 today. Since population stability is 2.1 births, poor countries have already come more than 80 percent of the way toward stability in one generation. The First World is below replacement, at 1.7 births per woman.

Trade and technology are making the Third World more affluent, and diet quality is rising rapidly toward First World levels. The demand for meat and milk is soaring as a result. We might be able to get adequate protein from nuts and tofu, but few of us seem willing to, if we can afford meat. China's meat consumption is rising by 10 percent per year. Indonesia is clearing tropical forest to grow low-yielding corn and soybeans for chicken feed. India is stripping leaves and branches from its forests to feed 400 million dairy animals.

Less than 0.2 percent of Americans are vegans, forgoing all livestock calories, and the percentages are similar in the rest of the affluent world. There may be good nutritional reasons for our passionate pursuit of meat and milk. Livestock protein is complete in amino acids and no vegetable proteins are. Livestock protein can also be digested with less energy expended per calorie. Plant foods are typically low in some key nutrients, especially calcium, iron, zinc, and vitamins D and B_{12}. (That's why vegan diets can actually risk the health of infants and young people.)

Yet to save the world's wildlands by having people eat "lower on the food chain," we might need to have 80–90 percent of humanity eating vegan diets by 2030. This is extremely unlikely. There is no funding for a major global vegan campaign, let alone any historic success in convincing large numbers of people to permanently give up livestock products.

Our other alternative—and the one that has worked in the past—is using science and knowledge to raise our crop and livestock yields per acre still further. That's where biotechnology appears to be critically important.

MORE PROTEIN AT LOWER COST

The Food and Drug Administration (FDA) is expected to soon approve the use of a genetically engineered copy of the hog's natural growth hormone. The biotech version of this hormone will let us produce pigs with half as much body fat and 15 percent more lean meat—using 25 percent less feed grain.

The new technology will, in effect, provide the equivalent of about 25 million tons of corn per year for hog feed—from laboratory bacteria that produce the pork growth hormone, instead of from clearing more land for crops.

Ordinarily, when a farmer gives a pig more feed than its natural supply of growth hormone can turn into muscle, the extra calories go into fat production. With the additional growth hormone (coming from a tiny capsule behind the hog's ear) the pig grows faster and leaner. . . .

What about using a natural genetic mutation to get more meat with fewer resources? The famous Belgian Blue double-muscled cattle are the result of a natural gene mutation noted by European farmers in the early 1800s. These cattle have nearly 20 percent more meat per pound of carcass, and it's all tender. The only drawback is that Belgian Blue calves are so heavily muscled at birth that they often have to be delivered by cesarean section.

The same gene modified in the Belgian Blue cattle exists in other cattle, in hogs, and even in poultry. Could we manipulate the gene for a somewhat less drastic increase in muscling, for a more cost-effective increase in tender meat per animal? In poultry, would a heavily muscled chick emerging from the egg be anything but a productivity gain? Genetic engineering holds out these fascinating possibilities.

Genetic engineering contains enough ethical questions to keep a philosophy department debating for a decade. However, ethicists make two major points: First, the key to ethics within biotechnology is whether the changes remove the basic nature of the creature; legless pigs—stacked like cordwood on a shelf—would be unethical. Second, the ethics of plowing down wildlife habitat are even more troubling than the ethical questions of biotechnology.

FIRST WORLD BIOTECH FARMING

First World farmers are already using biotechnology, with American biotech companies and farmers in the lead.

The biggest impact to date has come from soybeans that tolerate herbicides with the lowest environmental impact (such as the glyphosates and sulfanylureas). This allows a farmer to suppress the weeds in his soybean fields with chemicals safe enough to be used around sensitive wild species like quail and trout. Millions of acres of herbicide-tolerant soybeans will be grown this year, mainly in the United States, Canada, and Argentina.

Farmers are also buying seed corn that contains a natural pest toxin called *Bacillus thuringiensis.* When corn borers start eating the stalks of the "Bt corn," they poison themselves. The first two years of field experience show that Bt corn is likely to control pests well.

Roughly 20 percent of American cows are now being given a biotech version of bovine growth hormone. The hormone improves feed efficiency about 10 percent.

English consumers are cheerfully buying cans of genetically engineered tomatoes because they are about 10 percent cheaper.

Most of the First World is eating cheese produced with the help of genetically engineered rettin. Previously, young calves had to be killed for the rettin in their stomachs.

CONSUMER REACTION

The introduction of the first genetically engineered farm products has stimulated antitechnology activists to frenzies of media gaming:

• Environmental groups have "quarantined" test plots of bioengineered soybeans in Iowa (with yellow crime-scene tape that shows up well on TV cameras).

• Greenpeace has used its famous rubber boats to prevent ships carrying bioengineered corn and soybeans from docking in Europe.

• Greenpeace and the World Wildlife Fund have gathered more than a million petition signatures in Switzerland to ban biotechnology from food uses.

In America, consumers haven't paid much attention to the activists. In surveys, 80 percent say they are aware of biotechnology. Nearly 55 percent say that biotechnology has already provided benefits to them or their families. Nearly 80 percent say they expect biotechnology benefits in the next five years.

With such high consumer acceptance, FDA regulations on genetically engineered products are predictably mild. A food has to be labeled as genetically engineered only if it (1) introduces an allergen or (2) substantially changes the food's nutritional content or composition.

The American approach to regulating biotechnology focuses on the product not the process. That seems to make sense. The park owner in the movie *Jurassic Park* got into big trouble because he was breeding predatory dinosaurs. If he'd used his genetic engineers to produce a better-tasting rabbit, the failure of his electric fence wouldn't have been very dangerous. . . .

It is difficult to forecast the future of biotechnology in farming, mainly because the technology is so young and its potential is so vast.

• If inserting wild-relative genes is already boosting yields in tomatoes by 50 percent and rice by 20–40 percent, it seems probable that there is major potential for using wild-relative genes in virtually every crop plant and every domestic bird and animal. This could well recapture the agricultural research momentum of the 1960s, when crop yields were rising twice as fast as today.

• Biotechnology offers real hope in the urgent drive to save the world's biodiverse wildlands. Without biotechnology, most of the wild genes would be useless to researchers, because the plants and animals carrying the wild genes can be crossbred with only close relatives. But with genetic engineering, virtually every wild gene is now a potentially vital and broadly applicable resource for helping improve the quality of our lives and achieve our conservation goals.

• Biotechnology will also radically speed up the traditional crossbreeding of plants and animals. It can eliminate the years of tedious back-crossing needed until now to take out the negative elements of a crossbreeding experiment.

• The development of aluminum-tolerant crops is a huge step forward. It means we can expect major increases in yields from tropical soils that until now have been barely adequate for subsistence farming. The tropics have hundreds of millions of acres of low-yield cropland that may now become lush with higher yields. Brazil and Zaire also have hundreds of millions of acres of acid savannas that have never been farmed; until now they have been covered with stunted brush and poor-quality grasses. High-yield crops on all this land could eliminate most of the food-production pressure on rain forests. (Third World people will still need jobs so they can buy food, instead of homesteading the rain forest.)

• Biotechnology will apparently also help reduce livestock disease losses and boost feed conversion efficiencies as the world moves from 1 billion hogs to 3 billion, and from 13 billion chickens to perhaps 50 billion. This, too, will help save wildlands.

SEIZING THE POTENTIAL OF GENETIC ENGINEERING

What should we do to ensure that biotechnology continues to provide progress for agriculture?

First, the affluent countries should double the current modest public investment in agricultural biotechnology. This is not a subsidy to farmers but an investment in low food costs and wildlands conservation. There should be a special focus on biotech research for the poorest countries.

Second, we certainly should eliminate farm subsidies and the accompanying farm trade barriers; they keep us from using the world's best farmland and farming systems to their fullest potential. Asia will have eight times as many people per acre of cropland as North America, and its tropical wildlands are home to a high percentage of the world's wild species. Free farm trade will encourage Asia to import some of its food rather than cut trees.

Third, we should ensure that regulators understand both the need for research safety and the environmental potential of biotech research, so that sustainable gains in yields are appropriately welcomed, not blocked.

If we do these things, then we can expect that biotechnology in agriculture will help to eliminate most of the remaining hunger in the world, even as it becomes one of our outstanding wildlife conservation triumphs.

CHAPTER 8

WHAT SHOULD GOVERN PUBLIC HEALTH POLICIES ON SMOKING?

Chapter Preface

Cigarette smoking and other forms of tobacco use are now widely acknowledged to have harmful effects on human health. The U.S. Centers for Disease Control and Prevention has estimated that 400,000 Americans die each year from lung cancer, heart disease, emphysema, and other diseases attributable to smoking—making it the leading cause of premature preventable deaths in the United States. Treating smoking-related illnesses cost the United States an estimated $50 billion in 1993 alone, according to the American Lung Association; adding the costs of lost work and productivity pushed the toll of tobacco to $97 billion.

Since U.S. Surgeon General Luther Terry issued a report linking cigarette smoking with lung cancer in 1964, government and health authorities have taken a variety of steps to discourage smoking. In 1965 cigarette makers were required to put warning labels on their product (these warnings were strengthened in 1969 and 1984). Cigarette advertisements were banned from television and radio airwaves in 1971. Health classes in schools taught students the dangers of smoking. Numerous states and communities banned smoking in public places. Such smoking restrictions in offices, restaurants, and other places became more widespread following the release of a 1993 Environmental Protection Agency report that concluded that smoking was dangerous for nonsmokers because of secondhand smoke.

In the wake of these education and anti-smoking efforts, smoking rates in the United States declined. The percentage of American adults who smoked fell from 43 percent in 1966 to 25 percent in 1996. Many have wondered why millions of Americans persist in or begin smoking, given the widespread acknowledgement of its health risks. An important reason according to some is the habit-forming quality of tobacco's main ingredient—nicotine—that is viewed by many as an addictive drug. David Kessler, head of the Food and Drug Administration (FDA) from 1991 to 1997, has stated that "77% of smokers desire to quit but cannot, primarily because of nicotine addiction."

The fact that smoking continues to cost the United States thousands of lives and billions of dollars annually, coupled with some surveys showing teen smoking rates rising in recent years, has led many health activists to conclude that the United States needs additional public health measures to combat smoking. Many argue that tobacco companies should be held accountable for enticing people to smoke and for the costs incurred by smoking. One debated avenue of reform is direct government regulation of cigarettes. In 1995 the Food and Drug Administration proposed measures to limit tobacco advertising and sales to youth. The FDA actions sparked an ongoing legal battle with the tobacco industry over whether the agency has the regulatory authority to oversee tobacco. Another popular idea among anti-smoking activists is raising taxes on cigarettes so as to discourage consumption.

A tactic that has gained recent prominence in the anti-smoking campaign is suing tobacco companies to recover smoking-related costs. In most past suits brought by individuals, tobacco companies have traditionally been successful in convincing juries that smokers knowingly assumed health risks when they chose to begin smoking (in part because of the required warning labels). However, in the 1990s the legal position of tobacco companies was damaged by the release of secret company documents and the testimony of former employees that suggested that tobacco companies: a) suppressed knowledge of the health dangers of smoking and the addictive nature of nicotine; and b) manipulated nicotine levels in cigarettes in an effort to intensify their addictive effect, according to critics. "What once seemed free choice based on informed consent to smoking's dangers," writes legal studies professor Jeffrey Abramson, "now seems like unwitting addiction based on misrepresentations about the ingredients inside the cigarette." In 1994 Mississippi became the first state to file suit against tobacco companies to recover costs of treating smoking-related illnesses through its publicly funded health programs; other states soon followed. In November 1998 a settlement was reached in which the tobacco industry agreed to pay the states approximately $200 billion over the next 25 years.

Some people, both smokers and nonsmokers, have argued that tobacco litigation and other anti-smoking initiatives go too far. They argue that smoking should not be viewed as a disease in and of itself, but instead as a viable and defensible choice made by millions of Americans. "To smoke is to engage in a risky personal life-style choice," asserts Thomas Humber, president of the National Smokers Alliance. "I smoke with full understanding of the risks—and the benefits—of that choice." Humber and other defenders of smoking question several key tenets of the anti-smoking movement. They argue that smokers already pay the social and health costs of smoking through existing tobacco taxes, and that more tax increases would be unfair. They also question whether nicotine is addictive to the extent of robbing people of free will to choose whether to smoke, and whether secondhand smoke has been proven to be a serious health threat to nonsmokers. Humber concludes that "smokers are being cast as the new pariahs," and that "the majority of smokers are asking only the fairness and tolerance that are required in any nation that respects individual differences." The viewpoints in this chapter highlight some of the current debates over smoking and the anti-smoking movement.

"The high-profile, large-scale traffic in tobacco is sufficiently harmful to society to warrant a deliberate effort to render it all but unprofitable."

PUBLIC HEALTH POLICY SHOULD EMPHASIZE CORPORATE RESPONSIBILITY

Joseph L. Andrews Jr.

Joseph L. Andrews Jr. is an internist and chest specialist in Concord, Massachusetts. In the following viewpoint, he argues that smoking has remained a serious public health problem in America largely because of the actions of the tobacco industry. Tobacco companies have suppressed knowledge on the carcinogenic and addictive properties of cigarettes, have manipulated nicotine levels in cigarettes, and have marketed them to young people. Andrews calls for a national campaign to reduce the sale and consumption of tobacco by making it less profitable for cigarette manufacturers to sell their product and by holding these companies financially responsible for the social costs of smoking.

As you read, consider the following questions:

1. What significance does Andrews attach to admissions made by the Liggett Group in 1997 concerning the tobacco industry?
2. What reasons does the author give for raising cigarette taxes?
3. What restrictions on tobacco sales and smoking does Andrews recommend?

Reprinted from Joseph L. Andrews Jr., "How to Kick a National Habit," The Humanist, May/June 1997, by permission of the author.

If successful, President Bill Clinton's election-inspired proposals to curb tobacco smoking by teenagers will help reduce the most preventable cause of ill health in America (an estimated 450,000 smoking-related deaths occur in the United States each year), as well as save more than $100 billion annually in federal, state, and private expenditures for health care and lost work. But revelations by the Liggett Group, Inc.—makers of Chesterfield, L&M, and Lark cigarettes—make it clear that much more action is needed. In its March 20, 1997, legal settlement with the attorneys general of twenty-two states seeking to recoup health care costs of treating smokers, Liggett admitted that it and other tobacco giants had known for decades that cigarettes cause cancer, they are addictive, and the tobacco industry had deliberately marketed them to teenagers to make up for slumping sales to adults.

It is thus time for the nation to adopt a comprehensive plan to dramatically reduce smoking and thereby improve general health. While those who still wish to smoke should be allowed to do so, the majority who desire neither this habit nor its high social costs are entitled to some relief. I believe my forty-odd years of experience in the trenches of the tobacco war have given me the necessary long-range perspective to offer a set of workable, constructive changes for the future.

EXPERIENCES WITH SMOKING

In the late 1940s, as a youth in suburban New York, I joined several other neighborhood kids in taking my first furtive cigarette puffs in a nearby, empty wooded lot. This rite, kept secret from our (smoker) parents (and followed by Sen-Sen and cloves), seemed to us to be an exciting way to assert our pre-pubescent independence. Ubiquitous cigarette ads in papers and magazines at the time heralded smoking doctors touting "safe" cigarettes, lauded the salubrious effect of smoke on your "T-zone" (throat), assured you that "L.S.M.F.T.—Lucky Strike Means Fine Tobacco," and, through celebrity testimonials, promised youth, glamour, vigor, and good looks to smokers.

In the 1950s, as a high school student serving the summer as an orderly at White Plains Hospital in downstate New York, I first encountered unfiltered the deadly ravages of smoking. After I wheeled the bodies of dead lung cancer victims to the morgue and watched as the pathologist sliced white golf ball- or melon-sized tumors out of blackened lungs, I reviewed the patients' charts. The conclusion was crystal clear even then: all the lung cancer victims had a previous history of heavy smoking for many years. I gave up cigarettes then and there. However, as a magazine editor at Amherst College in the late 1950s, I was only too happy to accept a small subsidy for including preprinted, color back covers that proclaimed: "Join the men [ranch hands] who know: nothing satisfies like the big clean taste of top tobacco—Chesterfield Kings" or "Live Modern: Change to Modern L&M."

But as a medical student at the University of Rochester, New York, in the 1960s, I learned that the components of tobacco smoke's 4,000 chemicals include at least forty-three different proven carcinogens (in humans and other animals) and more than 200 poisons, such as aromatic hydrocarbons and nitrosamines. I also learned that nicotine is addictive in the particulate phase and the gas phase delivers many more poisons—carbon monoxide (which displaces needed oxygen from red blood cells), formaldehyde, ammonia, nitrogen oxides, benzene, acrolein, pyridine, and hydrogen cyanide, to name a few—directly into the lungs' bronchial airways and alveoli (air sacs) and, thence, directly and quickly into the bloodstream.

Later, as an internal medical resident and fellow in pulmonary medicine at Boston City General, Boston Veterans Administration, and Massachusetts General hospitals, I tried to help long-term smokers, gasping from their smoking-induced emphysema, bronchitis, and heart disease. Many passed their final days in the intensive care unit, hooked up with tubes from a tracheostomy (incision in their wind pipe) to a ventilator machine. I often treated heart failure patients after their premature, tobacco-induced heart attacks. Many of the men—members of Senator Robert Dole's "experienced generation"—had started their smoking habits as soldiers during World War II after having received free or cheap cigarettes at the PX.

In 1964, the first surgeon general's report to note the link between widespread cigarette smoking and rapidly increasing rates of lung cancer appeared. Subsequent surgeon general's reports were to identify tobacco smoking as the major preventable cause of many disabling and often lethal diseases, including emphysema, bronchitis, and cancers of the lung, larynx, and bladder. They also identified smoking as a major contributing factor in deaths from heart attacks (coronary heart disease), in peripheral vascular diseases and strokes, and in incurring billions of dollars in lost work days, medical expenses, disability, and death. Secondhand smoke was also later implicated as a definite health threat to both adults and children. And Belgian scientists have found that newborns of mothers who smoked during pregnancy have adult nicotine levels in their bodies and thus need to be treated as ex-smokers.

As an Air Force physician during the Vietnam War era, I saw a new generation of soldiers—recruits who were too patriotic or too poor to be successful draft-evading hippies or yippies—get hooked on free cigarette samples or cheap PX smokes. When I started medical practice at the Lahey Clinic in Boston during the 1970s, I dealt daily with both men and women smokers—business executives, workers, and homemakers from all segments of society—who were fighting cigarette nicotine addiction and related illnesses. It became clear that smoking adversely affected almost every organ system in the body. Later, I started a comprehensive, ambulatory pulmonary rehabilitation clinic to aid tobacco-afflicted bronchitis and emphysema sufferers, who were often too winded to slowly climb one flight of stairs.

THE NEED FOR PREVENTION

After I witnessed daily the disabling results of long-term smoking, I realized that the need for prevention was just as great—or greater—as treatment. As chief of pulmonary medicine at the New England Deaconess Hospital in Boston, I fought to make the facility one of the first smoke-free hospitals in the country. I was aided by other anti-smoking pioneers, including Dr. Richard Overholt, a thoracic surgeon who, since the 1930s, had excised thousands of lungs riddled with smoking-induced tumors, and Dr. Theodore Badger, an experienced chest specialist. Unbelievably, we had to battle many angry nurses who complained that their personal freedom would be violated by policies to exclude smoking from the facility. Some prominent hospital and clinic administrators feared they would lose the business of nicotine-deprived patients, who they predicted would go elsewhere (though most didn't).

As a clinical researcher and teacher at Harvard and Tufts medical schools, I helped identify the growing menace of a cigarette-related lung cancer epidemic in women. Liberated women had begun puffing tobacco in the 1940s and slowly developed their lung cancers over the next twenty years. As a result, lung cancer death rates in women soon surpassed those of breast cancer to become the number one cause of cancer death in women—as it had been in men for many years. Indeed, women had truly "come a long way, baby" in dying by the tens of thousands from lung cancer. The American Cancer Society predicts that, over the next year, 192,000 Americans—110,000 men and 82,000 women—will be newly diagnosed with and 164,000 will die from lung and throat cancers, both strongly related to smoking, while another two million people worldwide will die from smoking-related diseases.

I also helped analyze diagnostic techniques to detect lung cancer and concurred with other researchers that the then-accepted, widespread screening techniques—such as chest x-rays and sputum exams (cytologies)—are very insensitive in detecting early, small, treatable tumors. Thus, by the time lung cancer is diagnosed, it has often metastasized elsewhere in the body. Thus I concluded once more: treatment is often too late; prevention is the key and should be the number-one priority.

In the 1970s and 1980s, I appeared as a consultant before the Boston City Council and elsewhere to help legislators formulate effective laws prohibiting smoking in restaurants and public buildings. After other health experts and I gave voluminous objective data about the multiple injurious health effects and costs to society of smoking-related illnesses, we were often followed by highly paid tobacco lobbyists, often ex-legislators. They assured their ex-colleagues that our health data, which implicated tobacco, was totally irrelevant because cigarettes were legal goods to be sold and smokers' freedom to smoke was protected by the Constitution and the Bill of Rights. Local laws restricting smoking were, therefore, legislated slowly at first and were often spotty.

Finally, in the 1990s, after more than forty years of accumulating vast scientific evidence proving the adverse and often fatal effects of long-term smoking, as well as of secondhand smoke, it is heartening to see grass-roots public opinion and most politicians supporting policies to prevent children from starting smoking and to encourage adult smokers to quit. However, in spite of the growing awareness of the dangers of smoking, an increasing number of teens (35 percent), as well as 26 percent of adults (down from over 40 percent in 1965), still smoke.

WORLDWIDE TRENDS

Worldwide, the figures and trends are more alarming. The World Bank's 1993 *World Development Report* declares, "Unless smoking behavior changes, three decades from now premature deaths caused by tobacco in the developing world will exceed the expected deaths from AIDS, tuberculosis, and complications of childbirth *combined.*" Epidemiologist Richard Peto of the Cancer Studies Unit at Oxford University estimates that, by 2025, tobacco use will kill at least ten million people per year—more than seven million of which will be in developing countries. The World Health Organisation states that tobacco use now constitutes "a global health emergency that many governments have yet to confront."

So President Clinton's efforts to reduce smoking among teen-agers and to recognize nicotine as an addictive drug under the jurisdiction of the U.S. Food and Drug Administration are a wel-comed start. But much bolder, more creative, and more ambi-tious measures aimed at peacefully phasing out a major destruc-tive industry are the next step.

The ethical reality we must face is this: the high-profile, large-scale traffic in tobacco is sufficiently harmful to society to warrant a deliberate effort to render it all but unprofitable. We don't need to prohibit tobacco entirely. Those individuals—after receiving complete and accurate consumer information—who still wish to avail themselves of tobacco products should be free to do so. And others should be free to manufacture and sell, at a fair profit, that which satisfies any lingering demand. Nor do we need to destroy the fortunes and livelihoods of tobacco farmers and workers. The aim should simply be to bring a gradual end to the active and knowing destruction of the public health.

A TWELVE-STEP AGENDA

The matter can be approached in much the same way we ap-proach other harmful substances and products. And this is the spirit behind the following twelve-step agenda to break Amer-ica's smoking habit:

1. *Create business incentives for farmers to make the transition from tobacco to alternative crops.* As long as farmers keep growing tobacco, manu-facturers will market tobacco products. Only when we approach the problem at its *source* and effectively scale down tobacco pro-duction will we succeed in decreasing tobacco consumption. While federal price supports for tobacco, which began in 1909, were terminated in the 1930s, current hereditary acreage allot-ments make it advantageous for certain farmers to continue spe-cializing in the crop. Right now, about 124,000 tobacco farmers in the United States depend upon a federal system that parcels out shares of the total tobacco production. This restriction of cultivated tobacco acreage has the paradoxical effect of artifi-cially making the crop highly profitable.

But the government doesn't have to keep doing things this way. Alternative incentives can replace current ones. Wayne Ras-mussen, who was historian for the U.S. Department of Agricul-ture for fifty years, has suggested a possible replacement policy of providing a subsidy to tobacco farmers who convert to food crops like wheat and corn. According to the Worldwatch Insti-tute's *State of the World 1997* report, in the face of world hunger, governments would do well to question the practice of using farmland for nonessential crops. "For example," it says, "the 5 million hectares [12,350,000 acres] of cropland used to produce tobacco could produce 15 million tons of grain for human consumption."

2. *Encourage economic incentives for consumers to quit smoking and disincentives for their habit to continue.* Actuarial analyses showing much higher morbidity and mortality for smokers, and hence higher insurance payoffs, provide a factual foundation for the widespread life insurance industry practice of charging higher premium rates for smokers and lower rates for nonsmokers. Health insurance policies have been similarly affected. But what about fire insurance premiums? They, too, could reflect lower payouts for nonsmokers and, hence, become lower for businesses and institutions with effective no-smoking policies.

3. *Increase cigarette excise and other tax rates enough to cover the social costs of smoking.* In 1997 there was a significant gap between the high cigarette taxes in some states (82¢ per pack in Washington, 76¢ in Massachusetts, 75¢ in Michigan), and the low rates in tobacco-growing states (5¢ in North Carolina, 3¢ in Kentucky, 2.5¢ in Virginia). Given a uniform federal tax of 24¢ per pack, this variation makes little sense. According to the American Cancer Society and Action on Smoking and Health, there are a number of cogent reasons why both state and federal taxes of this type should be higher:

- Costs for health care and lost productivity come to about $100 billion annually in the United States. As argued in Worldwatch's *State of the World 1997* report, "It simply does not make economic sense for a government to promote smoking while at the same time bearing the brunt of health care costs caused by tobacco use." Tobacco taxes can thus be considered more of a "user fee."
- Each 25¢-per-pack tax increase is estimated to reduce adult smoking rates by 4 percent and youth smoking by 10 percent. In California and Massachusetts, where voters approved citizen initiatives to increase pack taxes, the average number of cigarettes smoked by adults fell annually by 2.7 and 2.2 percent, respectively (or a 17 percent drop in Massachusetts since 1993), compared to an 0.8 percent yearly drop in other states.
- Decreased smoking rates would reduce disease and death rates both in teenagers under eighteen (projected at more than five million future preventable deaths by the U.S. Centers for Disease Control and Prevention) and in adults. Thus, the currently projected 450,000 tobacco-related

deaths annually in the United States would be lower.

- Nicotine addiction in teenagers acts as a "gateway drug." Smoking teens are 100 times more likely to use marijuana and thirty times more likely to use cocaine, according to figures cited by the surgeon general.
- Taxes scaled to the level of tar and nicotine would encourage manufacturers to lower the percentages of these hazardous substances in their tobacco products.

4. *Encourage further lawsuits by states to recover from the tobacco companies taxpayer dollars already spent on tobacco-related health costs.* The recent out-of-court settlement by the Liggett Group, Inc., shows how states can recover millions of dollars in smoking-related Medicaid health care costs. This successful approach should therefore be repeated by all other states. And since Liggett has agreed to add a warning to its packaging stating that smoking is addictive and to aid the Justice Department in its criminal investigation of perjury, fraud, and conspiracy allegations against the tobacco industry, the potential gains through this type of action involve far more than money.

5. *Help individual tobacco victims recover their health care costs and compensate their families for tobacco-related deaths.* The tobacco industry has poured millions of dollars into teams of high-powered, high-priced lawyers to defend their interests against victims of tobacco-related illness and death. "In more than 800 suits, initiated since 1954, the cigarette companies have gone to trial only twenty-three times, lost twice, and paid not a dime in damage payments" to individuals, the *Nation* reported in its September 28, 1995, issue. An example is the Cipollone case in New Jersey, on which the tobacco industry spent more than $50 million, dragging the case out over a ten-year period, to deny damages to the family of a heavy smoker who died of lung cancer. It took the case to the Supreme Court, filed more than 100 delaying motions, and finally caused the exhausted plaintiff's firm, having futilely spent more than $5 million, to quit.

In 1996, a class action suit against the American Tobacco Company, now in the federal court in New Orleans, was launched by a world-class group of product liability lawyers, led by Wendall Gautnier on behalf of Peter Castano, a smoker since age sixteen who died of lung cancer at age forty-seven. If it goes before a jury, this case could represent ninety million current and former smokers and become the largest product liability suit in American history, with the potential of winning $40 billion in damages. The plaintiff's lawyers will attempt to defeat tobacco industry lawyers, who disclaim all responsibility and contend that all responsibility is the smoker's. The plaintiff's lawyers aim to prove fraud against the tobacco companies, which they allege withheld secret data about the addictive and injurious effects of smoking. [Editor's note: In May 1996 a U.S. appeals court dismissed the lawsuit *Castano v. American Tobacco et al.*, ruling that it involved so many people as to be too unwieldy for a class action suit. The plaintiff lawyers later filed similar class action lawsuits on a state-by-state basis.]

6. *Promote divestiture of tobacco company stocks.* When the pension plans and investment firms of teachers, executives, workers, and government employees do not divest their tobacco stocks, they give dollars to support disability and death from smoking. For example, Fidelity Investments of Boston encourages its many mutual funds to invest $7 billion in Philip Morris, the largest holding of many of its mutual funds. Fidelity also invests another $1 billion in RJR Nabisco, Joe Camel's home base. Fidelity touts Philip Morris' "strong growth attributes, despite future litigation threats." Years ago, South Africans and their U.S. supporters fought successfully against apartheid by promoting divestiture of its formerly segregated firms. All individuals and corporations should be encouraged to similarly divest all equities based on selling nicotine, tar, and carcinogens. A divestment restriction bill for state employees was passed by the Massachusetts House in 1996.

7. *Reward honesty for revealing and penalize dishonesty for covering up cigarette ingredients and corporate research results regarding the addictive and health perils of smoking.* Tobacco companies reportedly have a long history of concealing scientific studies that demonstrate the addictive quality of nicotine and the many adverse health effects of smoking. Documentation has appeared in the *Journal of the American Medical Association*, the *Nation*, Dr. Stanton Glantz's *Tobacco Papers* (1996), and elsewhere. Effective laws would require tobacco companies to make public their scientific studies and list all chemical ingredients on packaging, as is done with most other consumer products. A tobacco disclosure law, requiring full listing of all ingredients, was passed by the Massachusetts legislature in 1996 and, not surprisingly, is under a challenge from the tobacco industry.

8. *Expand education about the injurious consequences of smoking.* The tobacco industry spends more than $6 billion annually to entice youngsters to start smoking and to keep smokers from quitting. Joe Camel grabs the attention of potential childhood smokers (90 percent of smokers started as teens), while the Marlboro Man spreads Madison Avenue macho across the United States and around the world. To counter these enticing tobacco images, effective education programs for both children and adults should communicate facts about tobacco-induced illnesses, in-

capacity, and death, as well as teach effective techniques to quit smoking. For example, the Massachusetts Tobacco Control Program, funded by a 24¢-per-pack tax increase and approved by a voter referendum in 1992, gives grants to towns to fund educators who teach students why they should not start smoking and how to quit.

9. *Discourage tobacco company advertising and promotions.* Cigarette companies spend $6 billion per year for advertising and promotions. This includes their sponsorship of sporting events, such as Winston Cup Racing, and their use of billboards in baseball and football stadiums and basketball and hockey arenas. The latter are also seen "incidentally" by millions of television viewers. The tax-deductible status of this outlay saves the industry more than $1 billion in taxes each year. President Clinton's restrictions on cigarette advertising aimed at minors are being challenged by the tobacco industry on free speech grounds, but the administration is arguing a "substantial government interest to protect children."

Should this argument fail a constitutional test, however, other possibilities remain. Advertising media are often encouraged to voluntarily refuse to accept certain types of advertising. That's why we (unfortunately) don't often see condom ads on television—though they are perfectly legal and would generate lucrative advertising revenue. If similar pressure could be brought to bear on other media regarding tobacco advertising, the public could actually benefit this time. Additionally, just as anti-smoking public service ads produced by the American Cancer Society drove cigarette advertisers off television in the 1960s, a similar approach could be applied in other advertising venues. Meanwhile, the very fact that cigarette billboards can be seen on television during sporting events is sufficient reason for television public service anti-smoking ads to make an important comeback.

10. *Further restrict tobacco sales.* Just as states and municipalities can limit, through licensing and zoning, what sorts of stores sell liquor and where such outlets may be located (as well as limit and regulate other types of businesses in other ways), so various levels of government can restrict tobacco retailing. By this process, over-the-counter and vending machine sales of tobacco products can be prohibited at food markets, pharmacies, restaurants, workplaces, government facilities (especially military bases), hospitals, public schools, private universities, discount stores, and the like. Some local laws already exclude cigarette sales from many of these sites, but there is no systematic coordination between communities. Many businesses, such as Target stores, the nation's third largest discount retailer, have voluntar-

ily ceased to sell tobacco, but Kmart and Walmart are still engaged in the trade. The ultimate goal should be to limit all tobacco sales to specially licensed smoke shops.

11. *Ban smoking in all public places.* While most hospitals have been smoke-free for one or two decades, the great benefits of a totally smoke-free environment to both the smoker and the secondhand-smoke-inhaling neighbor should be extended by statute to all factory and office workers and students, as well as to all military personnel. The total ban on smoking in the country's workplaces proposed by the Occupational Safety and Health Administration in 1995 has been stalled in Congress by opposition from tobacco and restaurant interests.

12. *Discourage tobacco exports by American cigarette makers to other countries.* With the decline in the number of adult American smokers, stated strategic plans of American tobacco corporations call for increasing exports to "expanding markets"—such as China, Europe, and Africa. Reports from China today describe the omnipresence of large billboards featuring those exemplary American character models, Joe Camel and the Marlboro Man. Past U.S. government trade policy has actually mandated that other countries accept minimum quotas of U.S. tobacco exports and allow unlimited advertising of U.S. tobacco products abroad. What to do? President Clinton now has an election mandate to be as strict about limiting U.S. tobacco exports and disclosing health risks abroad as he does at home. He should be encouraged to follow through.

TOBACCO COMPANY OPPOSITION

This comprehensive twelve-step plan to break America's, and perhaps the world's, smoking habit will quite naturally lack the blessing of leading tobacco product manufacturers. But then marketers of infant formula in the Third World weren't pleased by the public boycott against them a decade ago. Major oil companies would do more offshore drilling and pollute more beaches if the public let them. And automobile emission controls and safety requirements remain a pain in the neck for car manufacturers.

Big tobacco has no intention of giving up without a fight, either. During the 1996 elections, two tobacco companies—Philip Morris and RJR Nabisco—gave more than $3.1 million to influence political parties ($2.6 million to Republicans and $523,000 to Democrats). Philip Morris hosted receptions for delegates at both parties' conventions. Many more millions of dollars are spent on lobbyists to argue the tobacco industry's viewpoints directly and to influence federal and state representatives.

So my twelve-step plan won't be easy to implement. But think where we once were in America. There was a time when just about everyone had to put up with smoking at work, in elevators, in every part of restaurants, and in an astonishing variety of other places. Television was saturated with uncriticized cigarette advertising. Smoking was the "in" thing to do, and people rarely asked if it was okay to smoke in another's presence. The public had no idea of the dangers, and government had no idea of the costs.

We've come a long way, baby! Now let's finish the job.

| "The strategy of blaming the [tobacco] industry for smoking is getting in the way of efforts to discourage smoking itself."

PUBLIC HEALTH POLICY SHOULD EMPHASIZE INDIVIDUAL RESPONSIBILITY

John E. Calfee

John E. Calfee is a resident scholar at the American Enterprise Institute. In the following viewpoint, he criticizes anti-smoking strategies espoused by some activists and government officials that, according to him, seem aimed more at punishing tobacco companies rather than reducing smoking. Past American public health campaigns succeeded in cutting America's consumption of cigarettes by emphasizing education on tobacco's health hazards and individual responsibility, he argues, but more recent anti-smoking efforts have been predicated on the assumption that smokers are helpless victims of a predatory tobacco industry. Proposed reforms such as raising cigarette taxes, banning tobacco advertising, placing cigarettes under greater regulation, and suing tobacco companies for damages will most likely fail to reduce tobacco consumption and may well incur significant social costs, Calfee concludes.

As you read, consider the following questions:

1. Why have media anti-smoking campaigns been ineffective, according to Calfee?
2. What are some of the social costs of attacking the tobacco industry, according to the author?
3. What recommendations does Calfee make for reducing smoking and its effects?

The war on tobacco has turned upside down. For decad[es] new information emerged about the health effects of smoking, public policy relentlessly emphasized individual decision-making. This brought real achievements—notably, a 40 percent reduction in U.S. per-capita cigarette consumption between 1975 and 1993.

Some half dozen years ago, however, the battle over tobacco entered a new phase. The focus shifted from smoking to the tobacco industry. A new view took hold. In this view, smoking is caused primarily by deceptive advertising targeted at young people, the manipulation of nicotine to maintain addiction, and the suppression of information on the harm caused by smoking. Smokers should be seen as victims of these forces. And the solution is drastic reform of the industry itself.

This new vision rapidly coalesced into policy. Several states raised tobacco taxes in order to protect smokers from their own preferences and to fund anti-smoking campaigns and research. Federal action followed, notably the attempt of the Food and Drug Administration (FDA) to regulate cigarettes as nicotine-delivery devices. At the same time came an astonishing barrage of litigation, generating multi-billion-dollar settlements in Mississippi, Texas, Florida, and Minnesota. A June 1997 agreement among plaintiff attorneys, state attorneys general, and the tobacco industry provided a model for comprehensive federal legislative proposals, over which debate continues to this day.

All of this activity tends to focus on a concrete goal and a specific set of tools. The goal is to reduce teen smoking rapidly by half or more, with a corresponding reduction in adult smoking as the teens get older. The tools: elimination of advertising seen by teens, price increases of up to $2 per pack, anti-smoking campaigns, litigation to penalize the industry financially, "look-back" penalties on the industry if teen smoking does not decrease, and FDA jurisdiction over the development of safer cigarettes.

SIGNS OF FAILURE

The new approach will almost certainly fail. In fact, disturbing symptoms of failure have already begun to appear. Teen smoking has increased substantially since 1991. That has caught people's attention, but probably more alarming is a little-noticed change in the trend of overall consumption. After 15 years of sharp annual declines, per-capita cigarette consumption has hardly dropped since 1993.

Quite aside from these numbers, there are compelling reasons to believe that the central elements of the new plan cannot do what they are supposed to do. Consider prices, the single most important tool in the new thinking. Current proposals would raise federal taxes by a dollar or two—former surgeon general C. Everett Koop and former FDA commissioner David Kessler have proposed $1.50. This is expected to cut teenage smoking by a third or more. The logic is that teens don't realize they will get hooked on nicotine if they smoke, but they will react strongly to higher prices. This seems most unlikely. With teen smokers consuming an average of eight cigarettes a day, there is little reason to expect an extra five or ten cents per cigarette to stop them from smoking. And in fact, the biggest drop in teenage smoking—a nearly one-third decline in the late 1970s—occurred when cigarette prices were also going down (by about 15 percent). On the other hand, prices have been stable or slightly rising since 1991, even as teen smoking increased. In the United Kingdom, where cigarettes already cost twice as much as in the United States, teenagers smoke at about the same rate as they do here.

ADVERTISING AND SMOKING

What about advertising? Tell a teenager that advertising is the reason he smokes, and you will probably convince a teenager that you are out of touch with reality. Repeated statistical analyses have failed to detect a substantial effect on consumption from advertising. One may quibble about the details of individual studies, but the overall results are unmistakable. If advertising's effect on cigarette consumption were substantial, it would have been detected by now.

FDA regulation, if it comes to pass, will be institutionalized frustration. The new rules on advertising cannot reduce teen smoking, because advertising restrictions can hardly prevent what advertising never caused. Safer cigarettes (with less tar and nicotine) will be stymied, as the FDA vigorously implements policies reflecting the public-health community's hostility to safer smoking and new types of cigarettes.

There remain the anti-smoking campaigns. Often tried, they have generally had disappointing results. The people who design these campaigns tend to act on their own pet theories (they think teens are being duped by advertising) and to pursue political goals. Anti-smoking advertising, like the anti-smoking movement generally, has therefore become a vehicle for the new view that the proper target is the tobacco industry rather than smoking.

Thus in California, Massachusetts, and most recently Florida, government-funded campaigns tell kids they can't trust tobacco companies. This non-news is unlikely to cause kids to toss their cigarettes away, but it is consistent with political objectives such as new anti-smoking measures. Two anti-smoking scholars recently praised California's anti-smoking ads for challenging "the dominant view that public health problems reflect personal habits," and they noted that "it is political action and attitudes, rather than personal behavior, on which counter-ads are focused." In fact, the most effective anti-smoking ads probably come from the pharmaceutical firms that market smoking-cessation products. These firms have a financial incentive to communicate the information and strategies that will make people get serious about quitting smoking.

MISINFORMATION

Why do so many well-meaning people pursue measures that cannot achieve their goals? The short answer is that they are prisoners of their own preconceptions. They reject the idea that well-informed people ever choose to smoke; they believe advertising has a power that it has never had; they are ignorant of the history of cigarette marketing; and they give unquestioning credence to economic studies of the "price elasticity" of cigarettes that are of dubious value for the purposes to which they are put.

For the fact is that there is a deep conflict between what anti-smoking campaigners want to be true and what is true. This has fostered a strategy of deception and distortion. Such a strategy can succeed in the short run because of the peculiar circumstances of the tobacco market. Anti-smoking activists learned years ago that when they stretched the facts, those who corrected them were dismissed as industry hacks. This led to the amazing discovery that those who oppose smoking can wander far beyond the boundaries of good science (even in esteemed outlets such as the *Journal of the American Medical Association*) and still see their words accepted and amplified by an unquestioning media. Naturally, anti-smoking campaigners have seized this opportunity, introducing numerous absurdities into the everyday thinking of scholars, regulatory officials, journalists, and politicians. Thus we have been told that cigarettes are the most advertised product in America (wrong by more than an order of magnitude), that research has finally nailed down the connection between marketing and smoking by kids, and that secret industry documents show that the problem all along has been the targeting of youth. Such misinformation is routinely accepted and repeated as if it were the truth.

Here is a concrete example. One of the most often cited *JAMA* studies—in fact, the *only* non-governmental study the FDA cited in its regulatory initiative that actually used market data rather than surveys and the like—claimed to demonstrate that advertising for the first women's brands, in the late 1970s, caused a surge in smoking by teenage girls. The authors used sales data (not advertising data), took their figures from an unpublished student paper, dropped the three of six brands that did not fit their thesis, mistook billions of cigarettes sold for billions of *dollars* worth of cigarettes sold (a forty-fold error), and concluded to much acclaim that massive advertising had fundamentally altered the market. This utterly useless study is repeatedly cited as proof that advertising causes teen smoking This kind of thing would not happen in an ordinary intellectual environment.

Sometimes, history has been rewritten. Despite what the FDA says, the discovery that people smoke to get nicotine is not new, and neither is the fact that manufacturers strongly influence the amount of nicotine in cigarette smoke. In the late 1960s and early 1970s, maintaining adequate nicotine levels in low-tar cigarettes was widely believed to be the key to progress against the diseases caused by smoking. This belief—which originated with public-health scholars, not the tobacco industry—was so pervasive that Consumer Reports declared in 1972 that "efforts should be made to popularize ways of delivering frequent doses of nicotine to addicts without filling their lungs with smoke."

The National Cancer Institute and the Department of Agriculture maintained a large program devoted to developing improved strains of tobacco (containing more nicotine). A biotech firm hired by a tobacco company to cultivate one of those variants in South America (to avoid growing it in the United States) was recently accused of criminal behavior for doing so in violation of a law that was repealed in 1991. Amazingly, the FDA regarded this episode as a prime justification for regulating the tobacco industry. Again, this kind of thing would not happen in an ordinary intellectual environment.

THE COSTS OF ANTI-SMOKING MEASURES

Clearly, the new strategy of attacking the tobacco industry rather than smoking is producing little if any benefit. The costs, on the other hand, are large and growing.

First, there are costs to public health. We are abandoning the only approach to smoking-reduction that is likely to succeed: reliance on individual responsibility. This point was eloquently stated by a George Washington University physician, Larry H. Pastor, in a letter to the editor of the *Journal of the American Medical*

Association in 1996. Describing the dubious proposition that tobacco litigation will make people quit smoking, Pastor noted that exactly the opposite could easily happen,

> because some smokers will feel reinforced in externalizing blame onto "the tobacco industry" and thereby fail to take the difficult steps necessary to confront their smoking addiction. The more such personal injury litigation succeeds, the more some will comfort themselves with the rationalization that, if they develop tobacco-related illness, they can sue the cigarette makers and obtain a lucrative reward.

The strategy of blaming the industry for smoking is getting in the way of efforts to discourage smoking itself.

Second, there is the matter of who will pay the higher cigarette taxes. A hallmark of the U.S. market is that most smoking is done by people of modest means. And the idea that smokers impose financial costs on others has little foundation. To say that blue-collar smokers should pay more for their habit because they cannot protect themselves from manipulation by the tobacco companies—and then watch them continue to smoke while the nation collects billions of dollars from their pockets to spend on other citizens—is a sorry combination of paternalism and hypocrisy. Perhaps these smokers should simply be allowed to pursue their freely chosen course without financial penalty. At any rate, with teens buying only about 2 percent of the cigarettes sold, we know that a massive tax increase designed to stop teen smoking will be paid almost entirely by non-teens, most of them poor or lower-middle class.

The third cost of the new approach lies in the danger of creating a government stake in continued smoking. The Clinton administration wants to raise cigarette taxes so it can transfer tens of billions of dollars from smokers to its favorite domestic-policy initiatives. Far more dangerous than a mere tax-grab, this plan will work only if most smokers continue to smoke and pay the higher taxes. The public-health community should renounce any such plan. The history of the anti-smoking movement makes clear that the toughest places in which to make progress are countries like Japan, Thailand, and China—that is, nations with a large state investment in smoking.

Fourth, as the new approach is applied to products other than tobacco, it will be hugely disruptive—and it cannot easily be confined to tobacco. This is so for three reasons. (1) The underlying principle, that marketers are responsible for the behavior of anyone who buys their products, is indiscriminate. It is not intrinsically more relevant to tobacco than to, say, automobiles, alcohol, or red meat. (2) The tools of the new regime are too tempting. They operate by combining political opportunism with the legal means for extracting financial payments. Once launched, the process is self-perpetuating. The plaintiff attorneys who are engineering today's mass tobacco litigation honed their skills in asbestos litigation, and they are eager to move on to other arenas. (3) These methods and tools are not easily dismantled. They are greatly prized by the litigation community, advocacy groups, politicians who like to spend taxes, even academics in search of funding. Wresting such valuable tools away from those who have become accustomed to using them could be very difficult.

Finally, the new approach to tobacco carries the cost of degrading the intellectual environment. This is no trivial matter. The public-health community's power depends on information, credibility, and the consequent ability to persuade. That power can be dissipated if it is carelessly misused (as it has been), and once lost, it cannot easily be regained. As journalist Carl Cannon noted, after describing some grossly untrue statements from the White House during the debate over tobacco legislation in the Senate, "The problem is that in employing the devilishly effective—but not always truthful—language of political campaigns, the good guys risk losing the moral high ground." Deception is not—at least should not be, in a free society—a viable long-run strategy.

PERSONAL RESPONSIBILITY AND SAFER CIGARETTES

The time has come, then, for public policy toward tobacco to return to its roots. The only effective way of combating the harmful effects of smoking in the long run is to encourage an enduring sense of personal responsibility—among smokers, their families, and physicians. But that's not all. Two decades of an absurd hostility to safer smoking and safer tobacco must end. We have forgotten that in the 1950s, the pronouncements of cancer researchers created a demand for cigarettes with less tar and nicotine, and the cigarette manufacturers responded with a speed that in hindsight seems miraculous. Today, instead of talking about draconian taxes and sweeping infringements on commercial speech, we should let the competitive market again serve smokers—just as it does everyone else.

"There should be no doubt that smoke emitted from other people's cigarettes is a real and preventable health risk."

THE THREAT OF SECONDHAND SMOKE JUSTIFIES SMOKING RESTRICTIONS

John R. Garrison

John R. Garrison is chief executive of the American Lung Association, a voluntary health agency. In the following viewpoint, he argues that secondhand smoke, also called environmental tobacco smoke (ETS), is harmful to nonsmokers. Scientific investigations by the Environmental Protection Agency (EPA) and other sources have conclusively linked ETS with increased risks of lung cancer, heart disease, and other health problems. Such hazards justify stronger smoking bans in public places, Garrison concludes.

As you read, consider the following questions:

1. How many annual deaths does ETS cause among nonsmokers in the United States, according to Garrison?
2. What scientists and organizations does the author say have endorsed the 1993 EPA report on secondhand smoke?
3. According to Garrison, what are some of the effects of ETS on children?

The toxic effects of secondhand smoke have been so well-documented during the last 25 years that there should be no doubt that smoke emitted from other people's cigarettes is a real and preventable health risk. Secondhand smoke, also known as environmental tobacco smoke, or ETS, passive smoke or sidestream smoke is estimated to cause 53,000 deaths each year among nonsmokers in the United States. The Environmental Protection Agency, or EPA, estimates that secondhand smoke is responsible for about 3,000 lung-cancer deaths each year among nonsmokers; of these, an estimated 800 are due to exposure to secondhand smoke in the home and 2,200 from exposure at work or in social settings. A study from Harvard University reports that ETS may even double a person's risk of heart disease.

Unlike the dangers of cigarette use, the threat that secondhand smoke presents is especially insidious because it affects the health of adults and children who cannot always protect themselves: Children do not choose to live in smoke-filled homes, and nonsmoking adults can't control the smoky air they breathe at work.

COMPILING EVIDENCE

The scientific community began compiling evidence about the adverse health effects of secondhand smoke as early as 1972, when a report of the surgeon general concluded that "an atmosphere contaminated with tobacco smoke can contribute to the discomfort of many individuals."

Since then, several reports have been released outlining the toxic effects of secondhand smoke. They include the 1986 surgeon general's report which concluded that secondhand smoke can cause lung cancer in healthy nonsmokers and that children whose parents smoke have an increased frequency of respiratory infections and respiratory symptoms compared with children whose parents do not smoke. The National Academy of Sciences and the International Agency for Research on Cancer also issued reports in 1986 that offered similar conclusions.

In 1991, the National Institute for Occupational Safety and Health, or NIOSH, concluded that ETS is a potential occupational carcinogen. NIOSH recommended that employers take measures to reduce their employees' exposure to secondhand smoke by designating a separate area for smoking.

The final breakthrough came in 1993, with the publication of the EPA's definitive report, *Respiratory Health Effects of Passive Smoking: Lung Cancer and Other Disorders*. This report not only supported earlier findings regarding the risks of lung cancer, it also augmented previous reports with an exhaustive review of the health effects of secondhand smoke on children.

The EPA's report classified secondhand smoke as a Group A carcinogen that is responsible for an estimated annual toll of 37,000 heart-disease deaths and 13,000 deaths from other cancers in U.S. nonsmokers. Secondhand smoke was found to be a risk factor for the development of asthma in children. It also was found to worsen asthma symptoms for up to 1 million children already diagnosed with asthma. Annually, an estimated 150,000 to 300,000 cases of lower respiratory-tract infections, such as bronchitis and pneumonia, among children under 18 months of age were linked to secondhand-smoke exposure. The EPA report also concluded that infants and young children exposed to secondhand smoke experience increased cases of ear infection, coughing, wheezing and mucus buildup.

The EPA report was subjected to an extensive open review both by the public and the agency's Science Advisory Board, a panel of independent scientific experts. The board, the Department of Health and Human Services, the National Cancer Institute, the surgeon general and many other major health organizations, including the American Lung Association, have endorsed the EPA's findings.

Despite these endorsements, the tobacco industry continues to question the EPA's conclusions on lung cancer. While the industry neither acknowledges nor disputes EPA's findings on the respiratory effects in children, it continues to argue that the EPA manipulated the lung-cancer data to arrive at a predetermined conclusion. Furthermore, the tobacco industry argues that a nonsmoker's exposure to secondhand smoke is so minimal as to be insignificant.

The EPA's findings that secondhand-smoke exposure causes lung cancer in nonsmoking adults was not based on a single analysis but, rather, on the total weight of all the evidence available at the time. In addition, no claims ever have been made that minimal exposure to secondhand smoke poses a huge individual cancer risk. While the lung-cancer risk from secondhand smoke is relatively small compared with the risk from smoking, exposure to secondhand smoke often is involuntary and varies greatly among exposed individuals. Clearly, those who work or live with smokers experience a greater risk of lung cancer than those who are less exposed.

Several lung-cancer studies published since the release of the EPA report reinforce the link between secondhand-smoke exposure and lung cancer. They include a 1992 study by H.G. Stockwell et al., that found a group of Florida women whose husbands smoked experienced a 60 percent increase of lung-cancer risk. A similar study of Missouri women conducted the same year by Ross C. Brownson et al., found a significant increase in risk among women exposed to high levels of secondhand smoke from their spouses. Finally, a 1994 study by Elizabeth T.H. Fontham et al., found significant increases in lung-cancer risk among women in two California and three Southern cities who were exposed to secondhand smoke.

SECONDHAND SMOKE AND CHILDREN

There is no doubt today that smoking by parents is associated with a broad range of adverse effects in children. Tobacco use during pregnancy is responsible for an estimated 20 to 30 percent of low-birthweight babies, up to 14 percent of preterm deliveries and some 10 percent of all infant deaths.

A study reported by the *American Journal of Respiratory Critical Care Medicine* in 1992 found that even apparently healthy, full-term babies of smokers are born with narrowed airways and impaired lung function. Research released in 1994 found the children of mothers who smoked a half-pack of cigarettes or more during pregnancy had lower IQ scores than children whose mothers had not smoked. Studies also have shown that smoking in pregnancy can lead to delayed physical growth in children.

Clearly, pregnant women who quit smoking can contribute greatly to their child's health and well-being. However, recent findings reveal that quitting smoking may not be enough. Mothers need to protect their unborn children from other people's secondhand smoke as well. A 1995 study of 3,500 pregnant women found that nonsmoking women who were exposed to secondhand smoke during pregnancy had lower-birthweight babies than nonexposed expectant mothers.

TOBACCO INDUSTRY DENIALS

Americans most certainly should be worried about the toxic effects of secondhand smoke. What should worry them even more are the proponents of the tobacco industry who continue to deny not only the lethal effects of secondhand smoke but of smoking itself. For years, the tobacco industry has denied the health effects of smoking and secondhand smoke with accusations of poor science, questions about statistical significance and assertions of ignorance.

Perhaps Joseph A. Califano, then secretary of Health, Education and Welfare, responded most aptly to such tactics in his preface to the 1979 *Surgeon General's Report on Smoking and Health*:

> In truth, the attack upon the scientific and medical evidence about smoking is little more than an attack upon the science itself: an attack upon the epidemiological, clinical and experimental research disciplines upon which these conclusions are based. Like every attack upon science by vested interests, from Aristotle's day to Galileo's to our own, these attacks collapse of their own weight.

In 1992, a Gallup survey conducted for the Coalition On Smoking or Health, cofounded by the American Lung Association, found that nine in 10 adults were aware that secondhand smoke is harmful to infants and young children, pregnant women and older healthy adults. Women were more likely than men to believe that secondhand smoke is harmful to all of these groups. Nonsmokers also were more likely than smokers strongly to agree about the harmful effects of secondhand smoke. An important finding was that even eight in 10 smokers know that secondhand smoke is bad for the people around them. The good news is that an increased percentage of those surveyed supported total bans or restrictions on smoking in public places such as restaurants, workplaces, hotels, buses and trains.

SMOKING RESTRICTIONS IN PUBLIC PLACES

Forty-eight states and the District of Columbia have some restriction on smoking in public places. These laws range from designating a separate smoking area in schools to complete bans or restrictions on smoking in areas open to the public, including elevators, public buildings, restaurants, health facilities, public transportation, museums, shopping malls, retail stores and educational facilities. Among the states that limit or ban smoking in public areas, 43 restrict smoking in government workplaces and 23 restrict smoking in private-sector workplaces.

Since early 1990, smoking has been banned from almost all U.S. domestic airline flights. Most of today's travelers can barely remember the days of hazy, smoke-choked air travel. In recent years, many airlines have made some or all of their international flights smoke-free as well.

While progress certainly has been made toward reducing exposure to secondhand smoke, a great deal still needs to be accomplished. Thousands of corporate and restaurant employees throughout the country are exposed to harmful levels of secondhand smoke on a daily basis. In addition, a dangerous new trend in the form of "glamorous" cigar bars is exposing many to the harmful effects of secondhand cigar smoke.

Clearly, all Americans need to recognize and protect themselves and their children from the harmful effects of second-hand smoke. They should encourage the smokers in their lives to quit, and they should encourage their legislators to maintain or strengthen bans on smoking in public places. Only then can we breathe easy, knowing that our lungs and our lives aren't at risk from someone else's smoke.

"It's not reasonable to conclude that
ETS [environmental tobacco smoke]
is dangerous because smoking is
dangerous."

THE THREAT OF SECONDHAND
SMOKE HAS BEEN OVERSTATED

Jacob Sullum

In 1993 the Environmental Protection Agency released a report
that classified environmental tobacco smoke (ETS) as a "known
human carcinogen" and linked secondhand smoke to increased
lung cancer rates. The report was used in justifying numerous
smoking restrictions in offices and other public places. In the
following viewpoint, Jacob Sullum argues that the EPA report is
marred by reliance on faulty studies and mishandled statistics.
The threat of secondhand smoke has been overstated, he argues,
because of anti-smoking sentiment among policy makers and
public health officials. He contends that a closer examination of
the available evidence reveals that the link between secondhand
smoke and increased deaths by lung cancer and other diseases
remains unproven. Sullum is a senior editor of *Reason* magazine
and the author of *For Your Own Good: The Anti-Smoking Crusade and the
Tyranny of Public Health*.

As you read, consider the following questions:

1. What does Sullum say has been the impact of the 1993 EPA
   report on secondhand smoke?
2. Why is passive smoking not analogous to smoking when it
   comes to health risks, according to the author?
3. What comparisons does Sullum make between the evidence
   that secondhand smoke causes cancer and the evidence that
   smoking causes cancer?

"Secondhand Smoke Kills." So says a billboard on Pico Boulevard in Los Angeles that I pass every day on the way to work. I'm still not convinced. But most Americans seem to be: a CNN/*Time* poll conducted in March 1994 found that 78 per cent believe secondhand smoke is "very" or "somewhat" harmful.

That idea was endorsed by the U.S. Environmental Protection Agency in 1993, when it declared secondhand smoke "a known human lung carcinogen." Since then the EPA's report has helped justify smoking bans throughout the country: in cities such as Los Angeles and San Francisco (likely to be joined soon by New York); in Maryland, Vermont, and Washington state; and in government offices, including the Defense Department. On March 25, 1994, the Occupational Safety and Health Administration proposed a ban on smoking in workplaces, including bars and restaurants. . . .

Most supporters of such measures probably believe that the EPA's report presents definitive scientific evidence that "secondhand smoke kills." But a closer look shows that the EPA manipulated data and finessed important points to arrive at a predetermined conclusion. The agency compromised science to support the political crusade against smoking.

A MISLEADING ANALOGY

The first line of defense for people who want to avoid scrutiny of the case against secondhand smoke (a/k/a environmental tobacco smoke, or ETS) is to argue by analogy. "We know that tobacco smoke causes disease and can kill you," says Scott Ballin, chairman of the Coalition on Smoking or Health. "It makes sense that a person who doesn't smoke cigarettes, who's sitting next to a smoker and inhaling the smoke, is also at some risk." The EPA offers a similar argument, devoting a chapter of its report on ETS to the evidence that smoking causes cancer.

Although superficially plausible, this analogy is misleading. A smoker breathes in hot, concentrated tobacco smoke and holds it in his lungs before exhaling. A nonsmoker in the vicinity, by contrast, breathes air that includes minute quantities of residual chemicals from tobacco smoke. "ETS is so highly diluted that it is not even appropriate to call it smoke," says Gary Huber, a professor of medicine at the University of Texas Health Science Center, writing with two colleagues in the July 1991 *Consumers' Research*. Furthermore, since many of the compounds in tobacco smoke are unstable, it is not safe to assume even that a nonsmoker is exposed to the same chemicals as a smoker. Of 50 biologically active substances thought to be present in ETS, Huber and his colleagues report, only 14 have actually been detected.

Even if exposure to ETS were analogous to smoking, the doses involved are so small that it's not clear they would have any effect. Many chemicals that are hazardous or even fatal above a certain level are harmless (or beneficial) in smaller doses. James Enstrom, a professor of epidemiology at UCLA, estimates that someone exposed to ETS would be taking in the equivalent of a few cigarettes a year, perhaps one-hundredth of a cigarette a day. Yet studies of smoking have never looked at people who smoke that little; the lowest-exposure groups have been subjects who smoke up to five cigarettes a day.

THE EPA'S SMOKING GUN

So it's not reasonable to conclude that ETS must be dangerous because smoking is dangerous. You have to look at the research that deals specifically with ETS. The EPA's finding is based on 30 epidemiological studies that compared lung-cancer rates among nonsmokers (mainly women) who lived with smokers to lung-cancer rates among nonsmokers who lived with nonsmokers. None of the studies measured actual exposure to ETS; they simply assumed that people who lived with smokers were more exposed than people who didn't. In most of these studies, lung cancer was somewhat more common among the subjects living with smokers, but in only 6 cases were the results statistically significant.

This is a crucial point. In any study that compares a group exposed to a suspected risk factor with a control group, the luck of the draw may result in a difference between the two groups that does not reflect a difference between the populations the groups are supposed to represent. Researchers do statistical tests to account for the possibility of such a fluke. By convention, epidemiologists call a result significant when the probability that it occurred purely by chance is 5 per cent or less. By this standard, 80 per cent of the studies discussed by the EPA did not find a statistically significant link between ETS and lung cancer.

But the EPA, which had always used the conventional definition of statistical significance in its risk assessments, adopted a different standard for the report on ETS. It considered a result significant if the probability that it occurred purely by chance was 10 per cent or less. This change essentially doubles the odds of being wrong. "The justification for this usage," according to the report itself, "is based on the *a priori* hypothesis . . . that a positive association exists between exposure to ETS and lung cancer." Of course, the EPA was supposed to test that hypothesis, not simply assume that it is true.

Instead of presenting results from the epidemiological studies as they originally appeared, the EPA recalculated them using the less rigorous standard. As a report from the Congressional Research Service drily notes, "It is unusual to return to a study after the fact, lower the required significance level, and declare its results to be supportive rather than unsupportive of the effect one's theory suggests should be present."

Even after the EPA massaged the data, the vast majority of the studies still did not show a significant association between ETS and lung cancer. Of the 11 U.S. studies, only 1 yielded a result that was significant according to the looser definition. (According to the usual definition, none of them did.) To bolster the evidence, the EPA did a "meta-analysis" of these studies. Dr. Enstrom notes that this technique was originally intended for clinical trials that assess the impact of a drug or procedure by randomly assigning subjects to treatment and control groups. By contrast, the data analyzed by the EPA came from retrospective case-control studies that "matched" people with lung cancer to people without lung cancer. Enstrom says using meta-analysis for such studies "is not a particularly meaningful exercise," because the studies are apt to differ in the way they define exposure, the confounding variables they take into account, the types of cancer they include, and so on.

In any event, the EPA's conclusion—that living with a smoker raises a woman's risk of getting lung cancer by 19 per cent—is justified only according to the definition of statistical significance adopted especially for these data. By the usual standard, even the meta-analysis does not support the claim that ETS causes lung cancer. Furthermore, the EPA excluded from its analysis a major U.S. study, published in the November 1992 *American Journal of Public Health*, that failed to find a significant link between ETS and lung cancer. Given the large size of the study, it could well have changed the outcome of the meta-analysis, so that the result would not have been significant even by the EPA's revised standard.

A Weak Case

Despite this "fancy statistical footwork," as a July 1992 article in *Science* described it, the EPA was able to claim only a weak association between ETS and lung cancer. With a risk increase as low as 19 per cent, it is difficult to rule out the possibility that other factors were at work. "At least 20 confounding variables have been identified as important to the development of lung cancer," write Huber et al. "No reported study comes anywhere close to controlling, or even mentioning, half of these."

Smokers tend to differ from nonsmokers in many ways—including diet, socioeconomic status, risk-taking behavior, and exercise—and it is likely that the spouses of smokers share these characteristics to some extent. "If wives of smokers share in poor health habits or other factors that could contribute to illness," the Congressional Research Service notes, "statistical associations found between disease and passive smoking could be incidental or misleading."

Misclassification could also account for some or all of the observed differences between wives of smokers and wives of nonsmokers. It's possible that some of the subjects thought to be nonsmokers were actually smokers or former smokers. Since spouses of smokers are more likely to be smokers themselves, such errors would have biased the results. The EPA adjusted the data to account for this effect, but it's impossible to say whether it fully compensated for misclassification.

These issues are especially important when the relationship between a suspected risk factor and a disease is weak. Based on the 11 U.S. studies, the EPA concluded that a woman who lives with a smoker is 1.19 times as likely to get lung cancer as a woman who lives with a nonsmoker. This ratio did not rise above 2.1 to 1 in any of the U.S. studies. In previous risk assessments, the EPA has seen such weak associations as cause for skepticism. When the agency examined the alleged connection between electromagnetic fields and cancer, for example, it said, "the association is not strong enough to constitute a proven causal relationship, largely because the relative risks in the published reports have seldom exceeded 3.0."

This concern did not prevent the EPA from reaching a firm conclusion about ETS, even though the agency recognized the limitations of the data. The head of the Scientific Advisory Board that reviewed the report conceded: "This is a classic case where the evidence is not all that strong."

The evidence is especially unimpressive when compared to the evidence that smoking causes lung cancer. In the latter case, there are thousands of studies, and virtually all of them have found a positive association, statistically significant in the vast majority of cases. And the associations are sizable: a typical female smoker is about 10 times as likely to get lung cancer as a female nonsmoker; for men the ratio is more like 20 to 1; and among heavy smokers, the figures are even higher. "The data on active smoking are so much stronger," Enstrom says. "That should be the focus of attention, not something which is so small and has the potential to be confounded by so many different things. I personally am baffled as to why people give it so much credibility."

PROTECTED FROM THEMSELVES

The explanation may be that the EPA's conclusion about ETS is useful in a way that the evidence about smoking is not. Although the share of adults who smoke has dropped from about 40 per cent to about 25 per cent since 1965, some 50 million Americans continue to smoke. And as Duke University economist W. Kip Viscusi shows in his book *Smoking: Making the Risky Decision*, this is not because they are ignorant about the health effects. Rather, they are willing to accept the risks in exchange for the benefits of smoking. From a "public-health" perspective, this is intolerable; no one should be allowed to make such a foolish decision. But the idea of protecting people from themselves still arouses considerable opposition in this country. Hence anti-smoking activists and public-health officials need a different excuse for restricting smoking: it endangers innocent bystanders. . . .

If your main goal is improving "the public health," you may be inclined to shade the truth a bit if it helps to make smoking less acceptable and more inconvenient. Marc Lalonde, Canada's former minister of national health and welfare, offered a rationale for such a strategy in a highly influential 1974 report: "Science is full of 'ifs,' 'buts,' and 'maybes,' while messages designed to influence the public must be loud, clear, and unequivocal. . . . The scientific 'yes, but' is essential to research, but for modifying human behavior of the population it sometimes produces the 'uncertain sound.' This is all the excuse needed by many to cultivate and tolerate an environment and lifestyle that is hazardous to health."

Writing about the ETS controversy in *Toxicologic Pathology*, Yale University epidemiologist Alvan Feinstein quotes a colleague who appears to have been influenced by the Lalonde Doctrine: "Yes, it's rotten science, but it's in a worthy cause. It will help us get rid of cigarettes and become a smoke-free society."

"The nicotine in cigarettes is an addictive drug that makes quitting difficult."

SMOKING SHOULD BE TREATED AS NICOTINE ADDICTION

Tamar Nordenberg

Nicotine, a chemical substance found naturally in tobacco leaves, is absorbed rapidly into the bloodstream when smoking a cigarette. In the following viewpoint, Tamar Nordenberg argues that the addictive properties of nicotine make it extremely difficult for people to quit smoking even when they want to because of health concerns. Nicotine can be as addictive as heroin or cocaine for some people, she asserts. Nordenberg describes some products that the Food and Drug Administration (FDA) has approved to help people quit smoking. These products ease smoking withdrawal symptoms and cravings by supplying the body nicotine through chewing gum, nasal spray, or nicotine patch. Such nicotine replacement therapies, she concludes, can be used in conjunction with counseling, family encouragement, and support groups to enable smokers to break their smoking habit. Nordenberg is a staff writer for FDA Consumer.

As you read, consider the following questions:

1. What percentage of smokers desire to quit, according to Nordenberg?
2. What does the author list as being some of the symptoms of nicotine withdrawal?

Excerpted from Tamar Nordenberg, "It's Quittin' Time," FDA Consumer, November/December 1997.

"Habit is habit, and not to be flung out of the window by any man, but coaxed downstairs a step at a time."   —Mark Twain

Even in the face of withdrawal symptoms that can challenge the strongest of wills, millions of Americans have conquered their smoking "habit," step by step. According to the U.S. government's Agency for Health Care Policy and Research (AHCPR), for every one of the 46 million American smokers, there is an ex-smoker who has successfully quit.

True, it's not easy. The nicotine in cigarettes can command both a physical and mental hold that can be tough to overcome. For some, nicotine is as addictive as heroin or cocaine, according to AHCPR.

"There's no question about it; sometimes when you're trying to give up cigarettes, you think 'I've got to have one,'" says Denis Brissette of Madison, Wisconsin, who smoked about three packs a day for 30 years before quitting four years ago.

For many smokers who want to quit, willpower alone isn't enough to beat the yearning. For them, smoking cessation products the Food and Drug Administration (FDA) has approved may reduce the cravings and other withdrawal symptoms. To help him quit, Brissette used the nicotine patch, which is now available over-the-counter along with nicotine gum. Other stop-smoking aids, available only by prescription, include nicotine nasal spray and the nicotine inhaler, as well as a stop-smoking product in pill form.

While these products can ease the symptoms resulting from the physical addiction to nicotine, group or individual counseling and encouragement from family and friends are critical to help address the mental dependence.

"You really have to be committed to quitting," says Celia Jaffe Winchell, M.D., a psychiatrist and FDA's medical team leader for addictive drug products, "and when you've made the decision to stop smoking, commit to using whatever it takes to quit."

KILLER ADDICTION

Imagine: Two jumbo jets crash every day and not a single person walks away alive. That, then-Surgeon General C. Everett Coop told Americans in 1989, is the number of people who die each day from smoking.

Cigarettes alone kill more than 400,000 Americans each year—more than AIDS, alcohol, car accidents, murders, suicides, illegal drugs, and fires combined. And smoking can harm not just the smoker, according to the Environmental Protection Agency and other experts, but also family members and others who breathe "secondhand smoke."

Given that cigarettes are known killers, why do so many Americans continue to smoke?

Seventy percent of adult smokers want to quit completely, according to a survey by the national Centers for Disease Control and Prevention. But the nicotine in cigarettes is an addictive drug that makes quitting difficult, as confirmed by the 1988 Surgeon General's report on smoking and health.

"There is little doubt," wrote smoking researcher M.A.H. Russell in 1974, "that if it were not for the nicotine in tobacco smoke, people would be little more inclined to smoke than they are to blow bubbles or light sparklers."

As with other addictive drugs, people can experience withdrawal when they get less nicotine than they are used to. Symptoms can include irritability, frustration, anger, anxiety, difficulty concentrating, restlessness, and craving for tobacco.

One reason cigarettes in particular are so addictive, Winchell says, is that a person gets a "very rapid and effective dose" of nicotine by inhaling it. Within seconds of inhaling a cigarette, nicotine enters the lungs and then travels directly to the brain.

"Tobacco use in 1997 is not just some bad habit, but a powerful addiction that warrants appropriate medical treatment," says Michael Fiore, M.D., director of the Center for Tobacco Research and Intervention at the University of Wisconsin Medical School.

As a rule, Fiore says, people who smoke more than 10 cigarettes a day and want to quit should use an FDA-approved smoking cessation product.

THE OPTIONS

Most medical aids to smoking cessation are nicotine replacement products. They deliver small, steady doses of nicotine into the body to relieve some of the withdrawal systems, without the "buzz" that keeps smokers hooked.

Nicotine replacement products are available in four forms: the patch, gum, nasal spray, and inhaler. Although the products deliver nicotine into the blood, they don't contain the tar and carbon monoxide that are largely responsible for cigarettes' dangerous health consequences.

Studies show that the nicotine replacement therapies as much as double the chances of quitting smoking. Smokers should choose the method that appeals to them and try a different method if the first one doesn't work.

"It's an individual decision," Winchell says. "You really can't say that one of these products works better than another."

Like the nicotine substitution products, the newest option—an anti-smoking pill—seems to reduce nicotine withdrawal symptoms and the urge to smoke. But Zyban (bupropion hydrochloride), approved by FDA in May 1997, has one thing that sets it apart. It contains no nicotine.

"We don't know exactly how Zyban works," Winchell says, "but it seems to have an effect on the chemicals in the brain associated with nicotine addiction.". . .

PSYCHOLOGICAL SIDE

Despite the availability of Zyban and the other medical aids for smoking cessation, Winchell says, "If someone is serious about quitting, the drugs alone won't do it. They must have some kind of support, whether it's from a formal stop-smoking program or at least informal support from their friends and family."

This, Winchell explains, is because nicotine addiction isn't all physical. Smokers come to enjoy the smoking behavior and are used to lighting up in certain situations. "A smoker's whole day," Winchell says, "is filled with cues that could trigger the desire for a cigarette: the first cup of coffee in the morning, sitting down to check the e-mail, opening the paper, finishing a meal."

Before quitting, a person should change his or her environment. A good way to start, according to AHCPR, is by getting rid of cigarettes and ashtrays in the home, car, and workplace.

Setting a quit date, and sticking to it, is another important step toward successfully giving up cigarettes. A good date might be . . . [the] "Great American Smokeout." Each year, millions of Americans participate in the American Cancer Society event, which is designed to encourage people to give up the deadly pastime for at least a day.

Because being around smokers, being under stress, and drinking alcohol are some of the most common smoking triggers, AHCPR recommends that people avoid such difficult situations whenever possible while trying to quit.

As a distraction from thoughts of smoking, the agency says, taking time for a fun activity may help. Exercising may be an especially useful distraction. And exercising, along with eating healthier, low-fat foods, can minimize the weight gain (not more than 10 pounds on average) that sometimes goes along with quitting smoking.

Quit-smoking programs, self-help materials, and hot lines are available throughout the United States.

Also, family, friends, or a health-care provider can offer encouragement and support when the going gets tough. "The buddy system helped me," Brissette says. "My mother-in-law quit at the same time I did. We supported each other through it."

Some people have found hypnosis and acupuncture helpful in quitting, but these methods have not been proven to work.

Cigars and smokeless tobacco should not be viewed as safe alternatives to cigarettes. They, too, can be addictive and can cause serious health effects such as cancer and heart problems.

NOT EVEN A PUFF

Regardless of the method you decide to try, Fiore says, "hang in there." Most people who abstain from smoking for three months can be cigarette-free for the rest of their lives, he says.

Your risk of heart disease and lung cancer drop steadily after you quit. Three years after quitting, your risk of dying from a heart attack is about the same as if you had never smoked, according to the American Heart Association. And the American Lung Association estimates that in 10 years, the risk of lung cancer declines to about 30 to 50 percent of a continuing smoker's risk.

So when you try to quit, keep the rewarding health benefits in mind. Don't be discouraged if the first quit attempt doesn't succeed, because experts say it usually takes two or three tries. Think about what seemed to help during past quit attempts and what didn't, and each try will carry a better chance of success.

But even after you've abstained for a while, cautions Fiore, don't be lulled into letting your guard down. Because the nature of nicotine addiction makes it impossible for most people to be occasional smokers, "you need to treat cigarettes the way an alcoholic treats booze," he says. "Don't take even a single puff."

"If nicotine is so relentlessly
addictive, how can it be that 50
percent of all Americans who have
ever smoked no longer do?"

SMOKING IS NOT A SIMPLE MATTER OF NICOTINE ADDICTION

Richard J. DeGrandpre

Viewing the habit of smoking as a mere result of physical addiction to nicotine is simplistic and misleading, argues Richard J. DeGrandpre in the following viewpoint. Some smokers do not become addicted at all, while others develop a dependence because of psychological or social reasons. He asserts that nicotine replacement therapy has had limited success in helping people to stop smoking and that equating cigarette smoking with a chemical habit may actually impede people's efforts to quit. De-Grandpre, a scholar of drugs and culture and coeditor of *Drug Policy and Human Nature*, calls for a fuller understanding of the nature of addiction in order to improve anti-smoking policies.

As you read, consider the following questions:

1. How does DeGrandpre define the "classical model" of addiction?
2. What has been the success rate of the nicotine patch, according to the author?
3. According to DeGrandpre, what are the three levels of addiction?

During the 1996 presidential election campaign, Bill Clinton successfully cast Big Tobacco as a national enemy, with Bob Dole playing the role of collaborator by downplaying the addictiveness of nicotine. Meanwhile, the Food and Drug Administration has been asserting jurisdiction over cigarettes as "nicotine delivery devices," arguing that tobacco companies intend to hook their customers, just like schoolyard drug pushers. Hundreds of pending lawsuits, including class actions and cases filed by state governments, similarly allege a conspiracy to addict smokers. These developments represent important changes in our attitudes toward cigarettes. Though justified in the name of public health, the increasing emphasis on the enslaving power of nicotine may only make matters worse.

CONVENTIONAL WISDOM ON ADDICTION

Understanding why requires careful consideration of the conventional wisdom about tobacco addiction, which recycles mistaken assumptions about illicit drugs. During the latter half of this century, the classical model of addiction, derived from observations of narcotic abuse, increasingly has been used to describe the cigarette habit. The classical model states that consumption of certain chemicals causes a physical dependence, either immediately or after prolonged use, characterized by withdrawal symptoms—symptoms that can be avoided or escaped only by further drug use. As Steven Hyman, director of the National Institute of Mental Health (NIMH), opined in *Science*, "Repeated doses of addictive drugs—opiates, cocaine, and amphetamine—cause drug dependence and, afterward, withdrawal."

This cyclical model, in which the drug serves as both problem and solution, offers a simple, easy-to-grasp account of the addiction process, giving the concept great staying power in the public imagination. In the case of smoking, this view of addiction is central to the rationale for regulating tobacco and the concern that the cigarette companies have been doping their products with extra nicotine. But the classical model tends to conceal rather than elucidate the ultimate sources of addiction, and it is just as ill-suited to the cigarette habit as it has always been for understanding illicit drug use.

If a chemical compound can be addictive in the manner described by NIMH Director Hyman, we would expect anyone who regularly uses such a substance to become addicted. Yet only a minority of those who use illicit drugs—whether marijuana, cocaine, or heroin—ever develop a dependence on them. The prevalence of addiction, as defined by the American Psychiatric Association's *Diagnostic and Statistical Manual*, among users of alcohol and cocaine runs about 15 percent and 17 percent, respectively. Even in a sample of 79 regular crack users, Patricia Erickson and her colleagues at Toronto's Addiction Research Foundation found that only about 37 percent used the drug heavily (more than 100 times in their lives), and 67 percent had not used in the past month. A similar pattern holds for tobacco. In the 1994 National Household Survey on Drug Abuse, 73 percent of respondents reported smoking cigarettes at some time, but only about 29 percent reported smoking in the previous month, and not necessarily on a daily basis. Writing in the May/June 1996 *Mother Jones*, Jeffrey Klein manages to argue that nicotine enslaves its users and, at the same time, that Tobacco Inc. seeks to recruit young smokers to replace the 1.3 million Americans who quit each year. If nicotine is so relentlessly addictive, how can it be that 50 percent of all Americans who have ever smoked no longer do?

NICOTINE REPLACEMENT THERAPY

The classical model also suggests that the cigarette habit should be highly amenable to nicotine replacement therapy, such as the nicotine patch. Yet few of the tens of thousands of patch users have actually broken the habit (only about 10 percent to 15 percent succeed). In direct conflict with the classical model, most keep smoking while on the patch, continuing to consume the carcinogens in cigarette smoke while obtaining considerably higher blood levels of nicotine. A 1992 study of nicotine replacement therapy reported in the journal *Psychopharmacology* concluded that the "overall lack of effect [of the patch] on cigarette consumption is perhaps surprising and suggests that in regular smokers the lighting up of a cigarette is generally triggered by cues other than low plasma nicotine levels."

Most people who successfully quit smoking do so only after several failed attempts. If addiction is driven by physical dependence on a chemical—in this case, nicotine—relapse should occur during withdrawal, which for nicotine typically lasts a few weeks. Yet a sizable proportion of relapses occur long after the smoker has suffered through nicotine withdrawal. In fact, studies do not even show a relationship between the severity of withdrawal and the likelihood of relapse. As any former smoker could tell you, ex-smokers crave cigarettes at certain times and in certain situations for months, even years, after quitting. In these cases, the desire to smoke is triggered by environmental cues, not by withdrawal symptoms. This is one reason why people who overcome addiction to illicit substances such as heroin or cocaine often say they had more difficulty breaking the cigarette habit. Because regular tobacco users smoke in a wide array of circumstances (when bored, after eating, when driving) and settings (home, work, car), the cues that elicit the urge are more ubiquitous than for illicit drug use.

IGNORING PSYCHOSOCIAL FACTORS

These failures of the classical model illustrate how conventional wisdom over-simplifies the dynamics of cigarette smoking. This reductionist view is dangerous because it ignores the psychosocial factors that underlie addiction. In coming to terms with cigarette addiction as a psychosocial process, rather than a simple pharmacological one, we need to distinguish between cigarette addiction and nicotine addiction. Certainly no one (except perhaps the tobacco companies) denies that cigarette smoking can be addictive, if by addiction one means a stubborn urge to keep smoking. But it is quite a different matter to say that nicotine accounts for the addictiveness of smoking. Nicotine withdrawal notwithstanding, nicotine alone is insufficient, and may even be unnecessary, to create cigarette addiction.

This claim can be clarified by two dramatic case studies reported in the British Journal of Addiction in 1973 and 1989. The earlier article described a 47-year-old woman with a two-and-a-half-year-long dependence on water, one of several such cases noted by the author. The woman reported a nagging withdrawal symptom—a dry, salty taste in her mouth—that was alleviated by the persistent drinking of water (up to 60 glasses per day). This case of dependence on a nonpsychoactive substance contrasts sharply with the second account, which described an 80-year-old woman who used cocaine without incident for 55 years. The authors reported that "she denies any feelings of euphoria or in-creased energy after [snorting] the cocaine nor any depression or craving for cocaine when her supplies run out. . . . She appears to have suffered no ill effects from the prolonged use of cocaine in physical, psychological or social terms." So we see that not every addiction involves drug use and not every instance of drug use involves an addiction.

To say that cigarette addiction is a psychosocial process means that social, cultural, and economic factors play a crucial role in acquiring and keeping a cigarette habit. In fact, the tendency to reduce the cigarette experience to chemical servitude may be one of the most powerful cultural factors driving addiction. Cigarette lore wrongly teaches smokers (and smokers-to-be) that they will suffer badly if they attempt to quit, while at the same time freeing them of responsibility for their drug use once they begin. Such beliefs also help romanticize cigarette smoking, elevating nicotine to a sublime abstraction. This not only reinforces the forbidden fruit effect, it helps transform the habit of smoking into a cult behavior. Smoking thus acquires the kind of meaning that the youth of America are most in search of: social meaning. As Richard Klein writes in *Cigarettes Are Sublime,* "smoking cigarettes is not only a physical act but a discursive one—a wordless but eloquent form of expression."

To counteract the forces that give momentum to drug use, the public meaning of addiction needs to be broadened to include the many, changing facets of the psychosocial realm in which we develop. "Putting people back in charge" of their addictions, as John Leo puts it in *U.S. News & World Report,* will not work if we focus only on the naked individual. Rather than pushing the pendulum of public policy between scapegoating the substance and scapegoating the individual, we should seek a middle ground. Realizing that the addiction process has at least three levels of complexity is a good place to start.

LEVELS OF ADDICTION

First, at the basic and most immediate level, are the short- and long-term biological processes that underlie the psychological experiences of drug use and drug abstinence. Even with the same drug, these experiences vary greatly across individuals. Scientists and journalists too easily forget that every psychological process is built on biology. Discoveries of biological mechanisms and processes underlying addiction are not proof that the problem is biological rather than social and psychological. Eating rich foods has powerful biological effects in both the short and long run, but we should not therefore conclude that the rise in obesity in the United States is a biological problem. Indeed, attempts to alter the addiction process that emphasize biochemistry (such as the nicotine patch) have met with little success.

At the next level are psychological processes (social, motivational, learning) that, although rooted in biology, are shaped by personal experience. Because each of us has unique life experiences, we do not necessarily interpret the same events in the same way. The reasons for one individual's addiction may be altogether different from the reasons for another's. As the Scottish film *Trainspotting* makes clear, stories of addiction are no less complex than any other personal stories. Still, intervention at this level has had some success with users of alcohol or illicit drugs, and several research and treatment institutions are examining methods for "matching" addicts with different treatment strategies based on their social and psychological characteristics.

Drug effects and drug addiction also vary greatly across time and place, implicating cultural factors as the third and most general aspect of drug addiction. These factors are rooted in but not reducible to psychological processes, just as psychological processes are not reducible to biology. Patterns of alcohol use around the world, which show that the prevalence of drinking problems cannot be predicted by consumption alone, illustrate the importance of culture. Italians, for example, historically have consumed large quantities of alcohol with relatively low rates of drunkenness and alcoholism. The effects of alcohol on human behavior—violence, boorishness, gregariousness—also have been shown to vary dramatically across cultures.

Given the cultural role in addiction and the radical changes that have occurred in attitudes about smoking, it is quite possible that the young smokers of today are not at all like the smokers of 50 years ago. Those who begin smoking now do so with the belief that it is addictive, causes poor health (and wrinkles!), and can be deadly. If individuals are willing to start smoking despite such knowledge, it is likely that they will acquire and keep the habit, seeming to confirm the current, politically correct image of addiction. And if this self-fulfilling prophecy is realized, chances are that interventions aimed at the social realm will continue to miss their target and fail to curtail addiction.

ORGANIZATIONS TO CONTACT

The editors have compiled the following list of organizations concerned with the issues debated in this book. The descriptions are derived from materials provided by the organizations. All have publications or information available for interested readers. The list was compiled on the date of publication of the present volume; the information provided here may change. Be aware that many organizations take several weeks or longer to respond to inquiries, so allow as much time as possible.

Gun Control

Handgun Control, Inc.
1225 Eye St. NW, Suite 1100, Washington, DC 20005
(202) 898-0792 • fax: (202) 371-9615
website: http://www.handguncontrol.org

A citizens lobby working for the federal regulation of the manufacture, sale, and civilian possession of handguns and automatic weapons, the organization successfully promoted the passage of the Brady law, which mandates a five-day waiting period for the purchase of handguns. The lobby publishes the quarterly newsletter *Progress Report* and the book *Guns Don't Die—People Do*, as well as legislative reports and pamphlets.

Independence Institute
14142 Denver West Pkwy., Suite 185, Golden, CO 80401
(303) 279-6536 • fax: (303) 279-4176
website: http://www.i2i.org

The Independence Institute is a pro–free market think tank that supports gun ownership as a civil liberty and a constitutional right. Its publications include books and booklets opposing gun control, such as *Children and Guns: Sensible Solutions*, *The Assault Weapon Panic: "Political Correctness" Takes Aim at the Constitution*, and *The Samurai, the Mountie, and the Cowboy*.

National Rifle Association (NRA)
11250 Waples Mill Rd., Fairfax, VA 22030
(703) 267-1000 • fax: (703) 267-3989
e-mail: nra-contact@nra.org • website: http://www.nrahq.org

The NRA, with nearly 3 million members, is America's largest organization of gun owners. It is the primary lobbying group for those who oppose gun control laws. The NRA believes that such laws violate the U.S. Constitution and do nothing to reduce crime. In addition to its monthly magazines *American Rifleman*, *American Hunter*, and *Incites*, the NRA publishes numerous books, bibliographies, reports, and pamphlets on gun ownership, gun safety, and gun control.

Violence Policy Center
1350 Connecticut Ave. NW, Suite 825, Washington, DC 20036
e-mail: comment@vpc.org • website: http://www.vpc.org

The center is an educational foundation that conducts research on fire-arms violence. It works to educate the public concerning the dangers of guns and supports gun-control measures. The center's publications include the report "Cease Fire: A Comprehensive Strategy to Reduce Firearms Violence" and the books *NRA: Money, Firepower, and Fear* and *Assault Weapons and Accessories in America*.

Abortion

National Abortion and Reproductive Rights Action League (NARAL)
1156 15th St. NW, Suite 700, Washington, DC 20005
(202) 973-3000 • fax: (202) 973-3096
e-mail: naral@naral.org • website: http://www.naral.org
NARAL works to develop and sustain a pro-choice political con-stituency in order to maintain the right of all women to legal abortion. The league briefs members of Congress and testifies at hearings on abortion and related issues. It publishes the quarterly *NARAL Newsletter*.

National Right to Life Committee (NRLC)
419 7th St. NW, Suite 500, Washington, DC 20004
(202) 626-8800
e-mail: nrlc@nrlc.org • website: http://www.nrlc.org
NRLC is one of the largest organizations opposing abortion. The com-mittee campaigns against legislation to legalize abortion. It encourages ratification of a constitutional amendment granting embryos and fe-tuses the same right to life as living persons, and it advocates alterna-tives to abortion such as adoption. NRLC publishes the brochure *When Does Life Begin?* and the periodic tabloid *National Right to Life News*.

Planned Parenthood Federation of America
810 7th Ave., New York, NY 10019
(212) 541-7800 • fax: (212) 245-1845
e-mail: communications@ppfa.org
website: http://www.plannedparenthood.org;
http://www.teenwire.com
Planned Parenthood Federation of America, the world's oldest and largest voluntary family planning organization, believes that everyone has the right to choose when or whether to have a child. Nationally, Planned Parenthood affiliates operate 850 health centers, which pro-vide medical services and sexuality education for millions of women, men, and teenagers each year. Its publications include *Abortion: Commonly Asked Questions* and *What If I'm Pregnant?*

Women and Children First
e-mail: ertelt@prolife.org • website: http://www.prolife.org/wcf
Women and Children First is a pro-life Internet project created to dis-seminate information to the public about pro-life issues and to help find assistance for women who may be in crisis pregnancies or who are

in need of counseling after having had abortions. The website provides an extensive pro-life resource list, health information, and fact sheets.

Affirmative Action

American Civil Liberties Union (ACLU)
125 Broad St., 18th Fl., New York, NY 10004
(212) 549-2500 • fax: (212) 549-2646
website: http://www.aclu.org

The ACLU is a national organization that works to defend Americans' civil rights as guaranteed by the U.S. Constitution. It works to establish equality before the law, regardless of race, color, sexual orientation, or national origin. The ACLU publishes and distributes policy statements, pamphlets, and the semiannual newsletter *Civil Liberties Alert*.

Cato Institute
1000 Massachusetts Ave. NW, Washington, DC 20001-5403
(202) 842-0200 • fax: (202) 842-3490
e-mail: cato@cato.org • website: http://www.cato.org

The Cato Institute is a libertarian public policy research foundation dedicated to limiting the control of government and protecting individual liberties. It offers numerous publications on public policy issues, including the triennial *Cato Journal*, the bimonthly newsletter *Cato Policy Report*, and the quarterly magazine *Regulation*.

The Heritage Foundation
214 Massachusetts Ave. NE, Washington, DC 20002-4999
(202) 546-4400 • (800) 544-4843 • fax: (202) 544-6979
e-mail: pubs@heritage.org • website: http://www.heritage.org

The foundation is a conservative public policy research institute dedicated to free-market principles, individual liberty, and limited government. It opposes affirmative action for women and minorities and believes the private sector, not government, should be relied upon to ease social problems and to improve the status of women and minorities. The foundation publishes the periodic *Backgrounder* and the quarterly *Policy Review* as well as numerous monographs, books, and papers on public policy issues.

National Association for the Advancement of Colored People (NAACP)
1025 Vermont Ave. NW, Suite 1120, Washington, DC 20005
(202) 638-2269
e-mail: hshelton@naacp.net.org • website: http://www.naacp.org

The NAACP is the oldest and largest civil rights organization in the United States. Its principal objectives are to achieve equal rights and to eliminate racial prejudice by removing racial discrimination in housing, employment, voting, education, the courts, and business. The NAACP publishes a variety of newsletters, books, and pamphlets as well as the magazine *Crisis*.

American Heart Association (AHA)

7272 Greenville Ave., Dallas, TX 75231
(800) AHA-USA1 (242-8721)
website: http://www.americanheart.org

The American Heart Association is a not-for-profit, voluntary health organization funded by private contributions. Its mission is to reduce disability and death from heart attack, stroke, and related cardiovascular diseases. It publishes five scientific journals and numerous reports, including "Alcohol and Heart Disease" and "Heavy Drinkers Can Add Heavy Burden to Their Risk for Stroke."

Distilled Spirits Council of the United States (DISCUS)

1250 Eye St. NW, Suite 400, Washington, DC 20005
(202) 628-3544
website: http://www.discus.health.org

The Distilled Spirits Council of the United States is the national trade association representing producers and marketers of distilled spirits sold in the United States. It seeks to ensure the responsible advertising and marketing of distilled spirits to adult consumers and to prevent such advertising and marketing from targeting individuals below the legal purchase age. Fact sheets and pamphlets, including *The Drunk Driving Prevention Act*, are available at its website.

Mothers Against Drunk Driving (MADD)

511 E. John Carpenter Frwy., #700, Irving, TX 75062
(800) GET-MADD (438-6233)
e-mail: info@madd.org • website: http://www.madd.org

The mission of Mothers Against Drunk Driving is to stop drunk driving and to serve the victims of this violent crime. MADD seeks to involve communities, businesses, young people, educational groups, and concerned citizens in the fight against drunk driving, as well as underage drinking. MADD publishes the biannual *MADDvocate* magazine for victims and the feature-style magazine *DRIVEN*, as well as a variety of brochures and other materials on drunk driving.

National Council on Alcoholism and Drug Dependence (NCADD)

12 W. 21st St., New York, NY 10010
(212) 206-6770 • fax: (212) 645-1690
website: http://www.ncadd.org

NCADD is a volunteer health organization that helps individuals overcome addictions, advises the federal government on drug and alcohol policies, and develops substance abuse prevention and education programs for youth. It publishes fact sheets, such as "Youth and Alcohol," and pamphlets, such as *Who's Got the Power? You . . . or Drugs?*

Amnesty International USA

322 Eighth Ave., New York, NY 10001
(212) 807-8400 • fax: (212) 627-1451
website: http://www.amnesty-usa.org

Amnesty International is an independent worldwide movement working impartially for the release of all prisoners of conscience, fair and prompt trials for political prisoners, and an end to torture and executions. AI is funded by donations from its members and supporters throughout the world. AI has published several books and reports, including "Fatal Flaws: Innocence and the Death Penalty."

Death Penalty Information Center (DPIC)

1606 20th St. NW, 2nd Fl., Washington, DC 20009
(202) 347-2531
website: http://www.essential.org/dpic

DPIC conducts research into public opinion on the death penalty. The center believes capital punishment is discriminatory, excessively costly, and may result in the execution of innocent persons. It publishes numerous reports, such as "Millions Misspent: What Politicians Don't Say About the High Costs of the Death Penalty," "Innocence and the Death Penalty: Assessing the Danger of Mistaken Executions," and "With Justice for Few: The Growing Crisis in Death Penalty Representation."

Justice for All (JFA)

PO Box 55159, Houston, TX 77255
(713) 935-9300 • fax: (713) 935-9301
e-mail: jfanet@msn.com • website: http://www.jfa.net

Justice for All is a not-for-profit criminal justice reform organization that supports the death penalty. Its activities include circulating online petitions to keep violent offenders from being paroled early and publishing the monthly newsletter, *The Voice of Justice*.

National Criminal Justice Reference Service (NCJRS)

U.S. Department of Justice
PO Box 6000, Rockville, MD 20849-6000
(301) 519-5500 • (800) 851-3420
e-mail: askncjrs@ncjrs.org • website: http://www.ncjrs.org

For a nominal fee, the NCJRS provides topical searches and reading lists on many areas of criminal justice, including the death penalty. It publishes an annual report on capital punishment.

Euthanasia/Physician-Assisted Suicide

Choice in Dying (CID)

1035 30th St. NW, Washington, DC 20007
(800) 989-WILL (989-9455)
e-mail: cid@choices.org • website: http://www.choices.org

Choice in Dying is a national, not-for-profit organization dedicated to fostering communication about complex end-of-life decisions among individuals, their loved ones, and health care professionals. The organization invented living wills in 1967 and provides the only national hotline to respond to families and patients during end-of-life crises. CID also provides educational materials, public and professional education, and ongoing monitoring of changes in state and federal right-to-die legislation.

The Hemlock Society

PO Box 101810, Denver, CO 80250
(303) 639-1202 • (800)247-7421 • fax: (303) 639-1224
e-mail: hemlock@privatei.com
website: http://www.hemlock.org/hemlock

The society believes that terminally ill individuals have the right to commit suicide. The society publishes books on suicide, death, and dying, including *Final Exit*, a guide for those suffering with terminal illnesses and considering suicide. The Hemlock Society also publishes the newsletter *TimeLines*.

International Anti-Euthanasia Task Force (IAETF)

PO Box 760, Steubenville, OH 43952
(740) 282-3810
e-mail: info@iaetf.org • website: http://www.iaetf.org

The Task Force is dedicated to preserving the rights of the terminally ill and to opposing euthanasia. IAETF publishes the bimonthly newsletter, *IAETF Update*, as well as fact sheets and position papers on euthanasia-related topics. It analyzes the policies and legislation concerning medical and social work organization and files amicus curiae briefs in major right-to-die cases.

Not Dead Yet

7521 Madison St., Forest Park, IL 60130
(708) 209-1500 • fax: (708) 209-1735
website: http://www.notdeadyet.org

Not Dead Yet is a national grassroots disability rights organization that opposes the legalization of assisted suicide and euthanasia. The group believes euthanasia is a form of discrimination targeting disabled and chronically ill people. Court briefs and press releases about euthanasia are available on its website.

Genetic Engineering

Biotechnology Industry Organization (BIO)

1625 K St. NW, #1100, Washington, DC 20006
(202) 857-0244 • fax: (202) 857-0237
e-mail: info@bio.org • website: http://www.bio.org

BIO is composed of companies engaged in industrial biotechnology. It monitors government actions that affect biotechnology and promotes increased public understanding of biotechnology through its educational activities and workshops. Its publications include the bimonthly newsletter BIO Bulletin, the periodic BIO News, and the book Biotech for All.

Center for Bioethics and Human Dignity (CBHD)
2065 Half Day Road, Bannockburn, IL 60015
(847) 317-8180 • fax: (847) 317-8153
e-mail: cbhd@biccc.org • website: http://www.bioethix.org
CBHD is an international educational center whose purpose is to bring Christian perspectives to bear on contemporary bioethical challenges facing society. Projects have addressed such topics as genetic technologies, euthanasia, and abortion. It publishes the newsletter Dignity and the book Genetic Ethics: Do the Ends Justify the Genes?

Council for Responsible Genetics
5 Upland Rd., Suite 3, Cambridge, MA 02140
(617) 868-0870 • fax: (617) 864-5164
e-mail: info@fbresearch.org • website://www.fbresearch.org
The council is a national organization of scientists, health professionals, trade unionists, women's health activists, and others who work to ensure that biotechnology is developed safely and in the public interest. The council publishes the bimonthly newsletter GeneWatch and position papers on the Human Genome Project, genetic discrimination, germ-line modifications, and DNA-based identification systems.

Human Genome Program (HGP)
Oak Ridge National Laboratory
1060 Commerce Park MS 6480, Oak Ridge, TN 37830
fax: (423) 574-9888
e-mail: mansfieldbk@ornl.gov • website: http://www.ornl.gov/hgmis
The U.S. Human Genome Program's research project is the 15-year national coordinated effort to discover and characterize all of the estimated 80,000–100,000 genes in human DNA and render them accessible for further biological study. The program will also address the ethical, legal, and social issues that may arise from the project. It publishes the newsletter Human Genome News and several documents, which include "Your Genes, Your Choices" and "Department of Energy Primer on Molecular Genetics."

Smoking

Action on Smoking and Health (ASH)
2013 H St. NW, Washington, DC 20006
(202) 659-4310
website: http://www.ash.org
Action on Smoking and Health promotes the rights of nonsmokers and works to protect them from the harms of smoking. ASH was responsible for getting cigarette commercials removed from radio and TV; smoking banned on airplanes, buses, and in many public places;

and for getting the FDA to regulate cigarette advertising and sales. The organization publishes the bimonthly newsletter *ASH Smoking and Health Review* and fact sheets on a variety of topics, including teen smoking.

American Smokers Alliance (ASA)

PO Box 189, Bellvue, CO 80512
fax: (970) 493-4253
e-mail: derf@smokers.org • website: http://www.smokers.org

The American Smokers Alliance is a nonprofit organization of volunteers who believe that nonsmokers and smokers have equal rights. ASA strives to unify existing smokers' rights efforts, combat anti-tobacco legislation, fight discrimination against smokers in the workplace, and encourage individuals to become involved in local smokers' rights movements. It publishes articles and news bulletins, including "Smokers Have Reduced Risks of Alzheimer's and Parkinson's Disease" and "Lung Cancer Can Be Eliminated!"

Canadian Council for Tobacco Control (CCTC)

170 Laurier Ave. W, Suite 1000, Ottawa, ON K1P 5V5 CANADA
(613) 567-3050 • (800) 267-5234 • fax: (613) 567-5695
e-mail: info-services@cctc.ca • website: http://www.cctc.ca/ncth

The CCTC works to ensure a healthier society, free from addiction and involuntary exposure to tobacco products. It promotes a comprehensive tobacco control program involving educational, social, fiscal, and legislative interventions. It publishes several fact sheets, including "Promoting a Lethal Product" and "The Ban on Smoking on School Property: Successes and Challenges."

Fight Ordinances and Restrictions to Control and Eliminate Smoking (FORCES)

PO Box 591257, San Francisco, CA 94159
(415) 824-4716
e-mail: info@forces.org • website: http://www.forces.org

FORCES fights against smoking ordinances and restrictions that are designed to eventually eliminate smoking, and it works to increase public awareness of smoking-related legislation. It opposes any state or local ordinance that it feels is not fair to those who choose to smoke. Although FORCES does not advocate smoking, it asserts that an individual has the right to choose to smoke and that smokers should be accommodated where and when possible. FORCES publishes *Tobacco Weekly* as well as many articles.

BIBLIOGRAPHY

CHAPTER 1

Karl P. Adler et al.
"Firearm Violence and Public Health: Limiting the Availability of Guns," *JAMA*, April 27, 1994. Available from 515 N. State St., Chicago, IL 60610.

America
"New Gun Control Initiatives," February 20, 1999.

Jack Anderson
Inside the NRA: Armed and Dangerous: An Exposé. New York: Dove, 1996.

John M. Bruce and Clyde Wilcox
The Changing Politics of Gun Control. Lanham, MD: Rowman & Littlefield, 1998.

William F. Buckley Jr.
"Bloody Impasse on Guns?" *National Review*, May 18, 1998.

Dana Charry and Ellen Charry
"The Crisis of Violence," *Christian Century*, July 15/22, 1998.

Fred Guterl
"Gunslinging in America," *Discover*, May 1996.

Philip J. Hilts
"The New Battle over Handguns," *Good Housekeeping*, June 1997.

Don B. Kates and Gary Kleck
The Great American Gun Debate: Essays on Firearms & Violence. San Francisco, CA: Pacific Research Institute for Public Policy, 1997.

Don B. Kates et al.
"Public Health Pot Shots: How the CDC Succumbed to the Gun 'Epidemic,'" *Reason*, April 1, 1997.

Gary Kleck
Targeting Guns: Firearms and Their Control. New York: Aldine de Gruyter, 1997.

David B. Kopel
"The Untold Triumph of Concealed-Carry Permits," *Policy Review*, July/August 1996.

Earl R. Kruschke
Gun Control: A Reference Handbook. Santa Barbara, CA: ABC-Clio, 1995.

John R. Lott Jr.
More Guns, Less Crime: Understanding Crime and Gun-Control Laws. Chicago: University of Chicago Press, 1998.

New Republic
"Rusty Got His Gun," August 17/24, 1998.

Peggy Noonan
"Sins of the Fathers," *Good Housekeeping*, July 1998.

Grover Norquist
"Have Gun, Will Travel," *American Spectator*, November 1998.

Daniel D. Polsby
"The False Promise of Gun Control," *Atlantic Monthly*, March 1994.

Bruce Shapiro	"Going for the Gunmakers," *Nation*, February 22, 1999.
Josh Sugarmann	"Reverse Fire," *Mother Jones*, January/February 1994.
Gordon Witkin et al.	"Again," *U.S. News & World Report*, June 1, 1998.
Franklin E. Zimring and Gordon Hawkins	"Concealed Handguns: The Counterfeit Deterrent," *Responsive Community*, Spring 1997. Available from 2130 H Street NW, Suite 714, Washington, DC 20052.
Franklin E. Zimring and Gordon Hawkins	*Crime Is Not the Problem: Lethal Violence in America*. New York: Oxford University Press, 1997.

CHAPTER 2

America	"The Abortion Horizon Today," March 27, 1999.
Joyce Arthur	"Psychological Aftereffects of Abortion: The Rest of the Story," *Humanist*, March/April 1997.
Angela Bonavoglia	"Late-Term Abortion: Separating Fact from Fiction," *Ms.*, May/June 1997.
Elinor Burkett	"The Last Abortion," *Utne Reader*, May/June 1998.
Christopher Caldwell	"Why Abortion Is Here to Stay," *New Republic*, April 5, 1999.
Margaret Carlson	"The Passive Majority," *Time*, November 9, 1998.
Miriam Claire	*The Abortion Dilemma: Personal Views on a Public Issue*. New York: Plenum Press, 1995.
Charles W. Colson	"Why Max Deserves a Life," *Christianity Today*, June 16, 1997.
Guy M. Condon	"Fatherhood Aborted," *Christianity Today*, December 9, 1996.
Mark Crutcher	*Lime 5: Exploited by Choice*. Denton, TX: Life Dynamics, 1996.
Jonathan Dube	"After the Abortion: By Ceding the Counseling Role to Pro-Lifers, Pro-Choicers May Be Doing Their Cause More Harm than Good," *Washington Monthly*, March 1998.
Audrey Duff	"The New Scarlet Letter," *Mademoiselle*, May 1996.
Karen Frank	"Mourning Their Baby: Aborting Fetus with Heart Disease," *Glamour*, April 1997.
Laura Fraser	"The Abortion Pill's Grim Progress," *Mother Jones*, January/February 1999.
Janet Hedley	*Abortion: Between Freedom and Necessity*. Philadelphia: Temple University Press, 1997.
Heather King	"One Woman's Journey," *Commonweal*, May 3, 1996.

Patrick Lee	*Abortion and Unborn Human Life.* Washington, DC: Catholic University of America Press, 1996.
Frederica Mathewes-Green	"Beyond 'It's a Baby,'" *National Review,* December 31, 1997.
Eileen L. McDonagh	*Breaking the Abortion Deadlock: From Choice to Consent.* New York: Oxford University Press, 1996.
Anaye Milligan	"My Girlfriend's Abortion," *Essence,* August 1998.
Louis P. Pojman and Francis Beckwith, eds.	*The Abortion Controversy: 25 Years After Roe v. Wade: A Reader.* Rev. ed. Belmont, CA: Wadsworth, 1998.
James Risen and Judy L. Thomas	*Wrath of Angels: The American Abortion War.* New York: Basic Books, 1999.
Wendy Shalit	"Whose Choice? Men's Role in Abortion Decisions," *National Review,* May 18, 1998.
Nada L. Stotland	*Abortion: Facts and Feelings: A Handbook for Women and the People Who Care About Them.* Washington, DC: American Psychiatric Press, 1998.
Lisa Tolin	"The Effects of Abortion," *Psychology Today,* July/August 1997.
U.S. News & World Report	"Who Gets Abortions and Why," January 19, 1998.

CHAPTER 3

Clint Bolick	*The Affirmative Action Fraud: Can We Restore the American Civil Rights Vision?* Washington, DC: Cato Institute, 1996.
William Bowen and Derek Bok	*The Shape of the River: Long-Term Consequences of Considering Race in College and University Admissions.* Princeton, NJ: Princeton University Press, 1998.
James A. Burford Jr.	"Affirmative Action Works," *Commonweal,* June 19, 1998.
Commentary	"Is Affirmative Action on the Way Out? Should It Be? A Symposium," March 1998.
Kimberly Williams Crenshaw	"Fighting the Post-Affirmative Action War," *Essence,* July 1998.
George E. Curry, ed.	*The Affirmative Action Debate.* Reading, MA: Addison-Wesley, 1996.
Ronald Dworkin	"Is Affirmative Action Doomed?" *New York Review of Books,* November 5, 1998.
Christopher F. Edley	*Not All Black and White: Affirmative Action, Race, and American Values.* New York: Hill and Wang, 1996.
Walter Feinberg	*On Higher Ground: Education and the Case for Affirmative Action.* New York: Teachers College Press, 1998.

Richard D. Kahlenberg	"In Search of Fairness: A Better Way," *Washington Monthly*, June 1998.
Glenn C. Loury	"Color-Blinded," *New Republic*, August 17/24, 1998.
William H. Mellor	"Silence Treatment," *National Review*, September 28, 1998.
Albert G. Mosley and Nicholas Capaldi	*Affirmative Action: Social Justice or Unfair Preference?* Lanham, MD: Rowman & Littlefield, 1996.
Jeremy A. Rabkin	"Private Preferences," *American Spectator*, November 1998.
Peter Skerry	"The Affirmative Action Paradox," *Society*, September/October 1998.
Stephan Thernstrom and Abigail Thernstrom	*America in Black and White: One Nation, Indivisible.* New York: Simon & Schuster, 1997.
Vivian Valian	*Why So Slow: The Advancement of Women.* Cambridge, MA: MIT Press, 1998.
Sheila W. Wellington	"Cracking the Ceiling," *Time*, December 7, 1998.

CHAPTER 4

Ernest L. Abel	*Fetal Alcohol Abuse Syndrome.* New York: Plenum, 1998.
John Berlau	"Drink to Your Heart's Content?" *Insight*, March 3, 1997. Available from 3600 New York Ave. NE, Washington, DC 20002.
Consumer Reports	"Heard It Through the Grapevine: Is Wine Really Good for You?" October 1997.
Sharon Doyle Driedger	"Drink and Be Merry," *Maclean's*, October 27, 1997.
Gary D. Friedman and Arthur L. Klatsky	"Is Alcohol Good for Your Health?" *New England Journal of Medicine*, December 16, 1993. Available from 10 Shattuck St., Boston, MA 02115-6094.
Robert M. Hackman	"Flavonoids and the French Paradox," *USA Today*, September 1998.
Tony Hendra	"Prohibition: The Sequel," *Forbes FYI*, May 4, 1998.
John Hinman and Michael Criqui	"Should Wine Bottles and Liquor Labels Be Allowed to Carry Health Claims?" *Health*, May/June 1996.
Harold Holder and Griffin Edwards, eds.	*Alcohol and Public Policy: Evidence and Issues.* New York: Oxford University Press, 1995.
Annette Kornblum	"Should You Drink to Your Health?" *Better Homes and Gardens*, October 1997.

Albert B. Lowenfels	"Should Physicians Recommend Alcohol to Their Patients? No," *Priorities*, vol. 8, no. 1, 1996. Available from the American Council on Science and Health, 1995 Broadway, 2nd Fl., New York, NY 10023-5860.
Michael Mason	"The Truth About Women and Wine," *Health*, May/June 1997.
Stanton Peele	"Getting Wetter? (Regulation of Alcohol Consumption)," *Reason*, April 1, 1996.
JoAnne M. Rantz and Andrew L. Waterhouse, eds.	*Wine in Context: Nutrition, Physiology, Policy.* Davis, CA: American Society for Enology and Viticulture, 1996.
Marc A. Schuckit	*Educating Yourself About Alcohol and Drugs: A People's Primer.* New York: Plenum, 1995.
Dave Shiflett	"Here's to Your Health," *American Spectator*, October 1996.
Julia VanTine	"Should You Drink to Your Health?" *Prevention*, June 1998.
Sam Zakhari and Momtaz Wassef, eds.	*Alcohol and the Cardiovascular System.* Bethesda, MD: National Institute on Alcohol Abuse and Alcoholism, 1996.

CHAPTER 5

America	"The Death Penalty: An Outsider's View," June 6/13, 1998.
William C. Bailey	"Deterrence, Brutalization, and the Death Penalty: Another Examination of Oklahoma's Return to Capital Punishment," *Criminology*, November 1998.
Hugo Adam Bedau, ed.	*The Death Penalty in America: Current Controversies.* 4th ed. New York: Oxford University Press, 1997.
Sharon Brownlee et al.	"The Place for Vengeance," *U.S. News & World Report*, June 16, 1997.
William F. Buckley Jr.	"Miss Tucker's Plea," *National Review*, March 9, 1998.
Economist	"Does the Death Penalty Deter Murder?" December 12, 1994.
Charlotte Faltermayer	"What Is Justice for a Sixth-Grade Killer?" *Time*, April 6, 1998.
David Frum	"The Truth About the Chair," *Weekly Standard*, January 19, 1998. Available from PO Box 96114, Washington, DC 20077-7770.
David Gelernter	"What Do Murderers Deserve?" *Commentary*, April 1998.

Christopher Hitchens | "Scenes from an Execution," *Vanity Fair*, January 1998.

Jesse Jackson | *Legal Lynching: Racism, Injustice and the Death Penalty*. New York: Marlowe, 1996.

Jet | "Study Cites Link Between Death Penalty and Race," June 22, 1998.

Charisse Jones | "Old Enough to Pay the Ultimate Penalty," *USA Today*, April 13, 1998. Available from 1000 Wilson Blvd., Arlington, VA 22229.

Charles Lane | "Lethal Objection," *New Republic*, March 2, 1998.

Peter Linebaugh | "The Farce of the Death Penalty," *Nation*, August 14/21, 1995.

Debbie Morris et al. | *Forgiving the Dead Man Walking*. Grand Rapids, MI: Zondervan, 1998.

Louis P. Pojman and Jeffrey Reiman | *The Death Penalty: For and Against*. Lanham, MD: Rowman & Littlefield, 1998.

Helen Prejean | *Dead Man Walking: An Eyewitness Account of the Death Penalty in the United States*. New York: Random House, 1993.

Bruce Shapiro | "Wrongful Deaths: False Convictions and Capital Punishment," *Nation*, December 14, 1998.

Mark V. Tushnet | *The Death Penalty*. New York: Facts On File, 1994.

Marvin E. Wolfgang | "We Do Not Deserve to Kill," *Crime & Delinquency*, January 1998.

CHAPTER 6

Pieter V. Admiraal | "Euthanasia in the Netherlands," *Free Inquiry*, Winter 1996/97.

Jay Branegan | "I Want to Draw the Line Myself," *Time*, March 17, 1997.

Dudley Clendinen | "When Death Is a Blessing and Life Is Not," *New York Times*, February 5, 1996.

Rand Richards Cooper | "The Dignity of Helplessness: What Sort of Society Would Euthanasia Create?" *Commonweal*, October 25, 1996.

Nicholas Dixon | "On the Difference Between Physician-Assisted Suicide and Active Euthanasia," *Hastings Center Report*, September/October 1998.

Barbara Dority | "The Ultimate Liberty," *Humanist*, July/August 1997.

Jon Fuller | "Physician-Assisted Suicide: An Unnecessary Crisis," *America*, July 19, 1997.

Kevin P. Glynn	"'Double Effect,'" *Commonweal*, January 29, 1999.
Julie Grace	"Curtains for Dr. Death," *Time*, April 5, 1999.
Herbert Hendin	*Seduced by Death: Doctors, Patients, and Assisted Suicide.* New York: W.W. Norton, 1998.
Leon R. Kass and Nelson Lund	"Courting Death: Assisted Suicide, Doctors, and the Law," *Commentary*, December 1996.
Jerome P. Kassirer	"The Supreme Court and Physician-Assisted Suicide—The Ultimate Right," *New England Journal of Medicine*, January 2, 1997. Available from 10 Shattuck St., Boston, MA 02115-6094.
Michael Manning	*Euthanasia and Physician-Assisted Suicide: Killing or Caring?* Mahwah, NJ: Paulist Press, 1998.
Paul R. McHugh	"Dying Made Easy," *Commentary*, February 1999.
James D. Moore	"One Year Down," *Commonweal*, March 12, 1999.
Jonathan D. Moreno, ed.	*Arguing Euthanasia: The Controversy over Mercy Killing.* New York: Simon & Schuster, 1995.
Philip R. Muskin	"The Request to Die," *JAMA*, January 28, 1998. Available from 515 N. State St., Chicago, IL 60610.
Sherwin B. Nuland	"The Right to Live," *New Republic*, November 2, 1998.
M. Scott Peck	*Denial of the Soul: Spiritual and Medical Perspectives on Euthanasia and Mortality.* New York: Random House, 1997.
Timothy E. Quill	"In the Name of Mercy," *People Weekly*, April 7, 1997.
Joseph P. Shapiro	"Casting a Cold Eye on 'Death with Dignity,'" *U.S. News & World Report*, March 1, 1999.
Lonny Shavelson	*A Chosen Death: The Dying Confront Assisted Suicide.* Berkeley and Los Angeles: University of California Press, 1998.
Wesley J. Smith	*Forced Exit: The Slippery Slope from Assisted Suicide to Legalized Murder.* New York: Times Books, 1997.
Andrew Solomon	"A Death of One's Own," *New Yorker*, May 22, 1995.
James M. Thunder	"Assisted Suicide: The Violation of the Inalienable Right to Life," *Vital Speeches of the Day*, May 1, 1997.
Michael Vitez	*Final Choices: Seeking the Good Death.* Philadelphia: Camino Books, 1998.
Sue Woodman	*Last Rights: The Struggle over the Right to Die.* New York: Plenum, 1998.

CHAPTER 7

Garland E. Allen — "Science Misapplied: The Eugenics Age Revisited," Current, December 1996.

Ronald Bailey — "The Twin Paradox," Reason, May 1997.

Jimmy Carter — "Biotechnology Can Defeat Famine," New Perspectives Quarterly, Special Issue 1997.

Ronald Cole-Turner, ed. — Human Cloning: Religious Responses. Louisville, KY: Westminster John Knox Press, 1997.

Economist — "Hello, Dolly," March 1, 1997.

David Ehrenfeld — "A Cruel Agriculture," Resurgence, January/February 1998. Available from Small Changes, 316 Terry Ave. N., PO Box 19046, Seattle, WA 98109.

Eric S. Grace — Biotechnology Unzipped: Promises & Realities. Washington, DC: Joseph Henry Press, 1997.

Robin Marantz Henig — "Tempting Fates," Discover, May 1998.

Mae-Wan Ho — Genetic Engineering: Dream or Nightmare? Bath, UK: Gateway Books, 1998.

Leon R. Kass — "The Wisdom of Repugnance," New Republic, June 2, 1997.

Gina Kolata — Clone: The Road to Dolly, and the Path Ahead. New York: William Morrow, 1998.

Michael D. Lemonick and Dick Thompson — "Racing to Map Our DNA," Time, January 11, 1999.

Ruth Macklin — "Human Cloning? Don't Just Say No," U.S. News & World Report, March 10, 1997.

Charles C. Mann — "Genetic Engineering," Foreign Policy, Winter 1998/1999.

Glenn McGee — The Perfect Baby: A Pragmatic Approach to Genetics. Lanham, MD: Rowman & Littlefield, 1997.

Henry I. Miller — Policy Controversy in Biotechnology: An Insider's View. Austin, TX: R.G. Landes, 1997.

Henry I. Miller — "When Worlds Collide: Science, Politics, and Biotechnology," Priorities, vol. 9, no. 4, 1997. Available from the American Council on Science and Health, 1995 Broadway, 2nd Fl., New York, NY 10023-5860.

Mother Jones — "The New You," May/June 1998.

Gregory E. Pence, ed. — Flesh of My Flesh: The Ethics of Cloning Humans: A Reader. Lanham, MD: Rowman & Littlefield, 1998.

Michael Pollan	"Playing God in the Garden," *New York Times Sunday Magazine*, October 25, 1998.
Michael Reiss and Roger Straughan	*Improving Nature: The Science and Ethics of Genetic Engineering.* New York: Cambridge University Press, 1996.
Jeremy Rifkin	*The Biotech Century: Harnessing the Gene and Remaking the World.* New York: Jeremy P. Tarcher/Putnam, 1998.
Frederick B. Rudolph and Larry V. McIntire, eds.	*Biotechnology: Science, Engineering, and Ethical Challenges for the Twenty-First Century.* Washington, DC: Joseph Henry Press, 1996.
David Shenk	"Biocapitalism," *Harper's Magazine*, December 1997.
Lee M. Silver	*Remaking Eden: Cloning and Beyond in a Brave New World.* New York: Avon Books, 1997.
Paul B. Thompson	"Food Biotechnology's Challenge to Cultural Integrity and Individual Consent," *Hastings Center Report*, July/August 1997.
Craig Venter and Daniel Cohen	"The 21st Century: The Century of Biology," *New Perspectives Quarterly*, Special Issue 1997.
James Walsh	"Brave New Farm," *Time*, January 11, 1999.
Robert Wright	"Who Gets the Good Genes?" *Time*, January 11, 1999.

CHAPTER 8

Robert Bork	"Addicted to Health," *National Review*, July 28, 1997.
Janet Brigham	*Dying to Quit: Why We Smoke and How We Stop.* Washington, DC: Joseph Henry, 1998.
California Environmental Protection Agency	*Health Effects of Exposure to Environmental Tobacco Smoke: Final Report.* Sacramento: The Office, 1997.
Matthew Cooper	"Trying to Stop a Teen Epidemic," *Newsweek*, April 13, 1998.
Economist	"Blowing Smoke," December 20, 1997.
Jonathan Franzen	"Sifting the Ashes," *New Yorker*, May 13, 1996.
Nancy Gibbs	"Up in Smoke," *Time*, June 29, 1998.
Stanton A. Glantz	"The Anti-Smoking Campaign That Tobacco Loves," *Harper's*, July 1996.
Stanton A. Glantz et al.	*The Cigarette Papers.* Berkeley and Los Angeles: University of California Press, 1996.

Jonathan Goldberg	"Next Target, Nicotine," *New York Times Magazine*, August 4, 1996.
David R. Henderson	"Joe Camel: Brought to You by the FTC," *Fortune*, July 21, 1997.
Philip J. Hilts	*Smokescreen: The Truth Behind the Tobacco Industry Cover-Up.* Reading, MA: Addison-Wesley, 1996.
Richard Kluger	*Ashes to Ashes: America's Hundred-Year Cigarette War, the Public Health, and the Unabashed Triumph of Philip Morris.* New York: Knopf, 1996.
William D. Novelli	"Tobacco Control: The Dramatic Choice," *Science*, October 10, 1997.
William D. Novelli and Matthew Myers	"The U.S. Tobacco Legislative Imperative," *Multinational Monitor*, October 1998.
James L. Pirkle et al.	"Exposure of the U.S. Population to Environmental Tobacco Smoke," *JAMA*, April 24, 1996. Available from 515 N. State St., Chicago, IL 60610.
Dennis Prager	"The Soul-Corrupting Anti-Tobacco Crusade," *Weekly Standard*, July 20, 1998. Available from PO Box 96114, Washington, DC 20077-7770.
Robert K. Samuelson	"The Amazing Smoke Screen," *Newsweek*, November 30, 1998.
Jacob Sullum	*For Your Own Good: The Anti-Smoking Crusade and the Tyranny of Public Health.* New York: Free Press, 1998.
Mike Thomas	"Just Trying to Be Cool," *Reader's Digest*, March 1997.
Elizabeth M. Whelan, ed.	*Cigarettes: What the Warning Label Doesn't Tell You: The First Comprehensive Guide to the Health Consequences of Smoking.* Amherst, NY: Prometheus Books, 1997.
Elizabeth M. Whelan	"Is a Deal with the Cigarette Industry in the Interest of Public Health?" *Priorities*, vol. 9, no. 2, 1997. Available from the American Council on Science and Health, 1995 Broadway, 2nd Fl., New York, NY 10023-5860.

INDEX

on, 30–31, 43
    lower in states without death
        penalty, 192–93
    society negated by, 174
    see also Medina, Pedro; Sonnier,
        Patrick
Honolulu Heart Program, 139
Hopwood v. Texas, 129
Houk, Thomas, 205, 206, 211
Huber, Gary, 314, 315, 317
Hudson Institute, 276
Human Fertilisation & Embryology
    Act, 252
Human Genome Project, 245
Humber, Thomas, 286
Humphrey, Hubert, 25–26
Humphry, Derek, 232
Hungary, 29
Hunter, Janice, 187
Huxley, Aldous, 256, 266
Hyman, Steven, 325

I Accuse (film), 229
Illinois, 197
immigrants, 104
India, 279
Indonesia, 275, 279
Institute of Medicine, 155
International Agency for Research
    on Cancer, 308
International Life Sciences Institute
    (ILSI), 140
Iowa, 193
Iran, 165
Israel, 48
"Is There a Duty to Die?"
    (Hardwig), 236
Italy, 21

Jackson, Jesse, 195, 201
Jacobs, Jesse, 201
Jaeger, Marietta, 180, 181
James, Dorothy, 169, 173, 174
Japan, 29, 305
Joffe, Carole, 83
John Paul II (pope), 166, 182,
    210
Johnson, Lyndon B., 26, 85, 88,
    89, 101
Jordan, 49

Journal of American History, 18
Journal of Blacks in Higher Education,
    102
Journal of the American Geriatric Society,
    147
Journal of the American Medical Association
    (JAMA), 29, 152, 296, 303, 304

Kahlenberg, Richard, 131
Kaiser Permanente, 147
Kemp, Evan J., Jr., 239
Kennedy, John F., 85, 88
Kentucky, 29, 45, 48, 294
Kessler, David, 285, 302
Kevorkian, Jack, 205, 206, 209,
    229, 242
    one of many doctors assisting the
        dying, 211
Kilner, John F., 255
King, David, 251
King, Heather, 52
Kirscher v. McIver, 209
Kleck, Gary, 28
Klein, Jeffrey, 326
Klein, Richard, 328
Klein, Stephen, 203
Kolender, Bill, 39
Koop, C. Everett, 242, 243, 301,
    320

LaHaye, Beverly, 206
Lalonde, Marc, 318
Lamm, Richard, 236
Landes, William, 49
Las Vegas, Nevada, 128, 129
Layson, Stephen K., 193
Leadership Conference on Civil
    Rights, 86
LeBlanc, Lloyd, 180–81
Lerner, Sharon, 76
Lewis, C.S., 258
Lichtman, Judy L, 121
Life Dynamics, 77, 78, 83
Life's Dominion (Dworkin), 212
Liggett Group Inc., 289, 295
Lizotte, Alan, 27
Los Angeles, 314
Los Angeles Times, 18, 49
Lott, John R., Jr., 19, 37, 38, 41,
    47